JOHN MASEFIELD : A LIFE

JOHN MASEFIELD

—

A LIFE

Constance Babington Smith

MACMILLAN PUBLISHING CO., INC.

NEW YORK

© 1978 by Constance Babington Smith

Macmillan Publishing Co., Inc.
866 Third Avenue, New York, N.Y. 10022

Library of Congress Cataloging in Publication Data

Babington Smith, Constance.
John Masefield: a life.

1. Masefield, John, 1878–1967 — Biography.
2. Poets, English — 20th century — Biography.
PR6025.A77Z7553   821'.9'12 [B]   78–8648
ISBN 0–02–504600–4

First printing 1978

Typeset in Great Britain by Eta Services (Typesetters) Ltd.,
Beccles, Suffolk
Printed in the United States of America

To the Masefield family

Foreword

John Masefield's writings have already been the subject of several books, but no full account of his life has hitherto been published. As his first biographer, I have tried to bring the man himself to life – the son, brother, husband, father, the friend who opened his heart in multitudinous letters (although guarded in his published autobiographical writings he was often outspoken to his intimates).

Thanks largely to the help of his relatives, friends and acquaintances, who have most kindly shared their memories with me and permitted me to study letters, photographs and other documentary evidence, I have discovered Masefield at all the various stages of his life, some of which have remained obscure in the past. As a result, we can now get to know not only the orphaned country boy who fell in love with the sea and ships and yet abandoned the life of a sailor, but the poverty-stricken bank clerk who pined to be a writer, the romantic dreamer who worshipped – and married – a woman more than ten years his senior, the patriot in the First World War, the Englishman drawn again and again to America, the family man who loved the theatre almost as much as he loved the life of the countryside.

And finally we can see John Masefield in old age, an elder beloved for his courtesy and kindness, who faced up to the burdens of being a public figure, even to the extent of accepting that he would one day be the subject of a biography – an idea which had earlier caused him to shudder – and who remained till the end a devotee of beauty in all its forms, and a searcher for ultimate truths.

Constance Babington Smith

Cambridge
1978

Contents

Illustrations

John Masefield at the age of about three: *Mrs. Pamela Hugh-Jones*

Edward Masefield: *Mrs. Pamela Hugh-Jones*
Caroline Masefield: *Mrs. Hilary Magnus*
Miss Hanford-Flood: *Mr. Compton Whitworth*
Kate Masefield: *Mrs. Norah Parker*

Masefield as a *Conway* cadet with his sister Norah: *Mrs. Hilary Magnus*

Boys studying in H.M.S. *Conway*: *Mr. Max Hamilton*
The *Conway's* Captain: *Mr. D.G. Fletcher Rogers*

The *Gilcruix*: *National Maritime Museum*

One of the carpet mills of Alexander Smith & Sons at Yonkers, New York: *Local History and Genealogy Divison, The New York Public Library: Astor, Lenox and Tilden Foundations*

Masefield aged nineteen: *Miss Helen MacLachlan and Columbia University Libaries*

Masefield in his early twenties: *Mrs. Hilary Magnus*

Constance Crommelin (later Mrs. John Masefield) and Isabel Fry: *Mrs. P. Diamand*

John Masefield: *King's College Library, Cambridge*
Constance Masefield: *Miss E. Holmes*

Masefield during the 1914–18 War: *Humanities Research Center Library, Austin, Texas*

Constance Masefield and the children at Lollingdon: *Mr. J.B. Masefield*

Acknowledgements

In dedicating this book to the Masefield family I have had in mind those who helped me in many ways while I was writing it; I am deeply grateful to all of them. The reminiscences of John Masefield's two sisters, the late Mrs. Ethel Ross (who died in 1977 at the age of 101) and Mrs. Norah Parker, have been of unique value, especially in connection with his childhood and youth, and his daughter, Miss Judith Masefield, has also given me most useful information about family doings and friendships.

To Sir Peter Masefield, the poet's cousin, I am indebted for the initial suggestion that I should undertake the biography, and I want to offer my warmest thanks to him and to Lady Masefield for their constant interest and confidence, and also for their hospitality, throughout the years of my work on the book. Others whose kindness, encouragement, and hospitality I must mention with gratitude are Mr. and Mrs. Jack Masefield and Mr. and Mrs. Hilary Magnus. Furthermore Mr. and Mrs. William Masefield helped me with my researches at Ledbury, Mrs. Brenda Masefield lent me documentary material, Mrs. Prudence Barker shared with me her memories of her uncle (as did Mrs. Lavender Jackson), Dr. and Mrs. Geoffrey Masefield spoke with me of their recollections, Mrs. Pamela Hugh-Jones lent me family-album photographs (of which Mrs. Barker, as a professionally skilled photographer, made excellent enlargements), and Mr. Richard Masefield allowed me to study his researches on family history.

As regards the family of Masefield's mother, the Parkers, I was fortunate in being able to talk with Miss Kathleen Parker, Masefield's first cousin, during the last months of her life; after her death, her nephew, Mr. Vincent Desborough, kindly came to my assistance, and Major J.M. Smyth supplied additional information. My thanks are also due to the Misses Dorothea and Eileen Holmes, cousins of Constance Masefield, who lent me diaries and material on the Crommelin family.

Among Masefield's friends and acquaintances with whom I got in touch, Miss Kathleen Barmby was especially helpful in briefing me about his final years, and Miss Rose Bruford about his activities in the cause of poetry-speaking, while all of the following contributed interesting recollections concerning various periods and aspects of his life: Miss Helen Binyon, Mrs. Margaret Bottrall, Miss Nancy Brown, Mrs. Catherine Cobb, Professor Nevill Coghill, Mrs. Laura Franklin, Lord Gore-Booth, Mrs. Alma Heavens, Professor Kenneth Muir, Mrs. Diana Oldridge, Dr. Audrey Richards, Mrs. Marie Sharpe, Miss Jean Smith, the late Dame Sibyl Thorndike. Others, who kindly gave me access to Masefield letters in their possession, were Mr. Wilfrid Blunt, Mrs. Mary Challis, Mrs. P. Diamand, Mrs. Gwyneth B. Edmunds, Mr. Stuart Fawkes, Mrs. Basil Gray, Dr. John Kelly, the late Mrs. Lucie Nicoll, Mrs. Leon Quartermaine, Mr. Clive Sansom, Mr. G.T. Sassoon, Mrs. Tamara Talbot Rice, Miss Ethne Thompson, Mr. Laurence Whistler, Mr. Compton Whitworth (great-nephew of Miss Hanford-Flood), and Senator Michael Yeats.

I also want to record my gratitude to those who advised me and provided specialized information of many kinds. Outstanding among these was Mr. D.G. Fletcher Rogers, Secretary of the Conway Club, who not only supplied me with a wealth of detail about Masefield's connections with the *Conway*, but also helped me to discover the facts about his voyage. Lt. Cdr. J. Brooke Smith, R.N., Mr. Max Hamilton, Captain A.R. Hallett, R.N., and Mr. Alex A. Hurst also assisted here. Dr. E. Martin Browne advised me on religious drama, Mr. Rex Doublet on Iquique, Mr. K.L. Perrin and Miss Anne Emerson on Great Comberton, Lady Phipps on Paris during the First World War, Mr. Michael Jamieson on Elizabeth Robins, Miss Alice Stuart on verse-speaking in Scotland, Mr. Compton Whitworth on Woollas Hall, and in other contexts the following were also very helpful: Mr. H.G. Babington Smith, Mr. B. Fairfax Hall, Miss Rosina Kew, Mrs. Kewney, Mr. and Mrs. Rees Lloyd-Jones, Mr. J.R. Naish, Mr. Colin Smythe, Sir James Stephen, Bt., Miss Carina Robins, and Professor Francis West.

I should like to acknowledge the help I received, during my researches in Britain, from a number of libraries and institutions. Foremost was the Bodleian Library, Oxford, where an extensive archive of Masefield letters and other documents is held in the Department of Western Manuscripts (Mr. D.S. Porter and Miss Margaret Crum gave me every assistance). I must also mention King's College Library, Cambridge, where the late Dr. A.N.L. Munby and Mrs. Penelope Bullock were particularly helpful. Elsewhere I received information, access to documents, and other help, from the following: the British Library; the British Red Cross Society; the Library of the Fitzwilliam Museum, Cambridge; the Cambridge University Library; the National Library of Scotland; the National Maritime Museum; Newnham College Library, Cambridge; the Public Record Office; the Libraries of the Universities of Leeds, Liverpool, and London; and the Trinity College Library, Cambridge.

I also wish to put on record my warm gratitude to those who welcomed and helped me at libraries in the United States, notably to Mrs. Lola L. Sladits, Curator of the Berg Collection at the New York Public Library; to Mr. Kenneth A. Lohf of the Butler Library at Columbia University; to Professor F. Warren Roberts, Mr. David Farmer, Mrs. Sally Leach, and Miss Ellen S. Dunlap, at the Humanities Research Center of the University of Texas. Other American libraries which aided my research on this book were the Houghton Library at Harvard University; the Library of Hamilton and Kirkland Colleges, Clinton, N.Y.; the Library of the University of Iowa; the Elmer Holmes Bobst Library of New York University; the Pierpont Morgan Library; the Guy W. Bailey Memorial Library of the University of Vermont; the Beinecke Rare Book and Manuscript Library of Yale University.

The visit I made to the United States in 1976 for the purpose of Masefield research was only possible because of the generous support of Dr. Corliss Lamont. In his role as representative of the family of Masefield's closest American friends, Dr. Lamont took immense trouble to facilitate my work, and to introduce me to those with a special interest in Masefield and his writings. In addition, his hospitality in New York was memorable and I cannot adequately thank him. The visit was also made exceptionally enjoyable by the kindness of Mrs. Gallatin Cobb in New York, and of Professor and Mrs. Walt Rostow in Texas, while among others to whom I am grateful I would like to mention Mrs. Marie Bullock, Mr. and Mrs. B. Haxall, Mr. Russell Edwards, Mr. Ernest Hellman, Miss Helen Mac-Lachlan, Lady Pentland, Dr. Dallas Pratt, and Miss Karen Steele.

For permission to quote from Masefield copyright material I am indebted to The Society of Authors, as the literary representative of the Estate of John Masefield, and also to Masefield's principal British and American publishers, William Heinemann Ltd. and the Macmillan Publishing Co., Inc.

The work took considerably longer than anticipated, and I must express my sincere gratitude to the Arts Council for their grant which enabled me to complete it, and also to my publishers for their patience. During the four years that I worked on the book I was given encouragement (by letter), which counted for a great deal, by three of Masefield's most enthusiastic admirers, Professor Fraser Drew, Mr. Geoffrey Handley-Taylor and Professor G. Wilson Knight. Help and encouragement of other kinds, which I valued greatly, were also given to me by Miss Catharine Carver, Miss Lucile Hyneman, Mr. Andrew Phillips, and Mrs. Stephen Roskill.

1978   Constance Babington Smith

PART I

In Bud

Chapter One

PARADISE

John Masefield claimed, again and again and in all seriousness, that as a child he lived in Paradise. And the earliest years of his life were certainly spent in idyllic surroundings; his family lived in the little town of Ledbury, amongst the meadows and woodlands, orchards and hop-yards, of one of the most beautiful regions of Herefordshire, the countryside associated with Langland, Traherne, and Elizabeth Barrett Browning that lies to the west of the Malvern Hills, not far from the Welsh border.

In later life he set down many of his early memories, describing the places, things, and events that first impressed him, and by means of these we can get to know the joyful little boy he was up until the age of six-and-a-half, when the death of his mother led to the disruption of his home and the uprooting of himself and his brothers and sisters. In addition we have one valuable scrap of evidence, a photograph of 'Jack' (as his family always called him)[1] taken when he was about three. This shows that he was a child of exceptional beauty, with fair curls, and eyes that gazed out at the world with a look of wonder mixed with ruefulness, a child with an air of vulnerable sensitivity.

The Masefield home in Ledbury, where he was born on 1 June 1878, was a commodious Victorian house called the Knapp,[2] a mixture of red brick, black and white half-timbering, and massive gables, which had been recently built on the northern fringes of the town. The day nursery was on the first floor, and there was a window-seat under the big bow-window

---

1 He was baptized John Edward.

2 Although in *Grace Before Ploughing* (1966) J.M. wrote that he had 'some reason to suppose' that he was not born at the Knapp, his birth certificate gives it as his birthplace. The house's name derived from its topographical position (a knapp, in local usage, meant a little hill rather dwarfed by higher ground).

that looked out westwards over a magnificent sweep of country-side. Beyond the garden lay an orchard, a field, a long clump of elms with a great rookery, and then, just beyond the elms, there flowed a reach of the Hereford and Gloucester Canal.[1] Further off, miles of woodland stretched into the distance, though on clear days another land appeared beyond the woods to the west, and Jack was told that this land was Wales, and that those far-away mountains were the Black Hills.

In the nursery at the Knapp the little Masefields played with their toy soldiers, and rocked on the rocking horse which was sometimes supposed to be a ship at sea. Jack was the third in age; his eldest brother Reginald ('Reggie') was four years his senior, Ethel came between them, and Henry ('Harry') was younger than Jack by just a year. Charles was the baby, two years younger still. This nursery was also where Jack first became familiar with story-books. Ballads delighted him and he used to coax his nurse to repeat them. He knew by heart, before he could read, 'John Gilpin', 'The Three Jovial Hunts-men', and 'The House that Jack Built', and as soon as he could read he found other favourites, including one about Dick Whittington and his cat and another about Sir Francis Drake. He also loved Hans Andersen's stories and *Alice in Wonderland*. Yet despite all this eager reading, the supreme joys of Mase-field's childhood came not from books but from real life. 'In those days, as a little child,' he wrote long afterwards, 'I was living in Paradise, and had no need of the arts, that at best are only a shadow of Paradise.'

The Masefield children played constantly in the garden at the Knapp, especially around two great yew trees that had grown together, thereby providing a wonderful green tent and also an adventurous climb up one trunk and down the other. Cricket was also a favourite game. They were seldom taken into Led-bury itself, except on Sunday afternoons for the children's services at the Chapel of Ease in New Street,[2] but they often

---

1 For a time this canal was used for bringing coal to Herefordshire, but it was closed in the early 1880s, superseded by the newly constructed railway.

2 This was a corrugated iron building, known locally as 'the Iron Church', which had been put up by Ledbury parishioners who wished for a place of worship smaller than the vast parish church.

went for country walks, and Masefield's sister Ethel[1] recalled
long afterwards some of the local characters they used to meet:

> Everyone knew us and spoke to us . . . One of our greatest friends
> was Hollins who drove the bus from the town to the station. It was
> one of Jack's earliest ambitions to drive a black and yellow bus like
> Hollins . . . At another time he was to be a huntsman, the whip for
> preference . . . The Kennels were only just beyond the station and
> often the Hounds would be at exercise in the meadow and Hanes the
> kennelman would bring them close up to the fence so that we could
> put our hands through and stroke them. Or we would meet them on
> the road trotting off to a meet or coming home tired and muddy.

The comings and goings of the countryside were absorbing,
but some of the most vivid of Masefield's own memories were
of nature itself. Water, for instance, always had a compelling
attraction for him, wherever and however he found it. The
canal was to him one of the wonders of the world, and the
barges, as they came and went, seemed links with an eternity of
joy: 'barges that were sailing from Paradise to Heaven carrying
hearts of gold and cargoes of wonder, and always, always,
returning a salute, even at a distance.'

On walks by the canal the children were of course accompanied by a grown-up, but Jack did occasionally slip off alone
to favourite spots nearer home, in spite of terrifying warnings
about bulls, and about gipsies who tried to entice and kidnap
little boys. We know from his own assurance that the experiences of childhood which meant most to him were those which
occurred when he was solitary and undistracted amidst the
beauty of nature. Furthermore he gives an account of one of
these experiences which must be quoted in full; it tells of the
birth of creative imagination in him.

All that I looked upon was beautiful, and known by me to be
beautiful, but also known by me to be, as it were, only the shadow
of something much more beautiful, very very near, and almost to
be reached, where there was nothing but beauty itself in ecstasy,
undying, inexhaustible . . .
I was sure that a greater life was near us: in dreams I sometimes
seemed to enter a part of it, and woke with rapture and longing.

1 Later Mrs. Harry Ross (d.1977).

Then, on one wonderful day, when I was a little more than five years old, as I stood looking north, over a clump of honeysuckle in flower, I entered that greater life; and that life entered into me with a delight that I can never forget. I found suddenly that I could imagine imaginary beings complete in every detail, with every faculty and possession, and that these imaginations did what I wished for my delight, with an incredible perfection, in a brightness not of this world.

Something in the very reality of the joy told him that it could not be talked about, it was too intense; but from that day onwards, throughout the year or so that the family remained at the Knapp, he had a secret life of his own, into which he could enter at will, or almost at will, 'a realm of joy beyond all telling'.

2

As we look back with Masefield to his childhood, 'they', the grown-ups upon whom his day-to-day life depended, can be perceived chiefly through the pervasive influence they exerted – he wrote little about their looks. The people the children saw most of, with whom in fact they spent all their days, were of course the servants, especially their beloved nurse Mary Hopkins ('Maymie'), a young countrywoman from their mother's home village in Worcestershire. Their mother they normally saw each day between tea-time and bed at six o'clock. Masefield later admitted that his own memories of his mother were rather dim, and that his thoughts of her were coloured by what he had heard of her after her death. When he was 'a little lad' walking the country roads, people would stop him and tell him of her, so that he came to think of her as an uncommon woman, 'with that talent or power which wins love in the world'. Everybody who knew her, he became sure, must have loved her as he did.

In her early thirties Caroline Masefield – known to her own generation as 'Carrie' – was an attractive though not beautiful woman; she had a tall, slim figure and her auburn hair was piled up in a huge bun. Vivacious and full of energy, she enjoyed dancing as well as walking. Carrie was a conventional Victorian mother, and when the children joined her after tea she played the piano for them, sang lively songs, and told them stories of her own invention; there was one about a fox that lasted, evening after evening, for weeks. She delighted in poetry too, and Masefield later testified that the first poems which ever moved him were two which he had learnt by heart for his mother, Tennyson's 'The Dying Swan' and 'I remember, I remember' by Thomas Hood.

The children's father, Edward Masefield, a solicitor working in the family law firm in Ledbury, and also participating energetically in local affairs, did not see much of his children, though when he did he was gentle and kind. He sometimes took them for walks, and each summer – a great event – he used to take Ethel, Jack, and Harry to Malvern to ride on the donkeys. This meant passing through two longish railway tunnels, and he always lit matches to make the darkness less frightening for the children.

All four of Masefield's grandparents were still alive when he was small, and both his grandfathers were of special importance to him. His father's father lived in Ledbury and the children saw him often. A tall, thin, silent man then in his seventies, George Masefield was in temperament and build, as well as in his capacity for hard work, typical of the men of his family. He was also a great reader of history, a collector of books, and something of an antiquarian. As a young man in the 1830s he had come to Herefordshire from Newport in Shropshire, and had settled in Ledbury which was the home of his wife's family, the Holbrooks. Clever and untiring, he had built up a prosperous business as an attorney, which in due course became Masefield & Sons,[1] and he was also appointed Clerk to the Magistrates, a position he held for nearly fifty years. In the meantime he took and extended a Holbrook house adjoining the parish church, called the Priory, and thenceforth he lived there in a style befitting his position as a leading figure in the little market town.

Masefield had six uncles and aunts on his father's side, but only two of them, Uncle William (the eldest) and Uncle Basil (the youngest) lived in Ledbury when he was a child.[2] Uncle

---

1 His two eldest sons, William and Edward (J.M.'s father) joined him in the firm.
2 J.M.'s uncle Briscoe Masefield, a Cambridge graduate, had become a master at Eastbourne College, and his uncle Robert Masefield was in business in London. His father's two sisters both died before he was three years old, Henrietta Heane in 1880 and Frances Masefield in 1881.

Basil, a bachelor, suffered acutely from asthma and had to live the life of a semi-invalid; Uncle William, taciturn and dedicated to his work, was married, and his wife Kate was the children's only aunt who lived in Ledbury and was part of their lives. The daughter of a clerical family, Kate Masefield devoted herself to charitable deeds, such as weekly visits to the workhouse, and since she was also (as an admirer of Charles Kingsley) a believer in the ideals of muscular Christianity, she heartily despised intellectual interests. The children used to look forward to visiting her because she had a little dairy farm, and she allowed them to collect the eggs and watch her Alderney cows being milked.

When Jack was a child – while his mother was still alive – he was often taken to visit his maternal grandparents who lived about fifteen miles away beyond the Malverns, and their home was for him, like the Ledbury of his earliest years, part of the paradise of his childhood. His grandfather, the Revd. Charles Hubert Parker, had long been rector of Great Comberton, a quiet village of black and white thatched cottages set amidst the plum orchards and meadows at the foot of Bredon Hill, a few fields away from the River Avon. The old rector reigned benevolently over the villagers; he had spent the greater part of his private means on helping to restore the church, build new cottages, and maintain the schoolhouse: a parishioner once described him as 'Our King, our Father and our Priest'. In his distant youth, as an Oxford undergraduate, he had been a keen amateur artist, with a gift for exquisite little pen-and-ink drawings of churches and other ancient buildings, but in later life he devoted himself entirely to his parish, and when he died at the age of eighty-three (Jack was then five) he had ministered to the people of Great Comberton for a total of fifty-seven years.

Jack's mother was by far the youngest of a family of eight; her brothers and sisters might almost have belonged to an older generation. Except for 'Aunt Adelaide', who lived at Great Comberton, they are hardly mentioned in Masefield's reminiscences. But the influence of his Parker grandfather meant very much to him. In the country rectory of the 1880s the daily rhythm of family prayers, grace before meals, and bedside prayers at night, was taken utterly for granted, as well as the weekly rhythm of church-going. The Bible too; and although there is no specific mention of Bible-reading in Masefield's memories, the extent to which he used biblical language and allusions in his writings indicates that it first began to enter his consciousness at an early age.

3

A calamity with far-reaching repercussions – the first of a series of calamities – shattered the calm existence of the Masefield family when Jack was six and a half. On 20 January 1885 his mother died. A few weeks earlier she had given birth to a sixth child, Norah; she had then succumbed to severe bronchitis and finally to double pneumonia.[1]

The next disaster, which from the viewpoint of Jack and the others must have seemed comparable to a further bereavement, followed soon after this: their nurse Maymie had to leave to take care of her own mother. So when the children, who had been sent to stay with Aunt Kate when their mother was dying, came back to the Knapp and to their father, with their former nursery-maid Minnie[2] in Maymie's place, they came to a strangely unfamiliar life, especially because they found that a new arrival, a governess called Mrs. Broers, had been put in charge of the household. Mrs. Broers was a large and somewhat loud young woman and the children detested her; Masefield later referred to her repeatedly as 'the vulgar woman'.[3]

Then in the following spring, just over a year after Carrie Masefield's death, further sudden distresses, one after another, hit the family, resulting in upheavals for them all. In March 1886 both of Jack's Masefield grandparents died, and at about the same time the whole family suffered an overwhelming blow in connection with their financial prospects, which had hitherto

[1] J.M. later came to suspect that an accident in which his mother was involved shortly before Norah's birth contributed to her fatal illness (she had come by carriage, with other members of the family, to a meet of the local hunt; one of the horses took fright and shied and the carriage tipped over). The accident was not however reported in the local press, and there is no conclusive evidence that anyone was hurt.

[2] Minnie's full name was Minnie May Low, and J.M.'s poem 'Minnie Maylow's Story' (1931) was based upon a story she used to tell to the Masefield children.

[3] The odious governess in J.M.'s *The Midnight Folk* (1927) is an obvious caricature of her.

seemed excellent; Masefield himself later wrote that his grandfather had 'speculated wildly . . . His wealth did not exist.' For
Jack's father, with his six children, this was a catastrophe. And
in the family it later came to be assumed that the shock of
finding himself suddenly poor, combined with the prolonged
anguish after his wife's death, was what caused, at this time, an
ominous decline in Edward Masefield's health.

When Jack was eight, soon after his grandfather died, the
family at the Knapp moved to the Priory. The hated Mrs.
Broers came with them and continued to make life a misery for
her charges. 'I don't think she was ever kind to us', Masefield
later wrote, 'and we were little beasts to her. I was the worst of
them. I stabbed her once with a fork in the arm.' Yet the uprooting from the Knapp brought many compensations, and
despite the presence of 'the vulgar woman', the Priory was soon
to be the setting for much boyhood joy. 'Often I thank God for
letting me grow up in such a place,' Masefield wrote many
years later, 'I loved my life there.' For an imaginative child the
house was a place of high romance, though sometimes also of
terror. It was 'a rambling pretty house in a great garden . . . a
very, very, old house, full of passages, corridors, strange rooms,
strange noises . . . a strange, dark, uncanny place, with rooms
never opened, and cupboards and secret chambers.'[1]

At the Knapp, with its wide views over the countryside,
Ledbury itself had seemed remote. Now, at the Priory, the doings
of the town were an integral part of daily life. For although the
house was well shut away it was close to the centre of the town,
and within hearing of much that went on. Jack was given a
room on the top floor, which he shared with his brother Harry,
and since its little windows looked out towards the high street,
the two boys were able to enjoy the excitement of any distur-
bances which occurred after bedtime. Sometimes the great bell
which was the town's fire alarm would start clanging, and they
would hear the shouting and commotion as the engines were
rushed out and driven off. Another kind of pandemonium
burst out every now and again during the hunting season. When
at the end of a long day the hunt had to pass through the town

---

1 In fact the house had a core dating from the seventeenth-century or perhaps
earlier, but its character had been much altered by the red-brick extensions, in
Gothic style, which J.M.'s grandfather had added.

on the way back to the kennels all the dogs of Ledbury – and there were hundreds of them – used to set up a frantic chorus of barking.

For the first eighteen months at the Priory Jack's formal education consisted of the lessons which he shared every morning with Ethel and Harry in the schoolroom, and it was there that Mrs. Broers introduced him to English history, geography, arithmetic, and French. He also had to learn to spell 'long lists of very hard words', and to explain their meaning. But elsewhere at the Priory he discovered for himself a more alluring kind of learning, which was severely frowned upon by the grown-ups. Several rooms on the ground floor contained the many hundreds of books which had formed his grandfather's library, and he found that these included a wealth of bound volumes of illustrated periodicals with reports of recent events. He also came upon stacks of magazines full of serial stories, and soon became a 'swift, eager, gluttonous reader' of exciting fiction (he delighted especially in the tales of Red Indians by Thomas Mayne Reid). Often he slipped away with his finds to a favourite hiding-place, under the bed in a spare room that was seldom used, so as to savour the thrillers in peace.

Jack's avid reading bore rich fruit. He discovered that he could catch the interest of his two younger brothers by retelling the stories he had read. And when he was alone, stories of his own were always going on in his head; he found delight in imagining different landscapes, 'deserts, forests, crags, volcanoes, snowy peaks, cataracts', and in peopling these scenes with appropriate characters. But none of this, alas, was the secret world of beauty which had been revealed to him in the garden at the Knapp when the honeysuckle was in bloom. To Jack's bewilderment, and to his deep sorrow, he had lost – since his mother's death – the ability to enter into it.

Sometimes he wandered off alone to the churchyard beyond the garden, and gazed up at the church's majestic spire with wistful, sombre thoughts. What was religion all about? A note of yearning and regret at the lack of any spiritual guidance occurs again and again in Masefield's boyhood reminiscences – surely an indictment of the 'religious education' then meted out to children of his class. There are also repeated references to an obsession which tortured his mind, the conviction that he was damned. As a child, when his mother was alive, he had certainly believed in Heaven, for after her death he prayed to God to take him to her in Heaven, even though he could not sing (he thought one could go to Heaven only if one could sing). But as a boy he believed primarily in Hell. Each Sunday, when after learning the collect parrot-fashion he accompanied the party from the Priory to morning service in the parish church, he was confronted by a scaring reminder of everlasting torment. In the family pew his place was almost opposite a stone pillar on which was carved the startled, tortured face of a man in Hell. Each Sunday, therefore, throughout the long tedium of matins, Jack's thoughts were dragged back, again and again, to the anguishing fate that he knew awaited him in the world to come.

4

Looking out towards the Malverns from a shelf on the steep slopes of Bredon Hill in southern Worcestershire stands Woollas Hall, a tall, gabled Jacobean manor of grey Cotswold stone. Surrounded by splendid trees, it was always associated, in Masefield's memory, with the cooing of innumerable wood doves and the cawing of rooks. As a boy he visited Woollas almost every summer, and it stood for all the joys he loved best; beauty, mystery, adventure – and an atmosphere of affection. Woollas renewed for him each year the paradise of his childhood, especially because it had links with his mother.

The house belonged to the family of his godmother, Ann ('Annie') Hanford-Flood, who had been his mother's dear friend since girlhood; the two were almost the same age, and Woollas was only a short walk from Great Comberton. 'Miss Flood', as Jack always knew her, was the eldest daughter of a family of Irish Protestant gentry, the Floods, and with her father William Hanford-Flood[1] (and all his household) she came to Woollas every summer from Kilkenny. When Miss Flood was twenty-four her mother had died and her father did not re-marry, so for the next seventeen years, until his death in 1892, she assumed the responsibilities of eldest daughter at home. It was during this time that Jack was born, and that Carrie

---

[1] He had taken the additional name of Hanford in the mid-nineteenth century when his wife, born a Hanford, inherited Woollas and its lands.

Masefield died. Thenceforward, whenever Miss Flood was at Woollas, she made a point of keeping in touch with her godson.

Jack's brothers and sisters, who had mere relatives for god-parents, envied him Miss Flood, who seemed to them 'aloof, unknown, surprising, a figure of romance'. Miss Flood was, in fact, an ideal godmother for a boy of Masefield's temperament. Although she was serious in character, and unprepossessing in looks – she was very tall, with a long, rather heavy face – she had Irish charm and a way with children. She understood Jack, encouraged him, and laughed at him when he needed it. She also opened up new perspectives, for she was a woman of culture, with a love for Italy and a special interest in archaeology. Although she and her godson did not very often meet, her influence was potent in shaping his ideas and tastes.

Jack's first visit to Woollas was for a day during the summer of 1885, six months after his mother died. He was put into the train at Ledbury all by himself, under the care of the guard, with a pink aster in his buttonhole for identification; Miss Flood was to meet him at Worcester station. Then the following summer he and Ethel were invited to go over together, and in 1887, when Jack was nine, they stayed at Woollas for a whole week. That visit remained very vividly in Ethel's memory; more than fifty years later she liked to recall the drives in an Irish jaunting-car, the boating expeditions on the Avon, the picnicking on Bredon Hill, and the meetings with cousins and friends of their mother's.

Further visits to Woollas took place up until the time when Jack was thirteen;[1] in his memory the delights of the place merged into timelessness. At Woollas he was never scolded for spending so much time delving into books; the library, though small, contained old books that enthralled him, such as local histories and tales of ghosts and the macabre. He could satisfy to the full his appetite for stories of spectres and hauntings and witches, though when darkness came he wished he had abstained, and hid quaking under the bedclothes. The fearful had an irresistible fascination for him. On one of his earliest visits he was peering round the Great Hall when suddenly he

---

[1] In 1892 Woollas passed to Miss Flood's eldest brother, who never took up residence there, so the house was let.

saw that close to him was a terrifying 'relic'; fixed on to the panelling just below the ministrels' gallery was an immense bull's head, 'black, splendid and very terrible'. When he asked what it was, Miss Flood told him that it was one of the Black Bulls of Bredon, which in the past had roved the hill but were now extinct. Jack, already petrified of bulls, derived a strange relish from the terror that the huge head awoke in him.[1]

One of his delights at Woollas was wandering alone over the hillside above the house, with its curious hummocks and precipitous woods, and he was continually making exciting discoveries. After learning, for instance, from one of the volumes of local history, that somewhere near Woollas there had long ago been a small chapel or church, built in the time of Henry III and dedicated to St. Catherine, he set off armed with clues from Miss Flood to search for the site. And he succeeded in finding a place where he felt sure the chapel must once have stood.

But best of all was the wonderful old house itself, with its gallery and chapel and priests' holes (the Hanfords had for generations been Catholic) and its panelled rooms where, as Ethel later put it, 'you crept round tapping gently to see if they sounded hollow, and where you longed and feared to come upon the hidden spring which would open a door and reveal a winding stair, or a chest full of gold and jewels, or perhaps a skeleton bound in chains.'[2]

5

In March 1888, when he was almost ten, Masefield for the first time put verses on to paper; he wrote a poem about a pony called Gipsy, and another about a Red Indian (earlier than this he had often made up 'poems' in his head, but he had not written them down). Neither of these first two experiments in verse has survived, but the date when they were written gives us a clue as to the frame of mind that gave rise to them. 1888

---

1 A photograph of the Great Hall at Woollas, more or less as it was in Miss Flood's time, shows the gigantic head in question: the horns resemble those of Highland cattle.

2 Much in J.M.'s *The Midnight Folk* (1927) echoes his memories of Woollas, although some of the settings resemble the older parts of the Priory.

was for Jack a year of misery. In January he had become a boarder at Warwick School, an old foundation of the grammar school type, which during the previous decade had been rebuilt and reorganized on the model of the great public schools. 'I was wretched at first,' Masefield wrote looking back to this time. 'I was too young.'

And they found that I wrote poetry. I tried to kill myself once by eating laurel leaves but only gave myself a horrible headache. Once I ran away, and was brought back by a policeman and flogged . . .

Jack's school life was however transformed when in 1889 a Junior House was opened for the smaller boys, 'so that they might be under a milder regime by themselves'. He greatly enjoyed the remainder of his time at Warwick, where he stayed until he was twelve, for he made friends easily, and thrived on the cricket, the gymnastics, and the swimming. Summing up his memories of Warwick School he later wrote 'It was a good school, the masters were a fine lot, and the place had a high tone.'

The next poetry that Jack wrote was probably composed at the Priory when he was about twelve, and it included some fragments in imitation of Sir Walter Scott, a birthday poem to one of his brothers, a poem about a horse, and a satire on a clergyman.[1] Also at the Priory, during his holidays from Warwick, Jack started writing his first 'book'. But it was not, as one might have expected, an adventure story. It was a business-like record of a hobby which at the time was of obsessive interest to the four younger Masefield children. They had a craze for pet guinea-pigs, and between them they formed a little 'society' called the Guinea Pig Association. Jack, as honorary secretary, maintained a meticulous stud book, giving the animals' names, markings and appearance, details of when they were bought and sold, and their performances in the annual 'guinea-pig races'. At one time he also produced a mock newspaper, *The Guinea Pig Free Press*, in imitation of the local weekly, the *Ledbury Free Press*; it is an amusing reflection of the young Masefields' slightly cynical attitude towards the doings of their elders.

---

[1] None of these have survived.

During the Christmas holidays of 1889, at the time when Jack was settling down happily at Warwick, renewed insecurity and anxiety burst upon him and upon all the family at the Priory. His father had broken down completely. During the previous few years Edward Masefield had been able, although in poor health, to keep on with his work as a solicitor and had also remained for a time prominent in Ledbury affairs. But by the end of 1889 his mind had become so gravely unbalanced that he could not be left unattended. At the beginning of 1890 William Masefield, as the family's senior member, made the decision that his brother could no longer be allowed to live at home, and he was admitted to a Gloucester hospital (where he died in the following year at the age of forty-nine). William Masefield now became administrator of his estate, and he and his wife made the courageous decision to take on the guardianship of the six children, no light undertaking when they had no previous experience of managing a family (their only child had died as an infant). Full credit must here be given to Kate Masefield, especially as she had never liked the children's mother. Not everyone would have made such a gesture of unselfishness and loyalty, even though there was no one else in the immediate family to step in and take charge.

The William Masefields' first move was to give up their own house and establish themselves at the Priory. Mrs. Broers was dismissed, and shortly afterwards Jack was taken away from Warwick School – much to his disgust – as it was considered too expensive; the family finances were still very strained. For a time he found himself back at the Priory under a new governess, Miss MacFarlane, along with the younger members of the family. But it was a changed Priory, for Aunt Kate had rearranged everything. For Jack the most tragic change was that his grandfather's books had vanished. And Aunt Kate's personality was not conducive to a happy atmosphere. Her sense of duty, in which she took much pride, was not matched by an ability to win the confidence or love of her young nephews and nieces. Admittedly 'the Aunt' had a motherly side – she doted on little Charles and baby Norah – but to the elder children when they came home during the school holidays she was often brutally scathing, especially so to Jack, whose addiction to books roused her scorn.

The question of Jack's future was by now becoming an urgent one, and it was Aunt Kate who first suggested that he should be trained to go to sea, with the idea that it would toughen him up. The navy would have been too expensive, so the merchant marine was indicated. But what did he himself want to be? What did he want to do? He could not be sure. He longed to write stories, but he also longed to paint them in colours or to carve them in stone. But all these boyish aspirations met with crushing adult disapproval. For Aunt Kate, especially, the arts as well as books were a waste of time, and worse still they opened the door to an immoral life.

The turning-point, so far as Jack's future was concerned, came during the first holidays after his father had gone away. Jack and some of the others were temporarily banished from the Priory, under the care of a holiday governess called Miss Barnsdale, the daughter of a Weymouth parson, who utterly won their hearts. Few women, Masefield wrote of her later, 'could more swiftly endear herself to a group of children all feeling lost. She made it clear to them all that she liked them and would stand by them.' And it was the happy influence of Miss Barnsdale that reconciled Jack to Aunt Kate's plans for his future. For a brother of hers had been a cadet in the school-ship H.M.S. *Conway*, and from him she had gained a rosy idea of the life there. So her account of a *Conway* boy's lot was an inspiring one. Thus the initial impetus which attracted Masefield towards the sea sprang from that 'admirable woman', that 'priceless joy', Miss Barnsdale, one of the few women to show him real kindness in his boyhood.

Chapter Two

DOWN TO THE SEA

I

In the autumn of 1891, when Masefield was thirteen, he joined the school-ship H.M.S. *Conway*,[1] which was then moored in the Mersey (like other training ships she remained at her moorings and did not go to sea).[2] When he arrived at Liverpool he had only the sketchiest idea of what lay ahead, based chiefly on an article in the *Boys' Own Paper*, the ship's prospectus, and Miss Barnsdale's accounts of her brother's time on board. In addition someone had told him that the ship's company might be rather rough and ready, which he took to mean that he would be bullied. But he had been reassured by the cheeriness of a former Warwick acquaintance who had been in the *Conway* for over a year. 'She is all right,' he had written. 'On Saturdays we have no school, but scrub the decks, which is fine work. Mind you bring back plenty of tuck, as it comes in useful on board.'

Of ships and their ways Jack had no inkling. The only vessels he had hitherto set eyes on were barges on the canal and river craft on the Avon. His home, his former school, the places he visited in the holidays, had all been distant from the coast. And among the books which had taken his fancy only a few were sea stories. So it is hardly surprising that he was staggered – overawed – by his first sight of Liverpool, then the leading

---

1 The ship that J.M. joined on 24 September 1891 was an old wooden-wall ship of the line, H.M.S. *Nile*. She was one of the sailing vessels which were converted into school-ships in the mid-nineteenth century to provide initial training, for an average of two years, and also a certain amount of general education, for boys who hoped to become officers in the merchant service. Prior to this, many ships' officers, who had gone to sea as apprentices at thirteen or younger, had received hardly any formal education.

2 The *Conway* (the third training ship of that name) remained on station in the Mersey until 1940 when she was moved to the Menai Straits. In 1953 she was wrecked, while under tow for refit (the wreck was destroyed by fire in 1956), and the training school was then transferred to shore quarters where it continued until 1974.

seaport of the world's leading maritime nation, a port crammed with sturdy new steamships as well as sailing ships of breathtaking beauty. Masefield's first glimpse of a splendid sailing ship, the four-masted barque the *Wanderer*, was a sight that branded itself on his memory.[1]

The autumn half had started a fortnight before he arrived (he had been kept away by quarantine for chicken-pox) so he was plunged into the hurly-burly of shipboard life with hardly a chance to look round. Like all 'new chums' (as the first-term boys were called) he was gauche and self-conscious in his brandnew uniform; he was also very earnest and eager to do the right thing. The *Conway* boys, most of them the sons of officers in the merchant service, or of professional men or clergy, numbered about 150, and their time 'at school' was divided between classes under teachers who came on board each day, and practical instruction from seamen of long experience in sail. (Although at this time the transition from sail to steam was far advanced, a grounding in sailing-ship methods, and indeed apprenticeship in sail, was still considered the best preparation for a sea-going career.)

In class, Jack was put into the lowest place, because he had never done any navigation or nautical astronomy. On deck he belonged to a station as well as to a 'top',[2] responsible for sharing in the work of both, and he was also a member of a mess, with the obligations of the mess to fulfil. All this was far from easy when the shouted words of command meant nothing to him. Looking back to this time Masefield later described, in his book *New Chum*, how a shrill whistle would blow and someone would shout 'yow, yow', or 'yow, YOW', or 'YOW, yow-yow'. How was he to know what 'yow' meant? How was he to yow, unless he could see his shipmates yowing? As the term progressed he found himself being cursed rather less often, but he knew that he was being watched all the time and assessed as 'good' or 'bad'. 'GOOD: He does his stanchions and brass-work well. He sweeps honestly, and doesn't try to hide the dust in odd corners. He isn't as hopeless with his hammock as he was. We don't have

1 In *The Wanderer of Liverpool* (1930) J.M. related the story of this ship in prose and verse.
2 One of the ship's divisions.

to tell him again and again.' But then 'BAD: He is a rotten fresh-water pumper. He is no good on the bilge pump. He lost us half our butter, that time. He doesn't even know the tucks of an eye-splice, yet.'

Amidst the turmoil of his first few weeks on board Jack found one firm consolation to hold on to. In *New Chum* Masefield has described his hero-worship for a senior boy, H.B. Meiklejohn, who was very kind to him, and who also had a taste for ghost stories; he invited Jack – to his amazement and joy – to 'spin some ghost yarns' for him. Towards the end of his first term, too, another senior boy kindled his adoration. One Sunday after-noon, the appointed time for writing letters and reading or (for those with the talent – and Jack was one of them) for making sketches and drawings of ships in albums known as 'setting-in books',[1] the cadet who was petty officer of the deck[2] happened to take the desk next to him. Jack noticed that the title of one of his books was *Meteorology*, and thinking it must be about shooting stars and comets he shyly asked if he could look at it. For the younger boy this led on to a knowledge of clouds and weather which was a delight to him all his life.

Also during his time as a *Conway* cadet Jack learnt to row and to dive. Swimming from the ship was not allowed as the tides were too strong and the currents too dangerous, but there were frequent visits to the salt-water baths in Liverpool, and for all the boys this was bliss. Rowing was of course a constant part of life as well as the most popular of sports. The races between the cutter crews were desperate contests, and the annual boat race between *Conway* boys and boys from the rival training ship on the Thames, H.M.S. *Worcester*, was the climax of the sporting year.

2

Jack's second year in the *Conway* was a time of happiness for him. He had by now mastered the arts of shipboard life, and in class, under a sympathetic master, he was able to turn his mind

---

1 J.M.'s lifelong hobby of drawing and painting sailing-ships dates from this time. Some of his first efforts were pen-and-ink sketches in the 'annals' of the Guinea Pig Association (see p. 15 above).
2 Probably G.G. Lihou.

to subjects that really interested him such as English and history. For a while he assisted in the ship's library,[1] and in every spare moment he picked up a book. After *Treasure Island* he discovered Marryat, Herman Melville, and Mark Twain, and he soon became imbued with an intensely romantic attitude towards the sea and ships. Poetry was crowded out except during the holidays (at the Priory he took a great fancy to Macaulay's *Lays of Ancient Rome* and tried his hand at imitations of them).

Meantime by chance he had come into personal touch with a gifted story-teller. He had been put into a seamanship class under an instructor called 'Wally' Blair, who was 'a yarn-spinner of the old dog-watch kind'.[2] Wally awoke in him afresh a wistful ambition to be a teller of stories, although while still in the *Conway*, caught up in her non-stop round, he found that tales of adventure no longer came welling up within him, and if he was asked to yarn he would retell some old serial story. In his final summer as a cadet, however, he received an unexpected and very welcome piece of encouragement: he won an essay prize, a splendid telescope, for 'Proficiency in Writing, Spelling and Composition'. Perhaps, after all, he would one day be a writer.

In a photograph taken at the Priory, showing him posed with the telescope to his eye, he looks happy and eager. With his lanky good looks and gentle demeanour, his straight fair hair cut in a fringe across the brow, he was obviously an attractive boy, and it is not surprising that he was popular with his young cousins and their friends when they went skating at Eastnor in the Christmas holidays or made merry at the Ledbury dances (in the *Conway* there were hilarious dancing classes each autumn, when a dancing master with a little fiddle taught the boys to waltz and polka).

But Jack's happy state of mind was not merely a matter of youthful exuberance. We know that a serious side was developing in him when he was fifteen. Long afterwards Masefield testified that in his youth he had made a habit of a form of

---

1 In 1938, when J.M. opened a new library in Ledbury, he mentioned that as a boy in a training ship he had once held the position of 'fifth librarian'. One of his main tasks, he said, was to see that no one bathed from the library windows.

2 J.M. included several of Wally Blair's stories in *A Mainsail Haul* (1905).

meditation, 'the getting of tranquillity' as he called it, and he claimed that he originally began to practise it during his final year in the *Conway* – last thing at night, when he had turned in to his hammock. When he was tired out he did not attempt the process, and sometimes it did not work, but when it did it calmed and cheered him:

The process was very simple. I read a page of some thoughtful prose, then, shutting my eyes, I repeated to myself a couple of poems, and then sang to myself with a mental voice, one, two, three, or even four songs. Usually, before I reached the fourth, I had attained a mental quiet, in which I could sort out the experience of the day, annul its trouble as illusion and see its good as jolly.

Sometimes too, he said, he repeated the process in the early morning before turning out, 'so as to start the day with a quiet mind'.

Jack left the *Conway* in March 1894 – he was not quite sixteen – by which time he had been a senior petty officer for more than a term: in other words he had been recognized as a boy who could take responsibility, one of the leaders in his age group. He was not in any way a shining star; there was no question of his being nominated for the Royal Navy, though he was, in fact, among the twenty cadets of his year who after leaving the *Conway* were appointed midshipmen in the Royal Naval Reserve. But the conventional phrases inscribed on the *Conway* certificate that was awarded to him at the end of his time, 'Conduct very good. Ability good', show that he was rated well above average.

The reason why he stayed on for an extra six months after the two years of the normal training period was almost certainly because in his final examination, which he took in the summer of 1893 (when he won the essay prize, as well as a prize for proficiency in history), his mathematics was not yet up to the standard required for a *Conway* certificate. His marks for algebra, trigonometry, arithmetic, and physics were in each case less than 25 per cent; algebra was his worst subject with only seven marks out of a possible hundred (his papers on compass deviation, geography, practical navigation, and nautical astronomy were much better, however, and his seamanship, both theoretical and practical, was above average). But the additional time in the *Conway* was no disadvantage as far as the next stage of his nautical experience was concerned; Jack was, even so, younger than most of the 'men'[1] who in the spring of 1894 were taken on as apprentices by the sailing-ship companies.

3

The *Gilcruix*, a great four-masted barque belonging to the White Star Line,[2] lay in dock at Cardiff in April 1894, making ready for a voyage to Iquique, the principal nitrate port of Chile, with a cargo of 'patent fuel', blocks of compressed coal-dust. Before the Panama Canal and before radio this meant facing Cape Horn and being out of touch with land for at least three months.

Masefield was one of six apprentices in a crew of thirty-three,[3] and one of his duties was to record in a journal the events of each day. This he did conscientiously until the *Gilcruix* reached Cape Horn, and fortunately the journal has survived. So we can well picture the first part of the voyage, which for him consisted of hard work in hard conditions, a few excitements, many glimpses of the strange and beautiful, and also some days of real misery.

On 25 April the *Gilcruix* set sail, and no sooner was she at sea than Jack discovered, to his utter dismay, that he was a bad sailor: 'Was sick while passing Bull Point and felt very ill indeed until I went below about 9 p.m. Coming on deck at 12 p.m. I took the poop watch and was very sick all the watch. Captain and the mate were very kind.' For two days he felt as if he 'would like to die', but after that he got his sea legs, and thenceforth, day by day, he shared in the work of the ship, until later in the voyage (17 May) when the south-east trade winds began to freshen. Then he was again very sick – 'Was in my bunk all the night' – and yet again, on 11 June, 'the motion of the ship' made him seasick; but on this last occasion there may

1 All *Conway* cadets, even new chums, were referred to as 'men' not 'boys'.

2 The *Gilcruix* was an iron ship of 2,239 tons net, built in 1886 by the Whitehaven Shipbuilding Company. She was sold in 1895 to Knohr and Burchard of Hamburg and renamed *Barmbek*.

3 It has often been stated that J.M. served his time at sea 'before the mast'. This is not correct; as an apprentice, not a seaman, his berth was in the half-deck not the forecastle.

have been an additional reason, for he had recently partaken of shark for breakfast: 'Nice eating only rather strong and fishy.' In addition to his acute bouts of nausea there was one other occasion when Jack was overcome by illness. On 22 May, after he had been chipping rust in the heat of the day, he got 'a slight touch of the sun' which laid him out for forty-eight hours.

But in spite of all these attacks he was evidently able, most of the time, to play his full part in the labours that he shared with the two other apprentices on his watch, lads called Hely and Shaw who were both, like himself, *Conway* 'first voyagers'. Apart from the routine watch-keeping their work was largely concerned with the maintenance of the ship: at deck level they scrubbed paintwork with sand and canvas, washed down the decks, and stowed away sails that were not in use. Jack got to know Hely and Shaw exceedingly well, and also the apprentices on the other watch, Christopher[1] and Connorton (two further *Conway* men) and Hurst (a nineteen-year-old 'third voyager'). The half-deck, or apprentices' berth – a cramped and stifling deck-house, more like a kennel than a cabin – was home for all six of them throughout the voyage; there they slept, ate, and spent their time off-duty.[2]

The occasional encounters with other ships were important events during the voyage, and two of these made a special impression on Jack. In the South Atlantic, when a large steamer, the *Magdalena* – 'a fine looking steamer bound to Monte Video' – sighted the *Gilcruix*, she altered her course, bore down on the sailing-ship and spoke to her. 'The passengers were rather excited, waving handkerchiefs and kissing their hands while cooks and stewards waved their aprons.' Also in the South Atlantic, one day at dawn, the *Gilcruix* passed another four-masted barque, the *Glaucus* of Glasgow, and the loveliness of the other ship, the 'swaying delicate clipper' (as Masefield later called her) was something he could not forget.

---

1 George Christopher was J.M.'s special friend among the *Gilcruix* apprentices.

2 Six years after the voyage J.M. used his journal as the basis for some chapters of 'autobiography' (which have remained unpublished) using fictitious names. There is an interesting contrast between the impersonal tone of the journal and the colourfulness of the 'autobiography', which tells of brutality and non-stop blasphemy, revolting food, and feuds among the apprentices, who apparently regarded J.M. as 'an odd fish', 'a bit uncongenial' and 'a damned innocent'.

In the journal there are several mentions of natural pheno-
mena of strange beauty. On watch one night, when there was a
very fine moon shining and a slight squall had just passed over
the ship, Jack witnessed – to his wondering amazement – a
nocturnal rainbow. And on another night watch he noticed
'the great phosphorescence of the water': 'a cloud of spray
coming over the bows . . . looked like a shower of sparks'. He
also made a note whenever unfamiliar fish or birds came in
view: he saw 'about a hundred porpoises leaping out of the
water in gangs' and 'a very large flight of flying fish . . . a
beautiful sight, each fish shining like silver in the sun's rays'.
By moonlight he saw 'a lot of black fish (grampus)' which leapt
half out of the water when they came up to breathe, and made
a peculiar snorting splashing noise. And then far to the south
he heard some whales spouting quite close to the ship, and also
a penguin laughing in the night, 'the laugh is a queer sound,
something between a cough and a hen cackling'.

During the early part of the voyage the winds had been
favourable and the going easy; the *Gilcruix* had sped south-
westwards, leaving Madeira about a hundred miles to the east.
Indeed there was no adverse weather until she was south of Rio
de Janeiro; but then she and her crew had to undergo a short
but sharp test of endurance. 'We were now enjoying genuine
River Plate Squalls,' Jack wrote in the journal on 13 June.
'Blew very hard indeed in the morning watch. Ship under lower
topsails and reefed foresail rolling heavily.' A less laconic
account of a 'genuine River Plate Squall' was later given by
Masefield in one of his reminiscences of the sea:

To windward the sea was blotted in a squall. The line of the horizon
was masked in a grey film. The glory of the sea had given place to
greyness and grimness. Her beauty had become savage. The music
of the wind had changed to a howl as of hounds . . . 'Up there, you
boys, and make the royals fast'.[1] My royal was the mizen-royal, a rag
of a sail among the clouds, a great grey rag, which was leaping and
slatting a hundred and sixty feet above me. The wind beat me down
against the shrouds, it banged me and beat me, and blew the tears
from my eyes.

In the cross-trees I learned what wind was. It came roaring past

---

[1] The royals are the sails at the very top of the masts.

with a fervour and a fury which struck me breathless. I could only look aloft to the yard I was bound for and heave my panting body up the rigging. And there was the mizen-royal. There was the sail I had come to furl. And a wonder of a sight it was. It was blowing and bellying in the wind, and leaping around 'like a drunken colt', and flying over the yard, thrashing and flogging. It was roaring like a bull with its slatting and thrashing. The royal mast was bending to the strain of it. To my eyes it was buckling like a piece of whalebone.

I lay out on the yard, and the sail hit me in the face and knocked my cap away. It beat me and banged me, and blew from my hands. The wind pinned me flat against the yard, and seemed to be blowing all my clothes to shreds. I felt like a king, like an emperor. I shouted aloud with the joy of that 'rastle' with the sail.

Forward of me was the main mast, with another lad fighting another royal; and beyond him was yet another, whose sail seemed tied in knots. Below me was the ship, a leaping mad thing, with little silly figures, all heads and shoulders, pulling silly strings along the deck. There was the sea, sheer under me, and it looked grey and grim, and streaked with the white of our smother.

Thus the 'roaring forties'. And then after them the 'Cape Horn calm'. On 29 June Jack wrote in his journal 'It was a dead calm without a ripple on the water but a long oily swell,' and he then added: 'Everybody remarked on the wonderful fairness of the weather for Cape Horn.' But next day, in the icy first watch, came the frantic call which everyone knew would come: 'All hands on deck!'[1]

> It was all wallop of sails and startled calling.
> 'Let fly!' 'Let go!' 'Clew up!' and 'Let go all!'
> 'Now up and make them fast!' 'Here, give us a haul!'
> 'Now up and stow them! Quick! By God! we're done!'
> . . . .
> Ten men in all, to get this mast of theirs
> Snugged to the gale in time. 'Up! dam you, run!' . . .
> Fierce clamberers, some in oilskins, some in rags . . .
>
> They reached the crojick yard, which buckled, buckled
> Like a thin whalebone to the topsail's strain.
> They laid upon the yard and heaved and knuckled,
> Pounding the sail, which jangled and leapt again.
> It was quite hard with ice, its rope like chain,

---

1 After 30 June there are no more entries in the journal.

Its strength like seven devils; it shook the mast
They cursed and toiled and froze . . .
Water and sky were devils' brews which boiled,
Boiled, shrieked, and glowered; but the ship was saved,
Snugged safely down, though fourteen sails were split.

In *Dauber*, Masefield's epic of the sea, he thus described the start of the Cape Horn ordeal, that long drawn out westward battle with the elements at their fiercest. *Dauber* is not autobiographical in form, but the experiences of the doomed young painter mirror those of every Cape Horn first voyager.

        . . . below
He caught one giddy glimpsing of the deck
Filled with white water, as though heaped with snow.
        . . . soul, body, brain,
Knew nothing but the wind, the cold, the pain. . .

A cold sweat glued the shirt upon his back.
The yard was shaking . . .
He felt that he would fall; he clutched, he bent,
Clammy with natural terror to the shoes . . .
Darkness came down – half darkness – in a whirl;
The sky went out, the water disappeared.
He felt a shocking pressure of blowing hurl
The ship upon her side . . . she staggered, she careered,
Then down she lay . . .
Then the snow
Whirled all about – dense, multitudinous, cold –
Mixed with the wind's one devilish thrust and shriek . . .
The ship lay – the sea smote her, the wind's bawl
Came, 'loo, loo, loo!' The devil cried his hounds
On to the poor spent stag strayed in his bounds.

For thirty-two days, as the *Gilcruix* was battered, smashed and torn, Jack learnt what it was to be 'never warm nor dry, nor full nor rested'. 'We got caught in the ice off the Horn and had our bows stove in,' Masefield later wrote, 'and had thirty-two days of such storm and cold as I hope never to see again. The Horn is a hard place in the winter . . . Seas forty feet high and two miles long, and ice everywhere, on deck, in the rigging, and tumbling in the sea, and we fighting the lot of it.' But finally, miraculously, the *Gilcruix* emerged from the elemental chaos, and limped her way up the long Pacific coast. Eventually she reached her destination thirteen weeks after she had left Cardiff. For Masefield it had been an initiation not only into life at sea but into manhood. 'I shall always be glad of my short sea time,' he wrote some years later to a friend. 'It was real, naked life . . . At sea, you get manhood knocked bare, and it is a fine thing, a splendid thing.'

4

It was during the first week of August, a time of sweltering heat, that the *Gilcruix* arrived at Iquique, that well-known nitrate port which during only a few decades, despite a major earthquake and a local war, had grown from a little fishing village on a strip of shore below the mountains into a booming export centre, with clubs and a racecourse and a cricket ground, as well as a stinking 'sailortown'. And there she moored at 'the tier', the offshore anchorage in the bay, alongside the scores of other sailing-ships that came and went.

The captains of the ships berthed at the tier seldom gave their seamen 'liberty days' on shore because of the menace of crimps, the kidnappers who got hold of drunken sailors and sold them on to outgoing ships. But the apprentices went ashore quite often; one of their main jobs was to row 'the old man' over to the landing stage and then wait for him till he was ready to return. So Masefield's first experience of a foreign land was the Iquique waterfront, where his companions were his fellow apprentices, or 'reefers' as they called themselves, whose chief aim was to acquire stocks of *anis* so as to get blind drunk whenever possible.

But when he later looked back to his time at Iquique he recalled one memorable liberty day when he slipped off alone, and climbed up into the steep hinterland behind the town. High among the hills, near a disused silver mine, he sat down to rest, to gaze out over the sea, and to ponder. There, far below him, were the anchorage and the ships and a few rocks with surf round them, and a train puffing to the station.

A barquentine was being towed out by a little dirty tug; and very far away, shining in the sun, an island rose from the sea, whitish, like a swimmer's shoulder. It was a beautiful sight that anchorage with the ships lying there so lovely, all their troubles at an end. But I knew that aboard each ship there were young men going to the devil, and mature men wasted, and old men wrecked; and I wondered at the misery and sin which went to make each ship so perfect an image of beauty.

It was at about this time at Iquique that Jack became seriously ill; he later wrote that he 'had a bad time, and nearly died'. Again, as on the voyage out, he was smitten by sunstroke, but it seems that he also suffered some kind of nervous breakdown. And since the Captain of the *Gilcruix* was a kindly man he evidently decided that Jack must be sent home. All he had to do was to discuss the matter with the local White Star agent, and then to recommend to the British Consul that 'John E. Masefield' should be classified as a D.B.S. (Distressed British Seaman) which would ensure him a passage back to England by steamship. An official document still in existence shows that on 29 August 1894, with the approval of the British Consul at Iquique, John E. Masefield was discharged from the crew of the *Gilcruix* 'on grounds of mutual consent'. No further details are given as to the cause of the discharge, but there is little doubt that illness was the reason.

For a time he was in the British Hospital at Valparaiso,[1] and later he described an incident during his convalescence there.

When I was in hospital in Valparaiso, I spent my evenings in the garden with an old lame sailor from Coquimbo. He was a very ancient shellback who had fallen down a hatchway, wrenching a muscle of his knee. His wound caused him much suffering, but at twilight, when the heat and the light became gentle, his pain was always less fierce than in the day, and he would then yarn to me of the sights and cities he had seen.

The place we chose for our yarns was among lilies, under a thorn tree which bore a fragrant white blossom not unlike a tiny rose. When we were seated in our chairs we could see the city far below us, and that perfect bay with the ships and Aconcagua snowy in the distance. A few yards away, beyond a low green hedge where the quick green lizards darted, was a barren patch, a sort of rat warren, populous with rats as big as rabbits. I was getting well of a sunstroke and my nerves were shaken, and the sight of these beasts scattering

[1] At that time the British Hospital at Valparaiso was situated on the Cerro Alegre, well up the hill, opposite the German Hospital. Subsequently, in the 1906 earthquake, it was burned down.

to their burrows was very horrible to me . . . My comrade watched me shudder as a rat crept through the hedge in search of food.

Eventually, when Jack was well enough to face the journey home, he was shipped off, probably in one of the fortnightly mail steamers that coasted northward to Callao, the port of Lima; from thence there was another, more frequent, service to Panama. Then to reach the Caribbean he would have had to take a train across the isthmus to Colon. And from Colon, as a D.B.S., he would almost certainly have been sent home on a Royal Mail steamship calling *en route* at various ports in the West Indies. We have no journal to establish the details of Jack's homeward voyage, but the Atlantic crossing probably took place in mid-October, for by the end of the month he was back at Ledbury.

This leisurely voyage, while Jack was still in the impressionable state of mind of a convalescent, was of crucial importance for his future. It gave him time to think; it gave him chances to observe innumerable vivid scenes at the ports of call; it also no doubt reminded him – as he tossed across the Atlantic – that he was a bad sailor. Before he set foot again in the Priory he had resolved that he was not going to finish his time as an apprentice. He was going to abandon all ideas of a career in the merchant service. He was, after all, going to be a writer.

Chapter Three

ADRIFT

I

They call me Hanging Johnny,
Away—i—oh;
They call me Hanging Johnny,
So hang, boys, hang.

. . . .

A rope, a beam, and a ladder,
Away—i—oh;
A rope, a beam, and a ladder,
So hang, boys, hang.

Jack had first heard this strangely beautiful chanty off Cape
Horn, in the thick of a blizzard, and it came back to him –
haunted him – during the months of misery that he spent at the
Priory in the winter of 1894. He was still jittery and far from
well when he got home from Chile. His sister Ethel, looking
back to this time, remembered him chiefly as lying full length
on the hearthrug singing sea-chanties to himself, and especially,
again and again, the sinister 'Hanging Johnny'. He also let fly,
in bitter verse, at the harshness of life at sea; there was a short
poem about a man falling from aloft, and another about the
incidents of a voyage.

Foremost among his torments during that winter was the
callous nagging of Aunt Kate, who had greeted him on his
return with taunts of having 'failed to stick it'. When she learnt
that he was once more hoping to be a writer she was scandalized. As soon as he was fit, she insisted, he must go back to sea.
And clearly he was forced to accept her tyrannical dictates, for
on 4 March he wrote to the Captain of the *Conway*,[1] thanking
him for introductions to various shipping lines, and announcing
that he had obtained a place on board the *Bidston Hill* (a four-

[1] Lieut. A.T. Miller, R.N.

masted barque, like the *Gilcruix*, but slightly larger) belonging
to W. Price & Company. She was currently in New York, he
said, 'loading I expect for Japan and Calcutta with oil', and he
would be leaving shortly by steamship to join her there.[1]

In Liverpool, the night before he sailed for America (on
board the White Star mail-ship *Adriatic*) he stayed at the
Sailors' Home. He felt utterly wretched, so he later confided to
a friend: 'Only a hopelessness. The sea seemed to have me in
her grip. I was to pass my life beating other men's ships to port.
That was to be "life" for me. The docks, and sailor town, and
all the damning and the heaving.' But how mistaken he was!
Once really out of range of Aunt Kate, once on the other side
of the Atlantic, he felt suddenly free to obey his own impulses.
On 30 March, when the *Bidston Hill* left New York, John E.
Masefield was not aboard her. 'I deserted my ship in New York',
he later wrote, 'and cut myself adrift from her, and from my
home. I was going to be a writer, come what might.'

News of Jack's desertion presumably reached Ledbury
through the *Bidston Hill*'s owners, and William Masefield
resorted to a firm of private detectives to try to locate his
nephew, but without any success. In the meantime Jack, who
had landed in New York with one pound in cash and a chestful
of clothes, had struck up an acquaintance with a drinking
companion whom he later described as 'a disreputable ruffian'.
Together they searched for work, but could find nothing in the
city. So they took to the roads and became homeless vagrants,
like innumerable others at this time of acute depression. For a
month or so in the spring and early summer of 1895 they
tramped and cut wood and did chores, and starved and slept
out, before finally getting temporary work on farms.

Little wonder that throughout his life Masefield sympa-
thized from his heart with the unemployed, the drifters, the
drunks, the menials – with 'the tramp of the road' and 'the
man with the clout'.[2] At the age of seventeen he himself had
briefly been all of these.

---

1 Masefield family friends evidently anticipated that J.M. would reach Japan, for
he was given a card of introduction to a lady at the Belgian Legation in Tokyo by
Prebendary Maddison-Green of Ledbury.

2 See 'A Consecration' in *Salt-Water Ballads* (1902).

2

As spring turned to summer Jack gravitated back to New York, to the squalor of Greenwich Village. For weeks he almost starved. Uncouth-looking and unkempt, he was spurned when he sought for work. But, so he later declared, he was 'marvellously happy' because he knew he was going to be a writer. He was already writing poetry. Then at last one day the chance of a job presented itself. He had gone at midday into a Greenwich Avenue saloon where those who bought a glass of beer were entitled to a free lunch and a sight of the papers. He had bought some beer and was busy studying the advertisements when to his amazement the proprietor, Luke O'Connor, came over and asked him if he wanted a good job. He needed a boy to give a hand behind the bar, and he could have ten dollars a month and free board and lodging.

After a haircut Jack was put into a white coat, and he at once started cleaning glasses and serving beer and cigars. But he very soon found that these were only a few of his multitudinous responsibilities. He had to see that the pipe through which the beer ran to the taps was kept packed with ice. He had to keep the bar icebox filled from the cold-storage cellar. He had to keep the free lunch counter supplied with food (sliced Bologna sausage, sardines, salt beef, rye bread, potato salad).

Above the bar was a hotel called the Columbian which also belonged to O'Connor and was patronized largely by drunks.[1] Whenever the electric bell buzzed Jack had to run upstairs – there was no elevator – to take their orders. Then in the mornings he had to go shopping for the ingredients (such as cherries, lemons, etc.) that Johnny, the expert bartender, needed for the concoction of fancy drinks – punches, cocktails, fizzes, and slings. Often during the afternoon he had to clean the bar windows or the great mirrors at the back of the saloon.

---

[1] An obituary in the *New York Herald Tribune* (20 February 1929) states that Luke O'Connor (1864–1929) was a pioneer in the New York cabaret business, and that the Columbian Hotel, 'or rather the Columbian Gardens', which was 'a combined hotel, bar and cabaret' situated at the junction of Greenwich Avenue, Christopher Street, and Sixth Avenue, had been under his ownership from 1888. The reference to 'cabaret business' cannot however be confirmed from other sources relating to the period when J.M. was there.

And in the evening, after about nine o'clock, when the regulars came in, he had to be once more behind the bar. 'The boys' stayed on till closing time at 1.00 a.m., drinking, singing, and telling the tallest of stories, and sometimes there were brawls. Then Jack had to separate the combatants – without causing any offence. And eventually, after the saloon closed, the whole bar had to be scrubbed. At about 2.00 or 2.30 Jack climbed the stairs to his little garret on the top floor of the hotel, clutching a tot of whisky.

It seems extraordinary that after such a day he had any energy left at all. But in the early hours of the morning he used to turn for consolation to the only book he had with him, the first volume of Malory's *Morte d'Arthur*: he had picked it up in a Sixth Avenue bookstore kept by an Englishman, Mr. Pratt. 'All the story-telling instinct in me was thrilled as I read,' he later recalled. 'It was pure joy, a British tradition that had passed into the imagination of the world.'

Jack saw a lot of Luke O'Connor, and also of his family, during the time that he worked in the saloon. Every day he joined them for breakfast, and also for their evening meal, at their home in West Fourth Street, a thoroughfare just north of the area that was then New York's red-light district.[1] He did not have Sundays off, for although Sunday opening was illegal, business at the bar of the Columbian Hotel continued as usual behind closed shutters, and Jack had plenty of opportunities to observe the crude methods of evading the law which were then the norm. Masefield later described how on Sunday mornings the main doors of the saloon were kept barricaded, and how 'John-na', the little Italian barman, was put in charge of a side door, with orders to admit only people he knew. One Sunday things went wrong. John-na had been tippling and was off his guard when two strangers came to the door. They pushed past him, and amid a stunned silence went up to the bar. But then 'the boss' took charge. 'He walked up to the two men and looked at them very straight, much as a doctor looks at a patient. The two men looked at him very straight, and shifted on their feet as though expecting something.' At last

---

1 According to an 1896 report there were three 'disorderly houses' on West Fourth Street, and two saloons which were 'resorts for disorderly women'.

O'Connor spoke: 'Say . . . won't you come upstairs?' The two men did not answer, but as the boss opened the door they passed out with him. 'Take off your coats, boys,' said one of the drinkers round the bar (the two bartenders had put on their jackets ready to go with the detectives), 'Them cops is on the make. You ain't going to be pulled.' Almost at once the electric bell rang from the boss's sitting room, and Jack was told to put a quart of champagne on ice. When the wine was cold he decked his tray and bore it upstairs. As he entered the boss's room he saw one of the detectives folding up a thick wad of dollar bills. He put down the wine and poured out three creaming glasses. 'Our case', so the story ends, 'never came before the magistrates.'

By mid-September, after Jack had worked at the Columbian Hotel for about two months, he decided to leave. He had heard of another job that would give him far more leisure as well as better pay. But he and O'Connor parted very good friends. The chance of the new job came up when Jack happened to meet a young tough from England, William ('Billy') Booth, who was employed in a carpet factory just outside New York, the Alexander Smith and Sons' mill at Yonkers. One evening when Booth was in Greenwich Village he visited a friend of his, an Irishman called Quinn, who was also an acquaintance of Jack's. While he was with Quinn, so Booth later recalled, a lanky English boy came in and sat on the foot of the bed. They chatted for a while about 'the old country', and Booth, who came from Shropshire, was delighted to learn that the newcomer's name was Masefield, for long ago in Shropshire he had lived near a family of gentry called Masefield, and he assumed that Jack was one of them. He was impressed by Jack's general appearance and his 'refined accent', and next day he spoke about him to his foreman, Mr. Picken, who was also, strangely enough, of Shropshire origin. And Mr. Picken said he thought they could take on the Masefield boy.

3

At dawn on 16 September 1895 Jack took the train to Yonkers. Years later every detail of that day remained sharp in his memory. It was a lovely crisp morning and he and Booth sang as they walked together to the factory, a vast complex about a mile from the station, employing, in those days, about four thousand men and women.[1]

The streets were crammed with people hurrying to work. There were 'printers' with red and blue and yellow arms (from working in dye) and a lot of awful toughs, with neither brows nor jaws, standing outside the mills, calling out at passing men and women. All sorts of filth. Presently we came to the gate.

Booth went in to work, and Jack was told to go into a little office where applicants for jobs were waiting – one or two men and a lot of 'hard-eyed women'.

The women stared at me with brazen eyes. I felt very much ashamed. There were so many, and they were so close. I blushed up to the roots of my hair; and one of them nudged another, and remarked 'Innocent'. But they behaved better when the boss came in to choose from them.

The name 'Masefield' was called, and after being greeted by Mr. Picken, Jack was guided to the department where he was to work, on an upper floor of one of the main buildings, the moquette mill.[2] In Masefield's autobiographical book, *In the Mill*, he described the impact that carpet manufacture made upon him as he was led through the great throbbing red brick building on that first day. 'Terack. Terack. Crash. BANG! Terack, Terack. Crash. BANG!' The air was thick with wool dust, and the din was 'a deafening, roaring, clanging clack in which one had to shout to make oneself heard'. More than a hundred power-looms were in full work on the lower weaving floor. The shuttles were stabbing and clacking, the belts were humming, the swords were coming back with a bang, and 'the appalling ceiling of advancing spools shook and jerked overhead'.

In the cutting shop where Jack was to work, the machines sliced off the ragged ends of wool before the spools were put into frames, or 'setts', ready for the looms. The cutting machines

---

1 The factory was subsequently much extended, and it was in operation for carpet manufacture until 1973.

2 Moquette carpet, somewhat resembling Axminster, was one of the two main types manufactured at the Yonkers works (the other was 'Tapestry').

made a good deal of noise – 'their belts hummed and the great knives within them clashed as the men pressed the pedals' – but it was nothing like the ear-splitting racket on the weaving floor.

Soon Jack had mastered his task; it was mostly quite easy. Immediately after the cutting he had to check that the tin tubes containing the spools of wool were in line; if they were not, the edge of the woven carpet would be uneven. To straighten them he used a special little tool called a 'tin opener'. But then came the tricky part. He had to make sure that each of the ten spools was in its right place, and that each ten was arranged in the proper order in the rack. When the spools were new and the colours bright it was easy to see that they were in their proper order. When they were not so new, when the colours were dimmed, this needed a special sense. But once the sett was in order, and he had initialled the card fixed upon it, the job was finished and he could drag the rack to the elevator nearest to the loom to which it had to go.

His first week at the mill was an anxious one because although he found the work easy he doubted whether he could keep the job. Within a few days however he knew that he was approved; someone had heard the section-boss saying that he liked the new lad, but there was one thing he couldn't understand about him; he went on working without being told; he didn't have to be watched: 'Gee, I don't understand it.' Soon Jack was on friendly terms with his fellow workers. They called him 'Masey', sometimes mocked him a little for his English accent, and teased him good-humouredly: 'Why do you call your little island Great? Gee, you can't hardly see it on the map!' They also occasionally vexed him, when the talk turned to national affairs. He himself was almost completely ignorant of American history, and their attitude towards England clashed with his patriotism. Boxing, or rather prize-fighting – a subject of universal appeal in the mill, which also fascinated Jack – was a safer topic.

Most of the men lived at home, or in boarding-houses in and around Yonkers, which was then little more than an overgrown village on the banks of the Hudson. But Jack at first failed to find accommodation in a boarding-house, and had to hire a room and eat out – this was called 'living on the European system'. Morning and evening he ate at a restaurant in the

square near the station, and at night he went to the home of one
of the mill's superintendents, James A. MacLachlan, where he
had been fortunate enough to get a room. During the week he
saw hardly anything of the MacLachlans, but at weekends he
sometimes joined in the family doings, and he told stories to
the superintendent's young son, Howard. As time went on
Mr. MacLachlan, who at first had been against taking a lodger,
evidently warmed to Jack, for he taught him how to shave
properly and also gave him an overcoat.

For Jack the only disadvantage of living at the MacLachlans'
was that it was a longish way from the restaurant, so that about
a mile and a half was added to his daily round. Nevertheless
during his first few months at the mill the walking that this
entailed was one of his main delights, especially in the early
morning:

It was still, exquisite blue September weather; the lovely River and
her cliffs lay just down the road . . . Upper New York was still un-
cleared and unbuilt. The woodland was much as it had been when
the Red Indians had it. Near the River there was modern industry;
elsewhere the land seemed untamed . . . the gray rocks stood up
among the sumachs and the maples.

Exceptionally memorable for Jack was his first Sunday at
Yonkers; he began it by reflecting with amazement that he
would have the entire day to himself. He went down to the
restaurant for breakfast, and then at once to the river, to gaze
across to the noble line of cliffs, the Palisades. He walked up the
river until he found a man who had boats to hire; he took a
boat and rowed across. To his astonishment he found the Jersey
shore almost untouched by man; no one seemed to have trodden
those screes or broken through the scrub.

The fair weather held for many weeks, and Sunday after
Sunday Jack made his way up the river on the Yonkers side,
dazzled by the brilliance of the fall. But as winter set in
all the colour and joy faded. In the mill they shut the great
windows and turned on the steam heat, which was snug, but
exceedingly unpleasant to Jack, who preferred to be frozen than
stuffy. Another snag in winter was that a mill-worker had no
daylight to himself except on Sundays. Jack went in the dark
to his breakfast, walked in the dark to the mill, and by the time

the whistle blew at six it was dark again. In the evening, back at the MacLachlans', he settled down with a book beside his little oil stove. But reading was not companionship, and during those winter evenings Jack was very lonely. At the mill, too, he now felt stranded. Having mastered his own repetitive work the novelty and challenge of the job had worn off, and he moved mechanically.

When spring came, by which time he had been six months at the mill, he began to take stock of his situation. What was the point of toiling away in a factory? Merely to make money? Yes, for more money would mean more leisure to read and write. One or two of the older men in the mill had encouraged him to believe that in time he could perhaps work his way up to be in charge of a floor, and his ambition was stirred when he learnt that a job he coveted would soon be vacant. But another man was chosen. It was a cruel blow, and he took it as a sign that perhaps he had better get out. Maybe he ought to go to sea again after all; or perhaps there might be something quite different, something really worthwhile. Perhaps he could study medicine, qualify as a doctor, and lead a life useful to others (he longed to do research in order to vanquish yellow fever). But he soon realized that ignorance as well as lack of funds barred him from a medical training; he had no glimmering of any science unconnected with the sea.

He talked things over with Billy Booth (by now he had left the MacLachlans' as he had been able to get a room at the same boarding-house as Booth) and Booth suggested that he should appeal to his family in England for financial help. Jack explained that in the circumstances he could not possibly write to his guardian, whereupon Booth volunteered to write on his behalf. In due course an answer came; it was a stern rebuff. William Masefield declared that he had washed his hands of Jack, that Jack would get no help from him, that Jack had made his own bed and he must lie on it.

4

Soon after arriving at Yonkers Jack had looked around for bookstores, and had discovered two. One of them, the Warburton Avenue Book Store, became a regular pay day haunt.

It belonged to a young American called William Palmer East, who ran it with the help of his sister Elizabeth. More than twenty years later, East was asked for his memories of Masefield. 'I was so busy then,' he recalled, 'I hardly noticed this boy who came in and out and had the run of the shop. He seemed at first almost a ragamuffin . . . It was my sister who really understood the boy's possibilities and mind, and who got well acquainted with him.'

Jack often chatted with Miss East and her brother, picking up scraps of literary information that helped to steer his reading, but he sometimes contributed ideas which Mr. East found strikingly different from his own. 'He was far more broadminded than I, and I was thirty,' East admitted. Apparently anything which had the word 'king' in it was repulsive to East at that time, but he found that Jack, although he always wanted to 'get close to the under man', also respected royalty. 'A man was a man to him, even then, and he had no class hatreds or preferences.'

For Jack one of the greatest joys of the factory job was that it gave him much more time to read, and books were then so cheap that he could easily build up a library. He had an insatiable appetite for reading, not only in English but in French, and he devoured Dumas and Molière as well as Sir Thomas Browne, de Quincey, Hazlitt, Dickens, Thackeray, Kipling, and Stevenson. At that time American editions of the best modern fiction often cost as little as five cents apiece, and Jack bought about twenty a week. One of his favourite novels was du Maurier's *Trilby*; his copy had the author's illustrations, and these tugged at his heart, for du Maurier's drawings in *Punch* had been familiar to him since childhood. As he read and reread *Trilby* it was as though an old and trusted friend was giving him his first taste of the Latin Quarter, of French poetry, of Bohemia.

One day when he was just over eighteen, Jack was browsing in the Warburton Avenue Book Store when his glance fell upon a shelf of books of poetry, both American and English. Among them was a Chaucer, price seventy-five cents, in a dull red binding. He knew nothing of Chaucer, except phrases about his being a well of English undefiled and the father of English poetry. He bought the book from Mr East, who said 'Ah, yes, last winter there were lectures on the old poets and Chaucer was asked for. This year it is all the classics, Keats and Shelley.' These words were very important to Jack. He had heard of Keats, and also of Shelley, but knew nothing of their writings. Now however that they had been named to him as 'the classics' he made up his mind to get to know them. He ordered both, and went home with the Chaucer.

On the following Sunday, in the afternoon, he decided not to walk in the woods but to read. 'It was a hot, beautiful day; and it seemed a pity to go into the woods while there were still so many mosquitoes' (he often suffered from malaria at this time). He stretched himself on his bed, and began to read *The Parliament of Fowls*. Chaucer's Middle English evidently presented no obstacle to his eager reading, and with the first lines he entered into a world of poetry until then unknown to him, a world 'boundless in liberty, inexhaustible in beauty, eternal in delight'.

> The lyf so short, the craft so long to lerne,
> Th'assay so hard, so sharp the conquerynge,
> The dredful joye, alwey that slit so yerne:[1]
> Al this mene I by Love, . . .

Transfixed, he wrote the date, 6 September 1896, in the margin of his Chaucer, and he then took out his watch, saying to himself 'I'll note the very minute, so that I'll remember it for ever.'

The Parliament of Fowls is a 'love-vision' in the Renaissance idiom, telling how all the birds assemble on St. Valentine's Day before the Goddess of Nature, in order to choose their mates, and how the royal eagle's choice is disputed, and then debated by the general parliament of the birds. Certainly the freshness, purity, and originality of Chaucer's language set an inspiring example which remained with Masefield all his life. But over and above this, one of the poem's central assumptions, that beauty in nature is no less than divine – 'this noble goddesse Nature' – coincided with one of his own most treasured

---

[1] 'that passes away so quickly'

intuitions. Furthermore the implication running through the poem, that courtly love is love's highest form, was in tune with the romantic ideals which had already captured Jack's imagination in the Arthurian legends.

Chaucer was only a beginning. Within a few days he collected his Keats and his Shelley from Mr. East. He began with Keats. He read one short poem, then immediately a second, then four lines of a third, but for that night he could read no more. He found himself in a new world 'where incredible beauty was daily bread and breath of life'. Everything that he had read until then seemed like paving-stones on the path leading to this Paradise; now he seemed to be in the garden, and the ecstasy was so great that the joy seemed almost to burn. He knew, then, 'that life is very brief, and that the use of life is to discover the law of one's being, and to follow that law, at whatever cost, to the utmost'. He knew then that his law was to follow poetry, even if he died of it – 'Who could mind dying for a thing so fair?'

For a sensitive Victorian boy of eighteen, who had suffered a good deal of knocking about, who craved for gentleness, and who lacked a spiritual anchor – although he groped towards God, the stilted killjoy religion of his upbringing had shut him off from any living Christian faith – here was a secret stronghold. On the rock of High Romance and Supreme Beauty he could build his life.

5

Of the two years that Jack spent at Yonkers, the first was a time of inner ferment and searching – up until the moment when he knew beyond any doubt that poetry was his vocation. The second, which took him to his nineteenth birthday, was a sequel to that great crux, a time of self-identification with the poets he worshipped, and of experiment in emulating their styles. It was also a time of seriously worsening ill health. He was, in fact, suffering from the onset of tuberculosis, though he did not know it at the time. Other factors also contributed to his deteriorating condition. Recurrent attacks of malaria afflicted him and his strength was ebbing, for he was deliberately starving himself, in the interests – so he thought – of his soul (he had adopted a minimal diet after being converted to vegetarianism by Shelley's Notes to 'Queen Mab').[1]

At the mill he had been promoted, and he now held the highly responsible position of 'mistake finder',[2] but he found that a day's work exhausted him. He became more and more bottled-up and solitary, and his fellow workers began to regard him as 'a little peculiar', while Jack on his side came to feel that most of the raw young Americans at the factory were definitely uncongenial.[3] Even Billy Booth, his only close friend, was not really a confidant, and in any case, after the end of 1896, when Booth got married, Jack saw much less of him. Yet at this particular stage isolation was in a sense a blessing. This is clear from the quotation that Masefield later chose as an epigraph for *In the Mill*, to convey the essence of his experiences while at Yonkers. It is one of the sayings of Gautama Buddha: 'Therefore . . . dwell as having refuges in yourselves, resorts in yourselves and not elsewhere . . . Whoever shall dwell as having refuges in themselves . . . shall reach to the limit of darkness, whoever are desirous of learning.' Jack was indeed 'desirous of learning', above all desirous of learning about poetry, not in the sense of acquiring academic knowledge about poems and poets, but in the sense of participating in poetry, of being led by it into the realm of beauty, and of setting down on paper the fruits of his own contemplation. After Chaucer, Keats, and Shelley he embarked upon Shakespeare and Milton. Shakespeare he loved 'for his fun and his beauty' and to Milton he returned constantly.

Before the end of 1896 he was composing sonnets, and as

1 He also cut down on stimulants; first he gave up tobacco, and next banned tea and coffee. An interesting point in J.M.'s account of this (in *In the Mill*) is the omission of any reference to alcohol. Perhaps, in 1896, he gave up drink at the same time as tobacco. But perhaps when he wrote *In the Mill*, forty years later, he did not wish to recall that a year prior to his experiments in abstinence he had spent most of his time in the company of alcoholics, and had himself often over-indulged. A further possibility is that he did not, at this time, abandon his drinking habits.

2 This meant taking a strip of carpet and comparing it with the pattern, for faults of setting or design.

3 In writing later to Miss Flood (12 August 1900) J.M. apologized for having got 'very rusty in the tongue springs', and added 'perhaps it comes from the seclusion I have dwelt in during my sojourn among the looms of Yonkers; a seclusion due to my hatred of Americans.'

soon as they were written he sent them off to his sister Ethel.[1]
She was a sympathetic recipient with whom he felt entirely at
ease. The earliest, dated 4 December 1896 ('Birthday Sonnet
to E.M.') is a poem of greetings to her on her twentieth
birthday.

> Time leans upon his scythe, the hours go by
> Making another day pass as they go;
> The days on wings of wind do quickly fly
> Making another year pass as they flow.
> Another year, with all its joys and woe,
> Its sickness, health, its happiness, and pain,
> Out on its journey sad doth swiftly go
> And brings us to the starting post again –
> So passeth life on earth – but unto Thee,
> To whom I write, may Time be very kind
> And give thee many years, and tenderly
> Erase the pain – and may he never find
> A fault in thee, and may you ever be
> Healthy in body, glad in soul and mind.

Not all of Masefield's early poems were sonnets. There is one,
for example, 'Winter', dated 24 January 1897, in a different
metre:

> The wind sings shrill, the leaves are brown and dead,
> The grass is withered, all the flowers flown
> And from the trees dry twigs and leaves are shed
>   By the wild tempest blown.
>
> A wild sad day, a stormy time of year –
> The limping hare crouches upon the ground
> In search of warmth – while all around you hear
>   The sad wind's mournful sound.
>
> And here I come to rest upon the sod
> With Nature holding wild communion sweet
> And in my loneliness approaching God
>   As is most right and meet.

---

1 She transcribed seventeen of these poems into a quarto notebook, and after J.M.'s
return to England she must have shown it to him, for inside the front cover, in his
own youthful hand, is written '"Roma non in diem aedificabat" ergo "nil desper-
andum"'. ['"Rome was not built in a day" therefore "never despair"'.] This
phrase shows that J.M. already knew some Latin although it was not taught in the
Conway. Presumably he acquired a smattering at Warwick.

As the spring of 1897 advanced, nostalgia for the sea and for past companionships brought him inspiration, as shown in a sonnet entitled 'By the Sea':

> I played beside the ocean, and a strain
> Of the loud-cadenced waves was borne to me,
> As if the sad, dark-haired, Parthenope
> Were singing, with a voice like autumn rain
> Falling midst pine-trees; and the soft refrain
> Woke Memory and like some quick-winged bird
> My Past drew nigh, and, listening, I heard
> The voices of lost friends to sound again.
>
> And all through noise of waters whose moist lips
> Kissed the ribbed sand. Or wind whose gentle breath
> Wakened Aeolian harps along the shore.
> Yet from these chords my weary soul drew store
> Of God, and though Sun, Moon and Stars eclipse
> This harmony shall light me down to death.

At about this time Jack's poetic ardour suffered a damping down. He had been able, 'through the kindness of a friend in England', to submit some of his poetry to 'a real author' for criticism. And apparently the only comment made by this author (whose identity we do not know) was 'He writes very young'. 'Even Keats found writing difficult at first,' Jack secretly protested. 'No one can put much into early work; he hasn't much to put.' The go-between friend had also added a piece of forthright advice on his own account: 'Get down from that high horse of yours.'

Smarting from these rebukes Jack turned towards another kind of writing, namely journalism. And when by chance he got to know a newcomer at the boarding-house who had sometimes written for newspapers, he showed him a few of his efforts. The stranger was kind, and said he thought that Jack would certainly be able to make a living by writing some day, but in the meantime he ought to take things more quietly. This was the first time that Jack had ever received any real encouragement concerning his writing. Thenceforward his daydreams centred more and more upon the idea of making a living as a journalist, though not in the United States.

London had become the focal point of his hopes. This was largely due to his regular reading of the *New York Sun*, which

under the editorship of Charles Dana gave much prominence
to the best in English culture and the newest in English thought.
By means of the *Sun* Jack came to know all the literary move-
ments of the time, and to think of London as the centre of the
world. For yet a further reason, his thoughts veered compul-
sively towards London. 1897 was the year of Queen Victoria's
Diamond Jubilee, and to an exile a time of poignant emotion.

Less than two weeks after the Jubilee celebrations, Jack's
moment of decision came. A row with his boss helped him to
make up his mind, and then there was no delaying. Before
finally leaving the boarding-house he sorted his writings and
discarded ruthlessly. He destroyed all that he had written of an
experimental novel as well as 'many poems'; all this, when
torn up, 'filled a large bucket, weighed astonishingly, and
burned with a clear flame'. He gave away some of his books,
sold others, and kept about nine to take with him.

His last day in New York was a scorching one in early July
(when he reached West Street there were several dead horses
and dogs lying in the street, and he saw two elderly men collapse
from the heat). His luck was in. A Liverpool steamer, long
familiar to him, was about to sail, and knowing the captain
was an 'old Conway' he bluffed his way on board and got taken
on as a steerage steward. He was at work on deck as the ship
moved down the harbour to the sea. Though he was busy
enough, he looked long at lower New York, wondering if, and
when, and how, he would see 'that marvellous town' again.
A pale, emaciated, run-down boy, in a miserable state of
illness, he was also 'unspeakably, radiantly and burningly
happy'. He had found his road.

PART II

In Flower

Chapter Four

TRANSITIONAL

I

'I landed in England with about six pounds and a revolver. I was going to try to get a job as a clerk (I knew nothing of business). Failing that, I was going to shoot myself. I was desperately ill and sick. I hadn't the strength to face more hardships.' Thus Masefield, in retrospect, described his arrival in Liverpool in July 1897. But at the time he wrote cheerfully to Ethel, from lodgings in Birkenhead, 'Oh it's grand to be in England again, I can tell you, and grand also to hear the mother tongue spoken without a nasal whine.'

The enthusiastic tone of his letter led his sister to think that he was in flourishing health, and she was shocked, when she came to see him a few weeks later, to find him looking wretchedly ill. He was also by then almost destitute, for he had failed to find work in Liverpool, even with the help of the *Conway*'s Captain, 'old Lippy Miller'. Yet her brother's main preoccupation, so she found, was nothing to do with earning his keep. While the weeks had been slipping by he had been living in an ecstasy, not only because poetic inspiration had been coming to him but because for the first time he had been discovering art. Years before, in his *Conway* days, the Walker Art Gallery had been a place of enchantment, chiefly for its paintings of ships. Now, as he explored it afresh, a new world of visual delight opened up for him as he feasted his eyes on the Pre-Raphaelites as well as on the old masters.

Looking back long afterwards, Masefield explained why the work of 'the moderns' had then, and ever since, entranced him. To one who was by nature a teller of stories, it was the 'story' behind each painting, and the fact that the painting helped to tell it, that counted for most. Precise form and vivid colour delighted him too, but the artists he came to worship were his idols because he had perceived that they were 'master storytellers'. For the nineteen-year-old Jack, however, contemplation and worship were not enough; he seized upon the role of amateur art critic, a role he was to cling to for many years, and to Ethel he complained loudly that 'the arm in Rossetti's "Beatrix" is badly foreshortened'.

Ethel Masefield was a clear-sighted and strong-minded young woman. By now she was working as a governess in Lewisham, and soon after her visit to Liverpool a job for her brother 'turned up' in London; there was a vacancy for a junior clerk at a pound a week in a small City office belonging to an acquaintance of hers called Mr. Pressland. So in the summer of 1897 Masefield came to London for the first time. Before leaving Liverpool he had given his gun to a friend who was leaving for the Klondyke, and for the next six months he set himself to learn 'business', although he was really too ill to work. By now he realized that he was 'on the way to consumption', and he was sure that he was soon going to die. Often he felt so weak that he could not add up figures, but his compassionate employer put up with his lapses. In one of his letters to Ethel, dated 11 December 1897, he wrote 'Things are so and so. I make Mr. Pressland very weary, I fear, but he is a kind fellow to work for.'

Meantime he lodged in the cheapest rooms he could find; by the end of 1897 he was in Fulham, at 36 Fairholme Road. There he was not without friends, for almost next door (at number 22) was a sea captain with Liverpool connections, Captain Robert Bartlett, and he and his wife Myra were both very good to him. Jack conceived a profound admiration for Mrs. Bartlett and dedicated two collections of verses to her, *Ballades of Myra's Drawing Room and other Rhymes, Chiefly Silly* and *Ballades of Cold Corpses*.[1] In the latter he dwelt obsessively on physical corruption (he later admitted that much of the verse he wrote at this time was unhealthy 'like all consumptive work') but the former shows that he also had moods of buoyancy, even of merriment.

In one such mood, in December 1897, he wrote an impulsive, slangy letter to Ethel (or 'Tettie' as he called her) on the occasion of her twenty-first birthday. His pen seems almost to

---

1 Neither of these has been published.

have run away with him as he launched out into the metres of
Swinburne and Rossetti: by now he not only imitated his
favourite poets but parodied them.

My dear Tettie,
  Why haven't you jolly well written? You don't deserve a birthday
letter but I suppose I've got to give you one allee samee.
  Many happy returns.

> Lilies and roses from the flowering years
> White snowdrops, sweet and pale as angel's tears
>   Gold threads the fates have spun
>   An aureate twenty-one
> Lit glad with harvest-sun that never sears.
>
> Blush-hued red roses girt about with may
> Whose hearts weep honey gold as breaking day
>   Flower-cups fulfilled of wine
>   And red-rose crowns atwine
> And all of these for thine with myrtled bay.
>   Hurray!

  What price this for an improvisatore 'Why Shakespeare's self is out
of it'?

> Pale flame-winged phantoms furrowing thro' still sky
> Stars shuddering into golden dawn to die
>   Red fire-formed hearts and souls
>   Wreathe round thee – aureoles –
> Fair, sinless banneroles no gold can buy.

  Aoi what ho the balmy Milton? We may as well do the birthday
in style.

> Red roses of deathless desire
> Wan waters and willow-woods white
> Fair flowers of venom-fanged fire
> Lips bloodless and voiceless that bite.
> Pale purple of poor poet's passion
> Wreathe soft round thy soul as a sea
> With white foam-flowers faultless of fashion
>   Crowning thee.

For Swinburne my name is Swinburning
The centuries harrassed and hoar
Music-chorus my mad choir churning
Brave billows unbooming before.
Till the sea becomes sterile and saltless
And the dimness of darkness be dead
May this aureate aureole faultless
Crown thy head.

At last Jack paused for breath, with the comment 'Much music makyth mad'. Yet he could not resist a final parody, this time of Richard le Gallienne.

All hail the twenty-wunner
It's a stunner
A penny bunner
And a treat
A balmy day's rejoicing
With the dinky thrushes voicing
A tinkle inkle joicing
Soft and sweet.

2

Between his moods of ebullience, indeed for most of the time, Masefield at nineteen was in a pitiful state. But at the beginning of 1898 one of his Parker uncles came to the rescue. His mother's brother John, who was a London solicitor, discovered his sad condition and tackled Uncle William and Aunt Kate. 'He screwed my guardians into advancing me a little of my father's money', Masefield later wrote, 'so that I could rest and get treated.' This was the beginning of the long slow road to recovery, although for several years Jack was never really well. He suffered from 'trances and night-sweats', and since malaria still plagued him he dosed himself with quinine, which brought on bouts of deep depression. As to the period of rest that he needed so badly, he may have had a few weeks off from work early in 1898, but with hardly a pause he started on a new job. Thanks to John Parker he was introduced to the Capital and Counties Bank,[1] who took him on at one of their London

---

[1] Later (in 1918) amalgamated with Lloyds Bank.

offices, probably the branch in King Street, Covent Garden; and so began three years of arduous grind as a bank clerk, which brought in just enough – but barely enough – to live on.

Jack's life at this time was much brightened by occasional visits to his Uncle John's family in Surrey.[1] There were four Parker daughters, all of them then at schoolroom age, who treated him like a brother, and the eldest of them, Kathleen – slim and delicate, with eyes of great beauty – was his special friend. To the four sisters and their parents he dedicated a booklet of 'ballades' (rather similar in vein to those he had given to Myra Bartlett) and he also gave his cousins a notebook containing two stories, a short fable concerning a rose, and a long romantic saga in six parts, 'The Tale of Elphin', based largely upon William Morris's *Earthly Paradise*, and written in poetic prose with an Arthurian flavour.

By now Jack had left Fairholme Road, and for the next couple of years he lived in a series of drab and grimy lodging-houses (from the window of one of his rooms he counted 323 chimney-pots) though for a while he lodged in the Islington area in the house of an Anglican priest, the Revd. Horace Townsend, at 98 Tollington Park. This was during the summer of 1899, at the time of his twenty-first birthday – a time when he had his first success as a writer. One of his sea poems, 'Nicias Moriturus',[2] was accepted by *The Outlook* and published on 3 June.

He loathed the feeling of being incarcerated in a vast city cut off from nature, and yet, paradoxically, he found himself falling in love with 'the capital of the world'. Although he missed the sparkle of New York, London inspired in him a kind of awe, and he took to going for long solitary walks of exploration. But before the spring of 1900 he had left the centre of the city and had given up his lonely way of life. He moved to Walthamstow to share rooms with two boisterous youths of about his own age, young relatives of Aunt Kate's called Denis and Jim Whatley (the latter a medical student). Naturally he found that sharing a menage had its drawbacks. He still read a great deal, and also

---

[1] In January 1898 the Parkers were living at Sutton, but not long afterwards they moved to Woking.

[2] 'Nicias about to die'. When published later in *Salt-Water Ballads* (1902) the poem was slightly revised, and retitled 'The Turn of the Tide'.

wrote many letters, as well as a few poems, but he was of course often interrupted. Nevertheless he cannot have objected too much, for we know that he took part with relish in pillow-fights and in experimental beer-brewing in a cellar full of black beetles, as well as in long walks with the Whatleys in Epping Forest on Saturday afternoons. There is little doubt that by now he was restored to fairly robust health and spirits.

Jack's association with the Whatley boys was probably one reason why his relationship with his guardians was now easier; although to a confidant outside the family he mentioned his dread at the prospect of a visit from 'that dire Aunt', he was now on sufficiently good terms with Aunt Kate to give her a book for her birthday – the hymns of Christina Rossetti. He was thus able, once again, to frequent the Priory, and visits to Ledbury became the background to a devoted friendship which grew up between himself and his younger sister Norah, now in her early teens; she was living at home and giving most of her time to music, especially the violin. By this time Ethel had married (in defiance of Aunt Kate she had eloped with one of the clerks in the Masefield office, Harry Ross) and the intimate correspondence between 'Tettie' and her brother had come to an end. This left a gap in Jack's life, but Norah ('dear Nono') was able to share in many of his interests, and since he soon decided that she needed educating in the arts, his letters to her are of much interest as reflecting his own ideas and preferences.

'You asked me some while back,' he wrote to her from Walthamstow, 'as to my favourite artist. The man I meant was Albrecht Dürer . . . I have some ten or twelve reproductions of his work hanging in this room, and I should say that no artist has ever had a greater mind, and for power of draughtsmanship I know none who can hang on the same wall with him.' To Masefield the charm of Dürer was his thoroughness: 'Every link in the chain has equal loving attention. He will draw a tuft of grass with exquisite wealth of detail, caring for it fully as much as for the Saint that treads it down. He resembles the great American who discovered that "to *him* every blade of grass was an unspeakably perfect miracle".'

But there were other great artists, for instance some of the earlier Italians, whose work he loved only a little less; of these he put Cima of Conegliano first, with Bellini and della Francesca next. Many others, too, enchanted him:

Vittore Pisano has always a great charm, and there is a little picture of Filippino Lippi which I greatly admire now hung in the National Gallery. Benozzo Gozzoli, Botticelli, Giorgione, Titian, Leonardo da Vinci, Carlo Crivelli, Garofalo, giants and pigmies – I care for all of them.

As to 'the moderns', so he asserted, 'Watts stands by himself. No one in England has done better . . . He is as moral as Albrecht Dürer (though weaker) and I believe that he and Turner are the only Englishmen who did not make asses of themselves in painting great subjects.' Jack also introduced his sister to his loves among the French 'moderns', notably those of the Barbizon school: they were 'a sort of French brotherhood of landscapists,' he explained. 'Millet . . . [who] painted "The Angelus", Daubigny, Corot, Rousseau and Diaz were the principal painters . . . All of them did some delightful work.' When he came home, so he promised, lapsing into slang, he would bring her a little book about them: 'It ain't very tonily illustrated but the letterpress is solid.'

3

Jack's links with Norah clearly meant a great deal to him, but he needed an older woman to whom he could open his heart. So it was by the greatest good fortune that his godmother Miss Flood (now in her late forties and no longer living at Woollas) reappeared on the scene at this time. As a boy he had taken her for granted; now he discovered her as a respected friend, and soon came to love and depend on her.[1] With the authority of a mature, cultured woman of twice his age she brought into his life – the two-sided life of an impecunious bank clerk and an aspiring poet and art critic – the stimulus of her independent outlook and her wide knowledge of the arts. Besides this she took a sincere and affectionate interest in her godson as a person and also in his writings; she succeeded Ethel as his most

[1] J.M. kept this treasured friendship quite separate from his family life; there is no reference to his godmother in his letters to Norah.

trusted critic.[1] Meanwhile she on her side obviously enjoyed
the friendship of such a zestful, unconventional, and adoring
young man. By mid-1900 the two were in intimate correspondence, and Miss Flood's kindness and understanding caused
Jack's reserve to melt away, thus releasing a torrent of un-
inhibited confidences:

In the rare moments of spiritual fizz which come to me I disburthen
myself to you . . . The letters must be a sort of written soda water
and I really feel sorry for you . . . having to read them . . . [But] I
know that even if I talk bosh to you by the liquid hour you will bear
with me patiently, to the end, enter into the spirit of the thing and
accord a relevant answer, and therefore I do not mind, I am afraid,
how I temper my hyperbole with sanity.

Miss Flood several times invited Jack to stay with her in the
country at houses which she took for short periods. One of the
places with which he thus became acquainted was Oulton Broad
near the Suffolk coast, and Oulton Cottage, where he stayed,
was on the very site of George Borrow's house. This link with
the interpreter of the wanderer's life was to Jack a delight;
he had a passion for *Lavengro* and *The Romany Rye*, and knew
both books almost by heart. Ever since he first read them
he had felt a spiritual kinship with Borrow: 'Here was a young
man who had wanted to write simple stories.'

Once in a while Jack and his godmother were able to meet
in London. In August 1900, when she was due to arrive from
Switzerland (earlier in the summer she had been at Oberammergau), she wrote in advance asking him to suggest a rendezvous. In reply he told her that since it was rather a slack time
in the office he thought he could get an afternoon's leave: how
about visiting the newly opened Wallace Collection? He
apologized however for raising this idea, since he doubted
whether the great assemblage of eighteenth-century art treasures
would in fact appeal to her – or indeed to himself:

I have not seen the Show yet and can only speak of its merits by
hearsay. And the reports I have heard testify more to its size and the
excellence of its appointments (carpets, chairs, catalogue sellers,

1 On 2 July 1900 J.M. sent two newly-written poems to Miss Flood for criticism,
'Over Seven Hundred were Transported' (a ballad about a Cavalier sent as a slave
to the West Indies) and 'A Ballad of John Silver, erstwhile Pirate'.

and handy umbrella-stands etc.), than to its intrinsic merits as a museum of objets d'art.

So why should they not, if she agreed, just sit and talk somewhere? But then he hesitated. Although so confidently garrulous in his letters he was diffident about the prospect of conversing with his godmother face to face: 'I know that I have so little to say, and that little so mediocre.'

Nevertheless he had already reminded her of a promise to take coffee with him at an establishment which he called 'my little coffee-house in St. Martin's Lane', and it seems very likely that during this visit to London she did in fact join him there. From the evidence of various contemporary photographs of Miss Flood we can picture her arriving, a tall, poised figure in sweeping voluminous skirts, encased up to the chin in a feminine blouse, a straw hat perched on her neat head, her heavy-featured face illumined by a gentle smile. And we can also see Masefield, who at twenty-two was extremely handsome, with straight unruly hair flopping over his brow, playing the part of host with awkward devotion. Furthermore we can guess, with a fair amount of certainty, what the two discussed for most of their time together, for art was one of the foremost interests they shared.[1]

The paintings that Masefield had most recently seen at the London galleries – the New, the Goupil, the French, Tooth's – were always one of the main topics for discussion with his godmother. One exhibition at the last-named gallery in the summer of 1900 spurred him to an excited outburst, for it included 'a big sea picture by Frank Brangwyn', and Masefield had, as might be expected, strong views on how sea life should be presented:

It will be a good thing for England when painters and poets leave off painting and ranting about fishing smacks and pirates and 'the dark blue sea', and take to showing with their best ability the real life of the poor fellows who bring them not only their luxuries but their very food. I myself hope some day to make a small plea for the sailors . . . What I want to do is to show the bitter torment of bad weather, the aching misery of perpetually freezing clothes and the state of cold sop one lives in 'when the stormy winds do blow'.

[1] Miss Flood herself was not a serious artist, although there was talent in her family; for a time her younger sister Alice took drawing lessons from Jack Yeats.

Then however he lamented that 'somehow the bite of sea misery' had 'lost its fang' with him: 'I suppose I have lived in flannel for too long. I cannot grasp the storm effects; my reminiscence is nearly always a reminiscence of Trade Wind.' Living in flannel was not the only hindrance. There were other aspects of sea life that allured and distracted him from his purpose of championing the seaman. 'If only', he complained, 'I could abstain from my romantic dreams of John Silver, the Spanish Main, and all the Tropic Island palm tree business I think I might succeed by and by.'

But to be a true poet of the sea was not Masefield's only ambition at this time. From his letters to Miss Flood there emerges a glimpse of a longing to dedicate his life more entirely to humanity; in essence it was the same longing that had fired him in America towards the unattainable ideal of becoming a doctor whose researches would quell yellow fever. From his godmother, when he was still a boy, he had first heard of Father Damien, the nineteenth-century missionary priest famed for his work among lepers in the Pacific Islands, and now his enthusiasm was rekindled, for he had come across an article on Father Damien by R.L. Stevenson, which made him feel, for a few fleeting moments, that there were aims in life more admirable than writing poetry. He even went so far as to confess that the work of a missionary doctor was his highest ambition of all, and that the cause of the merchant seaman came only second. But this was a passing avowal – he was soon making fun of his own dreams.

In Masefield's letters to his godmother he dodged from one topic to another with utter spontaneity – from art to Father Damien, from Father Damien to literature. He knew that she would always be interested to hear what he had been reading.

Books, a lamp-lit night full of books, still engage my spare moments. Elizabethan poetry in great measure. It is a subject no man can ever thoroughly exhaust and I have no great wish to essay the venture. I take it up greedily for a week or two . . . and then away to something Scotch and salted, something Celtic and hair creepy, to something French and decadent.

They were both reading a good deal of French and he was sorry, he said, that he had not applied himself more energetically to the study of the language when he was younger:

I find rather a difficulty in my reading now and again, rather a difficulty in construction than in vocabulary . . . Mallarmé plagues me
and so does Gustave Flaubert, yet old French, Ronsard, Villon and
Remi Belleau, I can read almost easily. I suppose their life and
methods were simpler, the artists aiming at simplicity of diction.
Their construction is not so involved, they do not *suggest*, they explain.

He also had much to tell her, and to discuss, about his English
reading: 'In prose I have read a lot of George Meredith . . .
Stevenson I have always with me and Sir Thomas Browne and
William Morris.' But aside from such favourites he had now
become disenchanted with English writing, especially with the
'higher class' journalism of the day, which he dismissed with
scorn as 'dusty, musty, loathsome, oleclothessome, undigested
English Erudition'. English poetry, too – his former love – was
now the target for equally sweeping censure: 'There is something lumbersome and cumbersome in our truly English poetry.
As if the poets drove up Parnassus in furniture vans instead of
flying up on wings in the manner of good man Puck.'

The reason for this new attitude was a compelling one.
Since the previous year Masefield had discovered the poetry of
W.B.Yeats. In the autumn of 1899 he had happened to see a
review of Yeats's collected *Poems* by H.W.Nevinson, and it had
moved him deeply. Immediately he had steeped himself in
everything that Yeats had written. Before long, writing to
Norah, he was describing the Irishman as 'the only living poet
whose heart has not got the money-grubs and who writes from
sheer joy much as a lark might sing'. The conviction that he
must henceforth be the Irish poet's disciple overwhelmed him
in the same way that the discovery of Chaucer had overwhelmed
him four years earlier.

4

In the late autumn of 1900 Masefield took courage and made a
direct approach to Yeats himself. Although the poet spent most
of his time in Ireland, for this was when he was deeply involved,
with Lady Gregory, in creating the Irish Literary Theatre in
Dublin, he usually came to London for the winter. And since
one of his axioms was 'I always encourage everybody; always',
Masefield soon found himself being invited to an evening meal
at 18 Woburn Buildings, the Bloomsbury lodging that was

Yeats's London home. Ever afterwards Masefield cherished memories of his first visit to number 18; it was on the evening of Monday 5 November, a cold, windy night, spotting with rain. The door was opened by Yeats's housekeeper, Mrs. Old, 'a tall robust country woman', and she conducted him upstairs into the dimness of the dark-walled living-room. It was an appropriate setting for a first encounter with the Irish poet.

Although he was not feeling well – he had a heavy cold – and had earlier thought of postponing the dinner, Yeats received Masefield cordially with the exclamation 'Delighted!', and the impact of his personality – his looks, demeanour, mannerisms – was later recalled by Masefield both in prose and in verse:

Perhaps the first impression was that of great personal distinction, and of a physical condition not robust. He was pale; he stooped somewhat; and as his eyes gave him much trouble then, he seemed to peer at one. His black hair was worn in a shock, very long. It came down to his brow and over his collar at the back. He had a characteristic way of tossing it back with a shake of the head. One saw at once that he was unlike anyone else in the world. The short-sighted eyes, peering through pince-nez from under the billow of hair, were full of fun and keen intelligence. The expression on his face, when not remote with speculation, was vivid with wit.

His hands, too, and his gestures, were most memorable:

> His hands were the most lovely of his time;
> His greeting, of the right hand gravely lifted,
> Half benediction, half old courtesy,
> Was such as Hector might have given in Troy
> These hands were portions of his eloquence,
> Quick with his wit, grave with his reverie.

On that stormy November evening, as Masefield and 'Mr. Yeats' dined together, the two of them alone, on stewed steak and apple pie, they talked mainly of the writers who were then most read by the young men 'in revolt against the times of their fathers':

William Morris, the most gifted and the most practical of the rebels, was the main guide and leader here . . . But the chief literary influences . . . were French or Belgian, and the greatest of these was Villiers de L'Isle-Adam, whose *Axël* was our standard. Yeats praised his *La Révolte*.

They also discussed the early plays of Maeterlinck (Yeats preferred *Les Aveugles*) and Verlaine, whom Yeats had met in Paris. Among the English, Yeats was pleased that Masefield had read and liked the poems of Ernest Dowson, and they also spoke of Beardsley, and of *The Yellow Book* and the *Savoy*, 'so bright with the talent of youth in protest'.

On a more personal note, Masefield then ventured to offer his thanks to Mr. Yeats for the intense pleasure that his work had given him. But Yeats, disconcertingly, seemed unwilling to speak of his past writings; he was interested only in the work of the moment. 'One must get all the fruit one can from every mood,' was his comment, 'for the mood will soon pass and will never return.'

Since it was Yeats's habit to be at home to his friends on Monday evenings, from eight o'clock until two or three in the morning, the tête-à-tête had to come to an end when they had finished the meal. First to join them was a short, rotund, middle-aged lady dressed entirely in black who evidently knew Yeats well, and thus (according to his own recollection) Masefield for the first time met Lady Gregory.[1] Then a few others came in, but on that particular Monday it was a small gathering, for only a few of Yeats's friends knew that he was back.

The talk ran upon Irish poets; then Lady Gregory, wishing to save Yeats's voice, read aloud some poems. She read very clearly and agreeably, with 'a just emphasis and a good sense of rhythm'. When she had finished, Yeats himself took up a book, and Masefield heard for the first time 'that wavering ecstatic song' which was to re-echo in his memory for years. 'His reading was unlike that of any other man. He stressed the rhythm till it almost became a chant; he went with speed, making every beat and dwelling on the vowels.'

---

[1] A notably different account of J.M.'s first meeting with Lady Gregory is given by her in her autobiography *Seventy Years*, ed. Colin Smythe (1973). Her account however lacks the precise date and meticulous details of J. M.'s own recollections, and it seems likely that her memory relates to a subsequent occasion. She wrote as follows:

I remember so well that evening, the beginning of a most pleasant friendship. Yeats was not well enough to come into dinner, and Masefield in his gentle and quiet way told me of his hardships and wanderings in his early life, and his search for work in America, and was listened to with delight and sympathy by me, but with evident disapproval by Yeats's old housekeeper as she changed the plates. Her back stiffened and her nose went up higher as she caught fragments of the reminiscences of one she no doubt considered to be no better than a tramp.

The evening ended earlier than usual because of Yeats's cold, but for Masefield it was an occasion of unforgettable joy as well as a promise of even better things to come, a secret assurance that as a poet he had found a lasting affinity. For as Yeats bade him farewell he invited him to come again on the next Monday.

Within the following weeks Masefield must have met Yeats quite a number of times, for by the new year their friendship was part of his life. This is clear from a telling reference in one of his letters to Norah. Alluding to the mystical prose and verse that had been published recently under the name of 'Fiona Macleod', Masefield hazarded a guess as to the writer's identity. 'I believe that her real name is Lady Gregory, but I have heard it said that "she" is really a quartette – Lady Gregory, George Moore, William Sharp, and' – here one can almost see Masefield swelling with happiness and pride as he wrote the final name – 'my friend W.B.Yeats.'[1]

5

> There was a strangeness and a poetry
> About that place . . .

The room where Masefield first met Yeats, 'that old room above the noisy slum', with its sombre furnishings, its portraits and Blake engravings, was soon to be a place of many further meetings for him, of new inspirations, new friendships, new opportunities. And it was chiefly through the gatherings and conversations there, during the first winter of the new century, that the twenty-two-year-old Masefield began to enter into the world which was to be his spiritual home for the rest of his life.

On Monday evenings, week after week, Yeats's friends made their way up 'that curved stair, lit by a lamp at the curve', drawn by the magnetism of the man who to his intimates was 'Willy' and to all of them was the revered Master.

> No man in all this time has given more hope
> Or set alight such energy in souls . . .
> Somebody said: 'All Willy's geese are swans
> To Willy': true; and lucky for the geese.

1 'Fiona Macleod' was a pseudonym used by William Sharp (1855–1905).

Who were they then, these 'geese', these disciples, devotees, friends, who cackled away on Monday evenings as they sipped wine from the dark brown and green glasses and smoked Virginian cigarettes? They were

> The writers and the painters and the speakers,
> The occultists, the visionary women,
> Astrologers with Saturn on their moons,
> And contemplative men who lived on herbs
> And uttered gentleness and sanctity,
> The poets of the half-a-dozen schools,
> Young men in cloaks, velvet, or evening dress;
> Publishers, publicists and journalists,
> Parliament men, who served the Irish cause,
> And every Irish writer, painter and thinker.

Sometimes too there were evenings when Yeats and only a few others would gather round the fire, and then was a chance to get to know the Master more intimately.

> In private speech, he was without any peer,
> For sudden, complete insight and swift judgement,
> For merry wit, game banter, lasting truth.
> His Irish voice would quicken with excitement,
> As he leaned forward, chuckling at his point.

The long evenings at Woburn Buildings, so earnest in tone and so deep in import, were not however Masefield's only evenings out at this time. And it is heartening to find, from one of his letters to Norah, that on occasion he was able to enjoy a little frivolity and nonsense. 'I went to a Ballad party the other night as "Lovely Spring",' he wrote to her on 17 February 1901, 'with a great watch-spring twirling out of my buttonhole. Very great success.'

As to his days, they passed in the usual toil at the bank; he was now in the Inspectors' Department at the Capital and Counties' head office in Threadneedle Street, which quite often meant working late. But he made good use of the little spare time he had. He told Norah that he had attended a conversazione at which Yeats had spoken on a subject very dear to him, 'a new method of speaking verse', and two ladies had given examples of the new method to a harp accompaniment. Apart from Yeats's followers, however, those present had been far from appreciative; the audience was chiefly composed of people with 'established ideals', and they were 'rather unsympathetic'. After the lecture there was a stormy debate and 'two old fogeys made genuine asses of themselves. Dr. Todhunter, an Irish poet of some note, made a splendid speech to refute their arguments and then we all had tea and so home to bed by lamplight.'

Such were the occasions when Masefield made new acquaintances and friends in the intellectual circle to which he had now been admitted. It is noteworthy that among them were many men considerably older than himself; poets and editors such as Arthur Symons and Ernest Rhys, artists such as Rothenstein and Strang, and foremost among them all, so far as Masefield was concerned, Laurence Binyon, 'the scholar poet of the British Museum'. Binyon, then in his early thirties and as yet unmarried, was soon to play an influential part in Masefield's life. When they first met he had already been in the Department of Prints and Drawings at the British Museum for five years and had published several books of poetry; he was also trying his hand at poetical drama, but the writings which established him as a leading connoisseur of Chinese art were yet to come. Spontaneously kind, he befriended Masefield in innumerable ways, welcoming him at the Museum on Saturday afternoons, inviting him to dinner parties, seizing every chance of introducing him to fellow writers and artists, and encouraging his poetic aspirations as well as his interest in art.

Meanwhile Masefield came to regard 'Mr. Binyon' not only with admiration and respect – his lyric poetry appealed profoundly to him – but with warm gratitude, indeed fondness; writing to Norah he several times alluded to him with touching affection as 'little Laurence Binyon':

Yesterday I had a singularly pleasant afternoon in the Print Room of the British Museum with little Laurence Binyon and Mr. Sturge Moore (the last an artist poet . . . a charming man) and I read Mr. Binyon's new play in manuscript and saw some genuine drawings of Albrecht Dürer, held them in my hand, and touched paper that Dürer himself must have held nearly four hundred years back.

Binyon probably first met Masefield at one of Yeats's Monday evenings, and at the beginning he doubtless accepted him

merely as one of Yeats's younger friends, although his curiosity
may have been stirred if Yeats introduced him – as it is said he
sometimes did – as 'my murderer' (Masefield had told him how
long ago he had attacked his governess with a fork 'with intent
to kill'). But soon Binyon was asking questions, and Masefield
was evasive, not wishing to reveal the shamefully unpoetical
nature of his current employment. This is clear from one of the
letters he wrote to Binyon from Walthamstow:

I have reproached myself, since our conversation, with having
shown, perhaps, something of a lack of frankness in replying to your
query as to my present occupation.
   I think I ought to have answered you in a more straightforward
manner.
   I am a clerk in a bank.

Binyon must have assured him that this appalling fact did
not jeopardize their friendship, for the tone of Masefield's
ensuing letters to him, written almost daily, was happy and
relaxed, as he confided to him on the subject of his favourite
poetry. 'Since I wrote to you yesterday', he told him,

I have re-read the most of your 'Odes', and am inclined to place the
modest chaplet of my affections upon 'Asoka', if for no weightier
reason, for that marvellously beautiful line

           And from black cedars a lone peacock cries

I do not know of any passage in any book I have ever read that has
thrilled me quite so completely as that single line. Perhaps a waif
strain of D.G. Rossetti (to my mind) runs its parallel

           They roam together now, *and wind among*
           Its bye-streets, knocking at the dusty inns . . .

'In a life before this life,' he went on, dropping precipitately
into American slang, 'I guess I heard the peacock, and in a life
before this I guess I beat up the dark alleys of some towered
city "by the light of the moon", and you and D.G. Rossetti are
helping me to recollect.' Reincarnation had evidently been one
of the subjects discussed recently at Woburn Buildings, for in
this same letter Masefield transcribed for Binyon a passage
from *Moby Dick* on the theme of metempsychosis, a passage

which he confessed he had quoted 'very faultily' on the occasion
of their last Monday evening meeting.

6

At twenty-three, in the summer of 1901, Masefield made two
major decisions. Firstly he resolved to leave Walthamstow, and
to live alone again, this time in central London, within closer
reach of his friends and interests. Probably at the encouragement of Binyon, who was one of the first to move into the colony
of writers and others in the little streets of run-down Queen
Anne houses behind Westminster Abbey, he established himself
in a room at number 8 Barton Street (Binyon's rooms were
close by in Smith Square). Secondly – and this decision was a
momentous one – he made up his mind to sacrifice the security
of a regular job, and to embark on the precarious life of a freelance writer. He hoped to find a market for the 'yarns' that he
longed to put on to paper, and Yeats had told him that he had
'a capacity for narrative'. So he abandoned his job at the
Capital and Counties Bank. His departure from Threadneedle
Street may, however, have been hastened by his employers, for
one of his contemporaries there subsequently put on record
that John Masefield 'left the bank after being reprimanded for
his frequent late arrivals'.

Masefield had reckoned that he would have to earn £75 a
year from his pen to survive, but he doubted whether he could
achieve even this, and it is abundantly clear that by August
his finances, as well as his health and his morale, were at an
extremely low ebb. With eczema on his neck, a painful mosquito
bite on his eyelid, and a hand that ached from writer's cramp,
he responded with heartfelt gratitude when Ethel sent him a
cheque for £25.

As to his writing, he was composing a few more sea ballads.
But encouraged by Yeats (who was then away for the summer)
he had been giving his main effort to a story which he called 'a
tale of piracy'. When he wrote to thank Ethel for the cheque
he had just made a clean copy to send to Yeats in Ireland, and
was anticipating the Master's comments with dread, because
'much needs to be done before the tale is fit for publication'.
The 'tale' never in fact attained to print, but one of his new

ballads, 'Trade Winds', was published in October by *The Out-look* (the literary and political journal which had already, three years previously, accepted one of his poems).[1] Norah, with whom he was still corresponding fairly regularly, hastened to congratulate him on 'Trade Winds', although she complained that one of his phrases, 'the soughing of the sail', had puzzled her, and she did not approve of his description of a fiddle as 'squeaking'. Her brother's reply showed that he was in a mood of deep pessimism and irritation. He wished he had burned 'that beastly ballad', so he declared crossly. 'It is a limp attempt and the last stanza is hateful to me. The sough in soughing rhymes with the feminine of boar. It derives from a Norse word signifying to murmur. "Squeaking fiddle". I repeat it.' In this same letter he frankly confessed to his state of depression; he did not dwell upon all its causes, but a few passing remarks convey the accumulation of miseries in his life, his poverty and ill health, the chronic anxieties of a writer's existence, the paralysing cold of his lodging. 'I shall be shifting house . . . these rooms being as draughty as sieves and as cold as eighteenth-century art.'

But by Christmas the tide had turned. Yeats was by then back in London, and Masefield had moved to a lodging in Bloomsbury (at 15 Coram Street) which was only a few minutes from Woburn Buildings. Zest welled up in him once more, inspiration returned, and although he still had such a cold that he could 'hardly hold up', his Christmas, so he told Norah, was 'a jolly one': 'breakfast with Yeats, dinner and tea elsewhere, and a second dinner and supper elsewhere'. The most joyful news of all however concerned his poetry: 'My ballads are being taken as fast as I can write them.' This referred chiefly to *The Outlook*, but a few weeks later he wrote again to his sister that his verses were also appearing 'on and off in different papers' (the *Tatler*, the *Speaker*, and the *Pall Mall Magazine*).

7

Masefield was by now becoming known to a widening circle, and it was at the Strangs' house in St. John's Wood, on one of

---

[1] J.M.'s contacts with *The Outlook* were initially with Albert Kinross, the assistant editor. He was also helped by F.W.H. Crosland, who joined *The Outlook* as sub-editor in 1899.

their Sunday evenings, that he first met William Rothenstein,[1] who later, in his memoirs, gave a lively description of the occasion. Laurence Binyon, who was a 'familiar' there, had brought with him a stranger, 'a quiet youth, with eyes that seemed surprised at the sight of the world, and hair that stood up behind like a cockatoo's feathers'.

As a youth he had run away to sea, Binyon whispered, and had had wondrous adventures; now he wanted to write; but he was very poor, and Binyon was helping him. After supper the stranger seated himself on the floor, and we sat round while he told us tales of adventure . . . A serious and romantic youth, I thought; and I got to like him. Indeed everyone liked him, and wished to be helpful; but to help is not always an easy matter.

For Binyon however it was not enough to wish to be helpful. Some sort of livelihood had got to be found for 'Jan', as his friends now called him (this was a diminutive that stuck to Masefield, among his intimates, for the rest of his life). Even though a few of his poems were being published, they could not bring in anything like enough for him to live on. It was typical of Binyon that at this point he helped to secure for Masefield not only one but two means of earning some money. One was in the field of poetry, and involved congenial research: Binyon was to edit a new edition of the works of Keats for Methuen, and Masefield was given the job of preparing the footnotes. But the other opportunity, though also most congenial, had nothing to do with poetry; it was a temporary job of an entirely unexpected kind.

1902 was the year when Wolverhampton, industrial capital of the northern Midlands, was to stage one of the trade exhibitions which during the latter half of the nineteenth century had become a fashionable means of promoting business, and the Wolverhampton authorities had decided that they must include an art gallery, where the main traditions of English painting, from Hogarth up until modern times, would be on show. They appointed as director of the project a local art enthusiast named Lawrence Hodson, a collector of Pre-Raphaelite paintings who had known William Morris. Soon Hodson was on the lookout

---

1 Later Sir William Rothenstein.

for an exhibition secretary, an intelligent, energetic young man with a good knowledge of art, to whom he could entrust the day to day organizing, and since he was acquainted with both Binyon and Rothenstein it is easy to see how the job was offered to Masefield.

It was an enticing prospect. For twelve months, from January to December, the work would bring in a steady income. In theory, too, once the pictures were assembled, the secretary would have plenty of leisure to read and write. But even more importantly, it was an opportunity to show what could be achieved by enthusiasm and will-power. 'If this show pans out pretty well I ought to make a big reputation,' Masefield wrote to Norah from Wolverhampton in March 1902. The exhibition was not to open till May but there was a mass of preliminary work to be done:

It means 1500 letters and dozens of personal interviews, [and] a fearful brain-racking in doing the letterpress of the catalogue. The tact of a Prime Minister, the blarney of a bagman, the courtesy of a King, and, for local artists and 'rotters', the mailed fist of a German Emperor, are essential. . . . Then you want the style of a Pater and the knowledge and memory of a Macaulay, the taste of William Morris and pretty much of his firmness with printers.

The starry-eyed dedication with which Masefield toiled away during the months before the opening certainly contributed much to the success of what he called in one of his letters to Norah 'my little show', although of course Hodson received the acclaim. According to the *Athenaeum*, then one of London's leading journals concerned with the arts (Roger Fry was its chief art critic), the Wolverhampton show was outstandingly good. 'For once in an English exhibition', the *Athenaeum* asserted, 'the appeals to cheap sentimentality and the love of theatrical display' had been severely excluded. There were four main rooms: the first was devoted to works by the earlier masters of the English school, Hogarth, Hopner, Reynolds, Gainsborough, etc.; the second contained paintings by artists of the second half of the nineteenth century (Legros, Watts, Millais); the third was given over to the Pre-Raphaelites; and the fourth was hung with contemporary work. It was here, in this 'modern room', so the *Athenaeum* pointed out with approval, that the shock to 'commonly received opinion' would be most felt, for the arrangements suggested that 'among modern artists it is Mr. Steer, Mr. Strang, Mr. C. Shannon, Mr. Ricketts and Mr. Rothenstein whose work really counts'. The writer had one (though only one) disagreement with the management – 'the use of Morris wall-papers for the walls of the galleries'.

The first half of Masefield's time as exhibition secretary was stimulating, exciting, and crammed with variety and action. But by early July his fervour was waning, and by the end of the month it was dead. Ever since the opening he had had to spend most of his time waiting about for long hours while the gaping visitors (about three thousand a week) flocked in, and stood and stared, and flocked out again. Soon he was bursting with impatience and aching to get away.

In October the exhibition closed. By this time his disillusion had given way to disgust, even though he had the consolation of knowing that the gallery had been the most popular part of the whole exhibition, and that it had won for him 'a spangled reputation'. Writing to Robert Trevelyan, with whom he had recently become friends, he castigated Wolverhampton and all that it stood for in his mind: 'From now until I leave this deadening and soul-crushing abortion of a misbegotten city, my time will be spent in packing and preparing to pack several hundred pictures covered with glass. God send they don't smash in transit, for any accident will delay my departure.'

8

Thus the year 1902 drew to an end, a year which might perhaps seem to have been an interlude, an interruption, in Masefield's life as a writer. Nevertheless during the time of busy scramble at Wolverhampton, and then during the time of tedium and misery, more and more of his writings were being published. His poems were now appearing fairly regularly in the *Speaker*, as well as various articles (he reviewed a book entitled *Sailor Tramp* by Bart Kennedy and Maxim Gorky's *Three Men*). Besides this, in the summer of 1902 the *Speaker* published a series of semi-autobiographical articles by Masefield, under the title 'A Measure of Shifting Sand' (they were based on his down-and-out experiences in America seven years earlier).

Yeats urged him to follow up these articles with a full auto-biography, but such an idea alarmed him. 'Writing plain narrative is the very devil,' he confided to Robert Trevelyan. 'I am too flamboyant and when I feel really "inspired" I write the most turgid slush that ever sickened a critic.' But a project of a different kind was taking shape at this time which was to have more lasting results for Masefield than his journalism. Writing to Trevelyan just after the Wolverhampton exhibition had closed he referred, almost casually, to 'my book . . . a book of verse to be published by Grant Richards and to be entitled *Salt-Water Ballads*'. The proofs had by now been corrected, he told him, and the book would be out, he hoped, before many weeks. He was not feeling very hopeful about its chances of selling, and he was doubtful, too, about what his friends would make of it. 'I don't know that my verses will please you very well. They are a rough and tumble lot of ballads dealing with life at sea and drunken sailors, and I can't say that there's much romance about them.'[1]

The title *Salt-Water Ballads* was not suggested by Masefield himself; it was his publisher's idea, and Grant Richards later came to realize that it was an unfortunate choice, for it implied, misleadingly, a parallel with Kipling's *Barrack-Room Ballads*. Certainly there was a superficial resemblance between the two books by reason of Masefield's use of the vernacular, but in spirit and purpose they were antithetic. Masefield's opening poem, 'A Consecration', made his purpose abundantly clear; in it he proclaimed that he had no intention of glorifying heroism or imperialism; his concern was with the outcasts, the despised, the despairing:

> Others may sing of the wine and the wealth and the mirth . . .
> Mine be the dirt and the dross, the dust and scum of the
>   earth!
> Theirs be the music, the colour, the glory, the gold;
> Mine be a handful of ashes, a mouthful of mould . . .
> Of the maimed, of the halt and the blind in the rain and the
>   cold.
> Of these shall my songs be fashioned, my tales be told.

[1] One of them was 'Sea-Fever', later to become J.M.'s most widely known poem.

As to style and manner, Masefield was vehement in rejecting the idea – put forward by some of the reviewers – that he had been influenced by Kipling. To Norah he wrote:

I have never been influenced in any way by Rudyard Kipling's verse (which I hate, and which I haven't read for three or four years). Our methods are quite distinct, and one might just as well say that Kipling got his manner from Burns as that I got mine from Kipling.

He did not deny, however, that he had been influenced by Yeats:

As to my debt to Yeats I am only too proud to admit it, but in one poem only ['The West Wind'] is there the slightest sign of imitation of his manner, and concerning that poem I talked with Yeats, and only put it into the book on his earnest recommendation.

Finally he named the models who really counted for him: 'Of the poets I have tried to emulate no-one seems to have heard. William Morris . . . the old ballad-writers, Keats, Chaucer, and some few songs in Shakespeare.'

To his brother-in-law Harry Ross, who had greeted the book with immediate enthusiasm, Masefield also wrote with much frankness:

Poet I'm not, and never shall be, but one or two of my rhymes have technical merits. Genius I'm not, but I'm pretty sure that I've kept my talents unrusted under pretty tough circumstances, and, by God's gilt-edged clouds, I'll have another smack at the shams and humbugs of this wicked world before I've done.

He also insisted to Harry, as he had to Norah, that he had not been 'under the influence' of other poets.

I've copied no-one, and no capable critic with any knowledge of modern verse can deny that I have a literary personality uncoloured by extraneous influences . . . Speaking quite impartially I think the book deserves the recognition of a maritime people. It is something new said newly . . . There is such a deal of cant, shoddy, humbug, drivel etc. going around, it is quite likely the book'll get killed before Christmas, but I feel that, in any case, I've said a straight word sure to be recognized as such by some few in the Lord's good time.

Recognition was not so tardy as Masefield anticipated. According to Grant Richards, *Salt-Water Ballads* attracted 'immediate if not considerable attention'. Within about six months of publication the first printing of five hundred copies (priced at 3*s*. 6*d*.) had been completely sold out.

Chapter Five

CONSTANCE

I

The dedication of *Salt-Water Ballads* reveals much of Masefield's state of heart at the age of twenty-four. He chose to dedicate his first book of poems to three women, all considerably older than himself, and two of them objects of his special regard and affection, namely Miss Flood and Miss Constance de la Cherois Crommelin (pronounced 'Lashery Crumlin') – the woman who within a year was to become his wife.[1] There is little doubt that Masefield was already in love with Constance Crommelin when *Salt-Water Ballads* was published. But at the time he worshipped her secretly and timidly, and he probably felt that by bracketing her with two others he could draw a discreet veil over his feelings.

Who was she then, this lady with an unpronounceable surname, for whom he had conceived a romantic passion? How did he get to know her and what was it that drew him towards sharing his life with her? What was her family, her background? What were her interests, temperament, looks? These were of course the questions that Masefield's family and friends were soon eagerly asking, and the reply he sent to a letter of congratulations from Ethel and her husband when they learnt of his engagement gives us a good idea of how 'Miss Crommelin' appeared to the starry-eyed gaze of her husband-to-be.

Description of Goddess

Height	5 ft. 6.
Hair	Perfect dark brown
Eyes	?[2]

---

1 The third of the trio, Helen ('Nellie') Heane, was a Masefield cousin who had been kind to him.

2 It is interesting that J.M. had not noticed the colour of Constance's eyes (they were hazel-brown).

Face   Very beautiful, of a rounded, calm and serious beauty, with a stateliness in it very fine to see.

              Her Christian name is Constance, and she is Irish/French . . . She is a very wise, learned and gentle woman and you'll like her . . . She is several years older than I am, God be thanked.

To Norah, too, Masefield stressed that he was glad of the difference in age. 'My lady is slightly older than I am, which, with such a bun-headed person as myself, is a jolly good thing.'

Constance was thirty-five when, at one of Laurence Binyon's dinner parties, she first met her future husband, who was eleven and a half years younger than herself. Binyon, who had wanted to return some hospitality he had received from her and her friend Isabel Fry, with whom she shared a flat, had invited them to meet 'the interesting new young poet'. This first meeting probably took place during the weeks just before Masefield left London for Wolverhampton, the blissful time at the end of 1901 when his poetic impulse yielded such abundant fruits. Both of Binyon's lady guests could be lively company and the evening was a success; furthermore Masefield evidently discovered his affinity with Constance almost at once. This is clear from his earliest surviving letter to 'Miss Crommelin', sent from Wolverhampton and dated 4 February 1902. It shows that Constance, who was a gifted teacher, with a passion for 'modern' English literature, was already taking a sincere and helpful interest in her young friend's writing. In this letter he transcribed for her his latest poem, 'The Dead Knight', to which he had been putting the final touches the day before. 'I hope you will like it,' he wrote. 'It took me a weary long time to do. The first draft was a good old grisly horror that would have stiffened a man's marrow and tied his nerves in a kink.'

The fact that Constance was Irish and an intellectual has sometimes given rise to the erroneous idea that she was one of the Yeats circle. But she was nothing of the kind. On her father's side she came of a family of Protestant gentry with origins in France and the Low Countries, who had brought the linen industry to Northern Ireland at the end of the seventeenth century, while through her mother she was connected with the Irish nobility.[1] Constance herself, who was born on 6 February 1867 – an unwanted child, the youngest of a large family – had always been remarkably intelligent. After schooling in Dublin she went up to Cambridge where she read mathematics at Newnham, and she stayed on for a fourth year to study classics and English literature. In the 1880s it was of course very unusual for a young woman of good family to attend a university, and equally so to embark on a career, but no sooner had Constance left Cambridge, in 1890, than she asserted her independence by taking a teaching post at one of the new boarding-schools for girls, Miss Lawrence's school at Brighton, which was soon to become famous as Roedean. There, as a senior mistress for seven and a half years (for the latter part of the time she was also a house mistress), she lived in an atmosphere of Unitarian earnestness, Spartan toughness, and intense enthusiasm for games and sports.

The main subject she taught was mathematics, but her 'Bible Classes', later mentioned by one of her pupils, were described as 'very thoughtful and open minded'. Many of her pupils adored her. The brilliant young senior mistress, with her strength of character, aloof good looks and calm demeanour, as well as her Cambridge attainments and her abilities as a tennis player and swimmer, could hardly fail to inspire heroine-worship. One of the girls who came under her spell was Margery Fry (a sister of Roger Fry, and latterly Principal of Somerville College, Oxford) and through her 'Miss Crommelin' first met Margery's elder sister Isabel, who was then twenty-two. At this time Isabel, to her great frustration, was living at home, and Constance suggested that although she had not been to a university she should join Miss Lawrence's school as a

---

1 The Huguenot Crommelins had once been great landowners in Northern France; for centuries they had been flax growers in Picardy before Samuel Louis Crommelin emigrated to Ireland in 1696, and started building up the linen industry on efficient lines. In the course of the next few generations, owing to the advent of the cotton trade, the family fortunes declined. When Constance was a child her father, Nicholas de la Cherois Crommelin, lived at Rockport, a 'small mansion' at Cushendun on the Antrim coast, but subsequently the estate was sold.

As regards Constance's aristocratic connections, her paternal grandmother was a daughter of the 2nd Lord Ventry, and through her mother, a Mulholland, she was a cousin of the 1st Lord Dunleath.

junior mistress. In 1891 she was taken on, and she remained on the staff for three years. Her time there was not a success. Her lack of college education made her touchy and unsure of herself, and her aggressive temperament upset the other mistresses as well as her pupils. Painfully self-conscious – although she had fine dark eyes she was short, thickset, and ugly – she had powerful emotions and no tact. Nevertheless Constance evidently found lovable qualities in her, and Isabel, in response to her affectionate solicitude, became intensely possessive.

After Isabel left, the two still kept in close touch, and although Constance stayed on at Brighton for a few years more, by 1897 she had given up her job in order to share in a tutoring venture with Isabel in London. She herself was going to coach pupils in English literature, composition, mathematics, and elementary Latin and Greek, while Isabel would 'assist' in the English subjects. This abandonment of a fairly secure career in favour of a precarious future as 'half governess, half coach', suggests that Constance's relationship with Isabel was at the time the decisive factor in her life. And five years later, when she first met Masefield, Isabel still dominated the scene.

2

Not long before his engagement Masefield paid a visit to the Cotswolds that marked the beginning of an important new interest for him. In January 1903 Charles Ashbee, an architect friend of the Strangs, staged an amateur production of Ben Jonson's *The New Inn* in the town hall at Chipping Campden, with a cast consisting of members of the Guild of Handicraft, a group he had launched under the influence of Ruskin and Morris.[1] The play was put on primarily for 'the village', but there were 'strings of visitors to keep the ball rolling', including, as well as Masefield, Strang and his family, and Goldsworthy Lowes Dickinson and his sister.

The New Inn was a seminal event for Masefield. He knew little of the theatre, for although through Yeats he had eagerly

---

[1] C.R. Ashbee (1863–1942) was a man of means as well as culture. His mother's family, the Jewish Lavys, were leading Hamburg merchants. As a young man his great enthusiasm was the revival of artistic handicrafts.

learnt a good deal about the Irish dramatic revival, his
knowledge was all at second-hand. When he witnessed the
Ben Jonson play it was the first time he had ever been really
moved by a theatrical production. It fired him with the idea
of a revivified drama, a poetical drama accompanied by a new
spontaneity in acting which would bring about a renewal in
the moribund English theatre. 'The play was first rate', he
declared (in a letter to Norah), 'on a stage without any beastly
tawdry scenery, and all the actors trying to speak verse poeti-
cally, not to gain applause by rolling their eyes and striking
attitudes . . . it was the finest thing I'd ever seen on the stage.'
Masefield's fervour, as he sat in the audience at Chipping
Campden, was clear for all to see. 'Our librarian', Ashbee
recorded in his journal, 'who is very observant, ran up to me
begging me to peep through a rift in the curtain during one
of the intervals with "I say, do look at old Masefield's eyes;
they're shining like silver." And they were that and more.'

During two or three months of the spring of 1903 Masefield's
new enthusiasm for drama was further stimulated. He discovered that John Millington Synge was lodging almost next
door to him in Bloomsbury (he himself was still in the room in
Coram Street which he had taken in order to be close to Yeats),
and for a time they saw one another often. Masefield had first
encountered Synge at one of Yeats's Monday evenings, and had
been immediately struck by his 'dark, grave face' and 'strange
personality'.[1] Synge, who was then thirty-two, was at an uneasy
interim stage of his career: his two earliest plays had not yet
been staged, and he had come to London from Paris in the hope
that Yeats could help him to find a publisher for his book on the
Aran Islands. But he soon had his 'first success', and Masefield
was among the dozen or so who witnessed it. The occasion was
in Yeats's rooms, where *Riders to the Sea* and *The Shadow of the
Glen* were read aloud very beautifully by 'a lady'. Afterwards
everyone applauded and, according to Masefield, Synge

1 Synge's 'strange personality' is also mentioned in a diary kept by Constance
Masefield in 1915 (when J.M. was 'enlarging his little sketch of Synge for the
Cuala Press'): 'Synge gave one awfully little. He seemed often gently malicious
about people and . . . never abounded in friendship or life. Yet one liked him, and
was conscious of liking him as he sat there quiet and cynical. His personality was
strange and I don't think anyone who hadn't known him could imagine him at all.'

'learned his *métier* that night . . . Until then, all his work had been tentative and in the air. After that he went forward, knowing what he could do.'

For Masefield, too, that evening's play-reading was an inspiration. He knew that Synge had heard the fables of those plays in lonely places in or near Ireland. 'There was something fresh and new about them: they came out of life.' Listening to the two plays, he was pierced by the realization that a wealth of fable lay still untouched in the lonely places of England as well as in Ireland. Then the thought came to him 'Someone ought to do something over here' and he reflected that he himself, in his Ledbury days, had known an out of the way part of England and had sensed 'its great, passionate, almost savage secret life', and that all of this was as yet unwritten.

3

In April 1903 Masefield stayed for two weeks in South Devon with Yeats's brother Jack and his wife. It was a happy time, for the three were on terms of warm friendship, and Masefield always responded joyously to surroundings of natural beauty. Their home was a remote thatched cottage, high above a stream in a lovely valley not far from the coast, and they had identified it with Ireland by calling it 'Cashlauna Shelmiddy' (an Irish rendering of 'Snails' Castle', an allusion to the abundance of snails in the vicinity).

From Devonshire Masefield wrote every day to Constance, and his letters show what a vital part was played by Jack and his wife – as confidants and advisers – at the moment when he was tending seriously towards marriage. 'The Yeatses are rare good folk', he wrote to Constance soon after his arrival at Cashlauna,

in a rare pretty house, and I talked over my worship of you, darling, in their pretty dining room last night, but I hardly like to tell you what they said as it is, I'm afraid, dear, too much in my favour. Darling Constance, they think this, that we ought to marry. Jack, who kept a very nice memory of you, was convinced of it.

'You know darling,' he wrote a day or two later, 'I must be a sore trial to Jack and Mrs. Yeats. I think I must bore them pretty nearly to desperation. Jack has drawn me in about a dozen melancholious poses, and labels them all "thinking of Her".'

One cause of his melancholy was that Constance was troubled over the discrepancy in their ages. 'About this question of age', he insisted, 'please believe me dearie that it *cannot* make any difference to my dear love of you.' He for his part had qualms on quite another point. Money problems loomed large now that he wanted to get married. Although by his standards (though not by hers) Constance was certainly well off, his own earnings from writing were paltry and so far as we know he lacked any assured private income.[1]

The fortnight that Masefield spent in Devonshire was by no means entirely a holiday; he had a pile of books to review for the *Speaker*, and his host and hostess did their best to make him keep to working hours. But in every spare moment he dashed off verses, including two ballads for *A Broad Sheet* (the lively little monthly 'page', consisting of ballads with hand-coloured illustrations, which Jack Yeats had launched in 1902). 'We were up late last night writing Cashlauna ballads,' he told Constance on Easter Monday. 'I made two or three about . . . a scoundrel named Theodor [*sic*] who comes into an old penny dreadful that is Sunday reading here.'[2]

In the meantime the spell of the countryside, as well as the chance of Jack Yeats's company, took Masefield much out of doors, and the two men went off several times for walks of twenty or twenty-five miles, though more often, so Constance was told, they spent hours amusing themselves by sailing home-made boats on the nearby stream, the Gara.

We stand on a great hillside . . . and have gorse in full bloom above, and below a fine wood that drops down to a brook that brabbles continually with a noise that goes to one's heart . . . Our great

---

1 In a letter to Ethel Ross (undated but probably written in 1904) J.M. mentioned a legacy he hoped to receive, but he gave no details.

2 Soon the 'Theodore' ballads led on to a Theodore cult. For years J.M. and Jack Yeats regaled one another with the adventures, feuds, amours, whimsies, and misdemeanours of their legendary buccaneer. Several Theodore ballads were published in the *Broad Sheet*, but for the most part his doings were recorded – both in doggerel and amusing sketches – in the letters between them, which were continually spiced with tales of Theodore and his ruthless lady-love the Lady Constanza, 'a wonderful she with black eyes, and hair like a jungle at midnight'.

delight is to build paper ships and set them afloat as targets for pebbles, and it is fine to see two such bad shots together . . . We have a wooden ship which has an engine room that smokes – real smoke . . .

I shall never forget this part of the world, and whenever I smell a faint smell of woodsmoke with a strong smell of primroses and wet grass I shall think of Cashlauna, and the toy boats skimming down the Gara towards the sea.

Back in London Masefield took stock of his prospects and concluded that intensified freelance journalism was his only hope. 'I am now going to grind out work like a barrel-organ on the August Bank,' he told Mrs. Yeats, when he wrote to thank her for his time at Cashlauna. 'And', he added, affecting the Irish idiom, 'if I can I'm going to the parson with herself in July. It's mostly a question now, alas, of dollars.' Shortly after this he wrote to Ethel that he was in touch with *The Times* and the *Daily Mail* as well as the *Manchester Guardian*, and he told Constance that he had been given help as well as useful advice by a friend at the *Speaker*:

He is going to introduce me to the *Daily News* and the *Pall Mall Magazine* and says that if I wish I can make 250 or 300 pounds a year, going easy all the time. He said that with an occasional book I could bring it up to 400. He gave me a small commission for *Speaker* articles of 1500 to 2000 words.

'Darling', he went on,

if I sell the autobiography[1] and am well established on various papers by July do you think you could risk your sweet future with me? I feel that I am better fitted for a literary life than for a more fixed position at a desk, and though I know that for your sake I ought to try to get the latter, I feel that with you by me I could keep you bravely (with lace too perhaps darling) without rusting that gold thread in my mind which you first found and made bright.

He realized that freelance journalism would mean slavery, and he was prepared for that. But in another letter to Constance he confessed that what he really yearned to do was to write 'a

[1] The 'autobiography' (see p. 71 above) was never in fact published, although later in 1903, so J.M. wrote to Jack Yeats (undated letter), Elkin Mathews were interested in the idea of producing it as an illustrated book, with woodcuts by Yeats.

simple story' for her, 'in white clean verse as wholesome as wheat, telling of man and his sorrows and all the joy of earth, and the beauty of friendship and gentle love, and all the strength and passion of noble angers . . . Dearie you must help me to do it.' Yet in spite of such wistful longings he was evidently persuaded, soon after this, to seek for some sort of steady employment. In the letter he dashed off to Ethel to announce his engagement he added 'Have got job, editorial-sub, on *Speaker*!'

4

The news that Masefield and 'Miss Crommelin' were engaged sparked off a variety of reactions amongst their friends and relations. Constance's decision to marry caused much anguish to Isabel Fry, but strange as it may seem Constance took the line that there was no need to sever the intimacy between them – in any case they were going to continue working together.[1] And in tune with this Masefield accepted Isabel quite happily, with no tinge of jealousy, as a friend – a very close friend – of the 'gentle lady' whose judgement he so utterly respected.

As to Constance's family (who had earlier left Ireland and settled near London, at Blackheath), they were very happy when they saw how happy she was, so she wrote reassuringly to 'Jan': 'Aunt Emily asked Isabel what were your views on Politics and Religion, and she said, "Oh about the same as Con's". Con is all right in Aunt Emily's eyes – in spite of her heresies, so you'll be all right too.' One of Constance's nieces, however, later recalled that when the news reached her family, her mother (Mrs. Holmes) announced with scorn, 'Your Aunt Constance is going to marry an obscure poet.'

---

1 This is confirmed by a 'declaration' which Constance set down in June 1903, i.e. a month before her marriage, in a small private notebook:

I want always to cherish, honour and protect Isabel. I will try always to have leisure for her every day and I know that in order to keep the bond of friendship as close as possible that I must keep absolutely parallel with her life.

I must always be as tender as I can, always remembering the dear character that I know so well, knowing that her temperament is melancholy and that it will never be any good pretending or assuming she has forgotten what she never can forget. I will try always to spend Easter with her, and we shall have one meal together daily whenever possible. I will pray for her always.

At the *Speaker* office the editor, J.L.Hammond,[1] 'gurgled with pleasure all day' after hearing the news (so Masefield told Constance) and kept repeating 'Well, I *am* delighted. Miss Crommelin is so *very* charming'. Masefield also had a 'charming letter' from Lady Gregory. But when he went to the British Museum, to share his rejoicing with Laurence Binyon, he was greeted with astonishment, even dismay. Binyon felt in a way responsible, since he had introduced the couple in the first place, and he was concerned about the difference in their ages.

Among the Masefields, Jack's brothers and sisters were glad that he was obviously so happy, although when they met Constance they found her intimidating. With Aunt Kate it was a different matter. When she invited Jack to bring Constance to the Priory for a weekend it proved to be the occasion of a distressing clash. The main reason was that Constance was thinking of a registry office wedding, and this utterly scandalized Aunt Kate. 'A registrar is as good a marrier as a parson,' Masefield later wrote in one of his novels, 'yet to country nostrils he leaves a whiff of brimstone about the lady's skirts.' Constance was a person who did not like giving in, but Aunt Kate, by dint of tireless bludgeoning, secured an assurance that the marriage would take place in church. She got her way, however, by means of such offensiveness that Masefield was still in a fury when he wrote a few days later to 'Con': 'Insolent and sneering treatment I have always had from her, but that she should extend the same treatment to you is a thing not to be suffered. It has made me more angry than I care to think about.' To Harry Ross he used stronger language:

We were down there last week-end, and a viler and more damnable reception than Con had could not be meted out in Hell to one of the worst of the lost. That sour curse in Eve's flesh nagged at her openly and covertly and I am not going to have anything more to do with a repulsive hag so dead to the requirements of decency, courtesy and

[1] J.L.Hammond (1872–1949) was a well-known journalist and social historian. In 1899 he undertook the editorship of the *Speaker*, a new Liberal weekly started in opposition to the *Spectator* after the Home Rule issue had split the Liberal Party: in 1907 the *Speaker* became the *Nation* under the editorship of H.W.Massingham. Hammond's most celebrated books are a trilogy covering the years 1760–1832, written in conjunction with his wife (*The Village Labourer*, *The Town Labourer* and *The Skilled Labourer*).

reverence ... For her to go spitting her venom at a dear lady who was also her guest is a thing I will take care she shall regret ... I shall put her into a ballad and into a book and into a curse in metre with seven sibilants in every line.

Masefield's devotion to his 'dear lady' caused him to welcome every suggestion she made for his good, and her instincts as a schoolteacher prompted her to make quite a number. While at Cashlauna he had tried to keep a promise to her to cut down on smoking, and after his return to London he dosed himself faithfully, on her advice, with a foul-tasting tonic. When she insisted that he must use a fountain pen instead of an ordinary nib he persevered accordingly, although he found this an irksome struggle. She also tried to help him to save; after his trip to Devonshire he wrote (4 May 1903) 'Now dearie, will you let me draw out the twelve pounds I lately gave you?'

A further instance of his willing subservience concerned the plans for the honeymoon. At the end of May he had written to Jack Yeats asking him to find rooms for them somewhere near Cashlauna. But shortly afterwards he wrote again.

It was very good of you to go over to Torcross but as things are I expect we shall go to Ireland, not Devonshire, for the honeymoon. You see Con is Irish and wants to go to Antrim, in which County she was born, and so to that county we shall probably go.

> In County Antrim near the sea
> How very happy I shall be ...
> Our married life will be begun
> Within the walls of Cushendun.

He then however added with some apprehension, 'I hope it will be fine on the sea, for sea sickness on a honeymoon seems a hellish prospect!'

As to the wedding, Isabel was in charge. The circumstances were unusual, in that the bride's family was not formally associated with the occasion, and Isabel stepped in to fill the gap. The invitations had been sent out in her name, and she had bidden the guests to come on 22 July to an at-home at her flat, 5M Hyde Park Mansions. They were also invited to come on the following day to St. Mark's Church, Marylebone Road, for the marriage ceremony.

In spite of the recent row Aunt Kate had been invited, and she was intending to come, but was prevented from doing so by a stratagem on the part of Norah. The two were staying at Eastbourne, and were supposed to come to London together for the wedding. Norah, who had witnessed the unpleasantness at the Priory and was dreading a further scene, decided to feign illness, and made a convincing pretence of having been stricken by sunstroke. As she anticipated, Aunt Kate refused to go to the wedding alone. They therefore missed the spectacle of Isabel weeping copiously in public.

And what of Masefield's emotions on his wedding day? He was deeply, blindly, passionately – and yet serenely – in love. On the evening before the wedding he wrote to Constance:

I thought my last night of bachelorhood would be a sad night . . . But I cannot think of the past and hardly of the dear days that are to begin for us tomorrow. I can only say God bless and keep you darling, and may he help me to be a better man, fitter to be your comrade, and your road mate, and may the ways be sweet to us, the hedges ever in leaf, and the larks singing until we reach the tavern where we rest.

5

For the first year of Masefield's married life, he and Constance made their home in the comfortable flat in Marylebone Road where Constance was already established. Soon she became pregnant. Meantime Masefield's working life was far from relaxed. After the publication in October 1903 of his second book of verse, *Ballads* (he himself thought it better than *Salt-Water Ballads*), he wrote poetry only sporadically, chiefly because of the overwhelming pressure of his other work.[1]

Perforce depending on his wife's income, he drove himself mercilessly. Clutching at anything he could in the way of journalism, he churned out articles for the *Speaker* and the *Manchester Guardian* (especially narratives based on his experiences at sea and in America) and at the same time contributed to the *Daily News* and various other newspapers and magazines.

1 At the end of his first year of marriage J.M. wrote to W.B. Yeats 'I cannot write prose all day, and verses when the prose is done. I have written 160,000 words (the length of two novels) this year.'

He also did an astounding amount of reviewing, mainly of novels. In a letter written at about this time he mentioned that he had got 'a page of reviewing 20 books weekly', and in others he referred to '24 books to review at once' and 'over 80 books to review'. It is hardly surprising that he became adept at summing up and judging a book's essentials, and a *Manchester Guardian* acquaintance later praised his novel notices as 'the shortest and most incisive that we had. He could pack an extraordinary amount of criticism into a small paragraph.'

Feverish journalism was not however Masefield's only work at this time. In the spring of 1904 he took a temporary job which came his way as a result of his success as Wolverhampton: under the aegis of William Rothenstein he helped to organize another art exhibition in an industrial town, this time Bradford. He did not, as at Wolverhampton, have to remain on the spot for months, since the Bradford exhibition lasted for only a week (to mark the opening of a new art gallery) but it was, in its way, equally an ordeal. The Bradford public was not prepared to accept Impressionism and presumably Masefield had to bear the brunt of their disapproval throughout what he called 'the abominable week'. 'But for you', he wrote afterwards to Rothenstein, 'I should have gone home long before the Saturday.'

When he did return to London, to slave away once more at his writing, it was to a flat where life now centred round a nursery; on 28 April 1904 Constance had given birth to a daughter (whom they decided to call Judith, or rather Isabel Judith Yeats). A lively description of the trio was written a few months later by Mrs. Ashbee (in her journal) after she had called at the flat to see them:

John Masefield has got a wife and a baby. An elderly wife and a very modern baby who at four months looks on the world with dangerously lustrous eyes, quietly and comprehensively out of a mature and well modelled face – and gives you a rather sad smile and a thin little hand to clasp. I suppose it is Mrs. Masefield's university learning and John's . . . romance and mysticism blended in this unexpected infant.

Our former starving poet is now in a better way of life, thanks to this wife who has money and a flat and a cat; Jan . . . (as he now calls himself) has to take the last in the bargain, and humbles himself much before the animal, coaxing him with creamy and fishy dainties. He has also learned to make excellent coffee, and to open the door for you, and is slowly realising which end of the baby Judith is to be held upwards.

Mrs. Ashbee then added a telling remark about the role that Constance had assumed:

She uses Jan as a sort of aide-de-camp to her generalship, and it seems the one chance of making such a dreamer achieve anything. He sits as of old in the chimney corner and gazes with grey-silver eyes into space, every now and then coming-to, to begin a story of a pirate called Slashing Roderick who sailed away in the good ship so and so – till he is brought to earth by his wife asking him to ring for tea.

An interesting conversation then took place, so Mrs. Ashbee recorded, which revealed Masefield's new devotion to Ireland[1] and also Constance's utopianism.

'London is hideous, horrible . . .' John murmured in his misty voice – 'the thing to do of course is to give up all this and go to Ireland and wander from hut to hut fiddling and telling tales to the Folk.'

'Janeen you're talking nonsense,' says his wife. 'I don't believe in this Folk of yours, you wouldn't find them there in this century – all that's dead and there's no going back to it. We must go forward; we know what we are making for.'

'Yes, we're making for a limitless Brixton, it's all Brixton – a hopeless waste of life. Never mind, someday we'll go to Campden and I'll make poems and you shall teach in the secondary schools.'

But the Masefields did not go to Campden, nor did they move to Ireland, when in the summer of 1904 they decided that they must acquire a house of their own. 'We are mightily plagued with house hunting,' Masefield wrote to Jack Yeats, '[but] we cannot tell where to go . . . Perhaps we may take a house in Greenwich, as there are some there, of great beauty, going cheap.'[2] Soon after this they did in fact settle on Greenwich, and took a semi-detached Regency house in a quiet byway called

---

[1] J.M. was recently back from a stay at Cushendun with Charles Ashbee.

[2] Constance had a special link with Greenwich because her brother Andrew Crommelin, the member of her family with whom she kept most closely in touch after she left home, had since 1891 been an Assistant at the Royal Observatory, a post he held for more than thirty years.

Diamond Terrace. Described by a friend as 'Churchwarden
Gothic and very sweet' it looked out over the river from the
steep slope to the west of the Park. 'We are going to live at
Greenwich', Masefield wrote to W.B. Yeats, 'in a little lonely
house not very far from the river, and I hope that sometimes,
when there are some fine ships to see, you will come with me
to see them.' But alas he was not enamoured of the Thames or
of the London docks.

It is a wretched river after the Mersey, and the ships are not like the
Liverpool ships, and the docks are barren of beauty. But the sailortown is yet the one human part of London, and I hope I shall find
happiness, if no ballad poetry, in wandering about among the crimps,
by the marine stores, with a sailor as a comrade, and a quid of jacky
in my cheek. But it is a beastly hole after Liverpool; for Liverpool is
the town of my heart and I would rather sail a mud-flat there than
command a clipper ship out of London.

Number 1 Diamond Terrace was at first only partially 'home'
for John and Constance, for hardly had they taken possession
than C.P. Scott, the editor of the *Manchester Guardian*, offered
Masefield an editorial job which would mean working in
Manchester. Much heart-searching ensued at Greenwich, but
eventually, in spite of Masefield's loathing for office work, he
accepted, and went north in October 1904. In the meantime
Constance, with baby Judith and her nurse,[1] reverted to living
most of the time with Isabel.

The Manchester job, which involved much night work –
Masefield's usual hours were 8.30 p.m. till 10 a.m. – proved to
be an anguishing strain. The autocratic Scott demanded utter
dedication from his staff, and after a couple of months Masefield
wrote to Jack Yeats that he was 'fairly sodden with want of
sleep'. Nevertheless he made a success of his main work which
was to comb the world press for news items of interest or
amusement and to present them in a daily column entitled
'Miscellany'.

From time to time he had to be in London, and could return
briefly to Greenwich. A vivid glimpse of life at Diamond
Terrace is provided in a letter written by Janet Ashbee to her
husband in January 1905, after she had stayed a night there. It

---

1 A countrywoman named Alice Rudkin.

was a bitter winter evening when she and Masefield made
their way to Greenwich by bus (Constance was to join them
later) and the house, when they reached it, was 'colder than
charity' being 'only intermittently inhabited . . . There was a
sort of spectral servant about, but Jan lit my bedroom fire,
brought in hot water, and apologized in his gentle courteous way
for absence of many things, including his wife and his baby.'
The two then had 'a dear little dinner' together, amid clouds of
frozen breath, and afterwards, until Constance finally arrived,
they huddled round 'a sort of bonfire', while Masefield read
aloud from his poems and stories and also from 'his latest plays'.
He evidently found Janet Ashbee a sympathetic listener, for
just after her stay he wrote to her: 'I hope you will come again
soon . . . when we are more settled . . . I am in the middle of
another play . . . It is hanging fire horribly.'

These references to Masefield's plays suggest that he had
already written quite a number. The plays themselves seem to
have vanished without a trace, but there are hints in his letters
that they were somewhat in the 'Theodore' manner. One of the
first to be mentioned was *The Buccaneer*, and there was also a
'meaty drama', *The Wrecker's Corpse*. It may seem amazing that
Masefield was able to compose plays, even juvenile melo-
dramas, when burdened by the unrelenting demands of his
journalism, but producing plays 'in his head' had long been a
delight to him – a rest and an amusement rather than a labour.
And while at Greenwich this long-standing habit developed
further. Inspired by the example of Jack Yeats, who had a
flair for producing blood-and-thunder dramas written specially
for the miniature stage, Masefield constructed a little model
stage for which he painted the scenery; he then cut out tiny
dolls to represent the actors, using chessmen as supers when he
needed a larger cast. Looking back to this time he recalled that
when he used to pull out his model stage with the little dolls
and work at a scene, it was 'not really work at all'.

6

Masefield stuck to the *Manchester Guardian* job for about five
months, but in the spring of 1905 he could stand it no longer.
'I have left Manchester,' he wrote to Harry Ross in April, 'as

the work was too awful, and the town wasn't possible as a residence.' He was writing to Harry to ask for some legal advice, for he had just had a rude jolt in connection with one of his *Manchester Guardian* narratives.[1] 'Anty Bligh', a ghost story in sailor's vernacular, had been pirated, title and all, by a would-be playwright called Moore. The first that Masefield knew of this was when he learnt that a one-act play entitled *Anty Bligh* was shortly to be performed in London, as a curtain raiser before a production of Sheridan's *The Critic* by the Mermaid Society. 'I never heard of a more cool piece of insolence,' he fumed, 'nor a deed more grossly unprofessional. I wonder if you would tell me of any Act by which the swine may be squelched.'

A few days later, having been briefed by Harry, he wrote a blistering letter to 'Moore', a Mancunian who had unexpectedly proved to be *Miss* Moore, 'a female girl, aged 18, very ignorant of the world'. 'Dear Madam,' he wrote,

I think you cannot fully understand how flagrantly your play will infringe my copyright.

I cannot consent to its production unless you undertake, in writing, (1) to pay me half of all money you receive for it; (2) to abstain from printing it; (3) to refrain from offering it to any other theatrical manager whatsoever. If you will not agree to these terms I shall call upon Mr. Carr[2] to stop the piece and obtain an injunction against you. I am a writer of dramatic pieces myself, and under no circumstances should I have allowed you to use my story had you approached me in the proper manner.

Terrorized by this onslaught the 'female girl' yielded to Masefield's conditions. But despite his victory, and despite some favourable publicity for himself which resulted from the play's

---

[1] J.M. often turned to his brother-in-law for legal help. Harry Ross had assisted with the legal arrangements at the time of his marriage, and also with drawing up a will. In an undated letter written in the spring of 1904, J.M. wrote:

I want you to make my will for me leaving everything including manuscripts, books and copyrights to Con, in case I predecease her. Should she die before me I would like to leave everything to be divided equally between Ethel, Jack Yeats and W.B.Yeats, and in this case I would like all my manuscripts to go to the brothers Yeats (Jack alone would be better perhaps) to burn or publish as he thinks fit.

[2] Philip Carr was President of the Mermaid Society.

production,[1] the incident continued to rankle. To Mrs. Ashbee he wrote at the end of April, 'A thieving pirate of a woman has just stolen a tale of mine and made an abominably silly play of it. I am fuming and furious for the law affords no remedy.'

The time at Manchester thus came to an end on a note of angry discord, and Masefield vented his abhorrence of town life and of office work upon the city itself. To Harry Ross, who often served him as a safety-valve, he wrote explosively, 'Good God, it is a hole!', and he then made a last swipe at the defeated plagiarist: 'No wonder Moore lives there!'

Shaking off the dust of Manchester and of the *Guardian* office, Masefield hastened away to Devonshire, to cleanse his spirit at Cashlauna, and afterwards made a trip to Ireland, where he stayed with Lady Gregory. This was not the first time he had been to Coole. He had stayed there the previous autumn, and his impressions of it then had been favourable; now, however, in contrast to Cashlauna, he found the place unconducive to psychic peace. 'Coole *has* a bad aura,' he wrote afterwards (1 May 1905) to Mrs. Jack Yeats. 'While I was there I had a continual feeling of something malignant and uncanny surrounding the house every night.'

> O there be ghosts both black and white
> And spectres long and short
> And there be ghosts that walk the night
> About the woods of Gort.
>
> And grim and grey as the darkness grows
> Their ghastly eyeballs burn
> When the twilight's hoarse with the cries of crows
> They slink from the clumps of fern.
>
> They walk the woods till the moon has set
> While the moonlight yet abides
> And they make the traveller cold with sweat
> As they wander down the rides.
>
> They gibber and wail in the woods of Gort
> They laugh ha ha at the moon
> If a wise man chance to watch their sport
> He turns to a crazy loon.

[1] G.K. Chesterton in the *Speaker* (29 April 1905), after mentioning that the play was 'founded on a story by Mr. Masefield', wrote that Masefield was 'certainly (as I think) a genius'.

Another visit that Masefield made in the spring of 1905, this time with Constance to Chipping Campden to stay with the Ashbees, left him in a very different mood. He loved the Cotswold village so much that after he left to return to London, he was overcome with melancholy.

> When I from Campden town depart
> I leave my wits, I lose my art,
> A melancholy clouds my face
> I feel as though I fell from grace.
> With morals sapped and manners gone
> I come to dingy Paddington,
> Sing willow   willow   willow.
>
> But when I come to Campden Town
> I've adjectives for every Noun
> I tire pretty patient Con
> With brilliant conversa-ti-on
> My virtues beam from every pore
> I feel myself a man and more
> Sing all a green palm bough
>   shall be my garland.

The life at Greenwich to which Masefield returned after departing from Manchester was infinitely more congenial than being chained every night to a desk in a newspaper office, but it did mean an empty house (Constance still had her teaching and often stayed with Isabel) as well as a 'loathsome mass of work'. For Masefield, at the age of twenty-seven, it was a time of deep pessimism. His work now included not only endless reviews and articles but editing commitments for several publishers and also his first prose book, a long historical essay, *Sea Life in Nelson's Time*, which exposed the brutality of life under sail (it was published by Methuen in September 1905).

Some months later he was grappling with his next historical book for Methuen, *On the Spanish Main*, and also editing a two-volume edition of *Dampier's Voyages* for Grant Richards. Meanwhile Constance helped him with the editing of two further books for Grant Richards, *Lyrists of the Restoration* and *Essays Moral and Polite, 1660–1714*, and he also edited for the same publisher *The Poems of Robert Herrick* and *Lyrics of Ben Jonson, Beaumont and Fletcher*.

When Ethel and Harry wrote begging him to come and see them he replied, 'I'm afraid I can't possibly manage a weekend. I work seven days a week alas . . . You taste real luxury, fifty-two Sundays, four or five Bank Holidays, and three weeks clear, or 70-odd days a year.' Yet although he claimed that he slaved from one end of the week to the other he did sometimes escape on Sunday evenings. In Diamond Terrace there was a Sailors' Home, a curious place, so Masefield told Jack Yeats, which could put up as many as seventy seamen at a time. 'They hold a sing-song there every Sunday night, and it is fine to hear "Rolling Home" again, after so long a spell.'

Chanties were much in his mind at this time, for along with all his other books he was compiling an anthology of sea poetry, *A Sailor's Garland*, and in it he included an article on chanties which had first appeared in the *Manchester Guardian*, and which had attracted considerable attention; it had spurred many old sailors to send in further specimens. But as far as Masefield was concerned it had more important repercussions; it proved to be a stepping stone towards a major new development in his life as a writer, for unexpectedly it opened a door into the world of the theatre. In March 1906 Shaw's play *Captain Brassbound's Conversion* was about to be produced at the Court Theatre, with Ellen Terry as Lady Cicely, and Granville-Barker was considering the use of chanties to enhance the nautical atmosphere. Masefield, who had suddenly become the acknowledged expert on the subject, was called in to advise.[1]

7

Masefield was already writing plays in all seriousness, and with a deliberate purpose.[2] To Rothenstein he explained that he was going through 'a mill of prose drama, the strictest discipline a writer can have', in order that his future work might 'keep more closely to life', 'and away from dreams and nightmares, and

[1] Shaw himself, however, had doubts about the chanty idea. On 14 March 1906 he wrote to Granville-Barker: 'I did not do anything about the chanty. We should have a special rehearsal of extras for it if we attempt it: it is impossible to stop a rehearsal for it. Unless they pick it up very easily it won't be worth the trouble.'

[2] Two prose plays, *The Sweeps of '98* and *The Locked Chest*, written by J.M. at this time, were not published until 1916.

the adornments and dress of life'. But contact with the Court Theatre and its personalities transformed his play-writing from a discipline into a living enterprise. *The Campden Wonder*, his first play to be actually staged, was produced at the Court for eight performances between 8 January and 1 February 1907.

Based on a shocking miscarriage of justice which had taken place at Chipping Campden in the seventeenth century, this short three-act play, in the Grand Guignol manner, was intended to appal – and indeed it did (the climax was a triple hanging, not shown, but implied off-stage). The *succès de scandale* that ensued launched Masefield as a playwright, despite the fact that the production at the Court had been a fiasco. Granville-Barker had presented the tragedy as the latter half of a programme in which it was preceded by a 'very light comedy' (*The Reformer* by Cyril Harcourt). 'I never saw a more hopeless failure,' Masefield lamented to Lady Gregory. Yet one of those who put all the blame on the producer, not the author, was Bernard Shaw himself. In a letter to Masefield remarkable for its kindness and understanding, he condemned Granville-Barker's juxtaposition of the tragedy and the comedy as 'one of those aberrations of which only clever people like G.B. are capable.' He added 'I have since exhausted every form of insult at my command to impress on him my opinion of the programme.'

At once Masefield set to work on another play, another rustic melodrama, *The Tragedy of Nan*, based on a tale which he had heard a few years earlier from Miss Flood. Nan's tragedy was said to have taken place in Kent in the early nineteenth century, but Masefield transposed it to a locality with which he was himself familiar, the banks of the Severn. There he showed Nan, a beautiful peasant girl, living miserably in the home of a cruel uncle and aunt. The aunt treats her with sadistic harshness. Nan is in love with Dick, and he loves her too – but only up to a point; when she tests his love he withdraws. Crazed by grief she stabs him and rushes out to throw herself into the Severn.

When *Nan* was published in book form, Masefield wrote a thoughtful introduction in which he claimed that tragedy is 'a vision of the heart of life'. And certainly *The Tragedy of Nan* contains a vision of the heart of his own life, the life which had been grievously wounded by a cruel guardian. In some of Nan's speeches – when she lets fly at her aunt – Masefield's heroine seems indeed to be giving voice to his own feelings:

Don't you speak. Don't you threaten. You'll listen to me. You 'ad me in your power. And wot was good in me you sneered at. And wot was sweet in me, you soured. And wot was bright in me you dulled. I was a fly in a spider's web. And the web came round me and round me, till it was a shroud, till there was no more joy in the world. Till my 'eart was bitter . . . and all choked.

Nan was first produced on 24 May 1908, under Granville-Barker's direction, by a theatrical society called the Pioneers, and it was an immediate success; it was revived as a matinée at the Haymarket Theatre in the following month. The production owed much to the performance of Lillah McCarthy in the title role: this fine actress (who had recently married Granville-Barker) was then triumphing as a creator of Shavian heroines. Her dark queenly looks and vigour of style gave to Masefield's poor country girl 'an intense and moving beauty'.

Masefield's professional association with the Granville-Barkers led on to a close friendship,[1] and Lillah McCarthy was one of the first of the beautiful and talented women who, throughout his life, inspired him, and at whose feet he worshipped. Yet his devoted dependence on Constance, and their mutual trust, remained unshaken, and she – loving, maternal, dominating – watched him and guided him at every step. 'I don't *think*, if I were you', she wrote to him apropos of Lillah,[2]

I should go on dining with Mrs. Barker any more. I fancy she rather loves having bevies of men round her when she is alone, and I don't think it is a very dignified position for the men. This is said in jealousy *for* you, and for the regard that I want people to have for you, not in any distrust or in the wrong sort of jealousy. But I know we neither of us like the people who 'hang around'. It is what makes people 'slight'.

1 J.M. sometimes stayed with the Granville-Barkers in Kent, and they helped him a great deal with his next play, *The Tragedy of Pompey the Great*.
2 This letter was probably written during one of Constance's sojourns with Isabel.

Chapter Six

BREAKTHROUGH

'I have just been painted (by William Strang), standing on one leg with a hat on my head and an overcoat over my shoulder. The sea is behind me, a celestial globe to my right, and a coloured cloth like a duster under my hand': so Masefield wrote to Miss Flood in the spring of 1909. The painting in question – 'John Masefield: the Discoverer' – shows him in a striking manner as he was at the age of thirty. No longer a 'starving poet' he is now a man in his prime, with a face that has filled out, and a wide moustache that gives him a look of maturity. His expression is reflective and sad and there was good reason for this melancholy; poetry was still crowded out of his life.[1] At the beginning of his thirties Masefield was still fighting the uphill battle of trying to make a living from his pen, mostly from journalism, and editing and introductory work, but also now from stories for boys and full-length novels.

At this time he employed a literary agent, C.F. Cazenove,[2] and according to Grant Richards, who until 1910 was Masefield's main publisher, Cazenove and he 'conspired' together, and as a result Masefield's two first novels were published in

---

1 J.M.'s third book of poetry, *Ballads and Poems*, was published in 1910, but the poems in it had almost all been written some time earlier. One of them, 'Cargoes' (written in 1902) subsequently aroused a perennial controversy. Its opening lines – 'Quinquireme of Nineveh from distant Ophir / Rowing home to haven in sunny Palestine' – have been repeatedly questioned by sticklers for topographical accuracy, on grounds that the site of Nineveh was 200 miles inland. J.M., when challenged, amused himself by producing good-humoured excuses. To the query of an Eton boy (probably in 1924) he replied 'I can only suggest that a Ninevean syndicate must have chartered the ship; even so it was odd.' To another enquirer, Mr. Stuart Fawkes, J.M. wrote (23 January 1930): 'It has often puzzled myself that a quinquireme owned in Nineveh should be rowing to Palestine, but perhaps before the Flood fully subsided such things were possible.'

2 Later, after Cazenove's death during the First World War, J.M. reverted to dealing directly with his publishers, relying much on Constance's advice, and helped by the Society of Authors.

1908 and 1909: *Captain Margaret* (a story of adventure and romance on the Spanish Main) and *Multitude and Solitude* (a contemporary novel centring round a scientist's campaign against sleeping sickness). Fiction on this scale did not come easily to Masefield at first; he later admitted that he had to force himself to compose these two full-length novels.

The foreground of Masefield's life during his early thirties – his work as a writer – thus consisted of an unending, and at times overwhelming, struggle to keep up with publishers and editors. The background – his personal life – was also at a particularly difficult stage. His general health was poor, and despite his hatred of town-dwelling the family had moved from Greenwich to a district closer to the centre of London; they now lived in the Paddington area, at number 30 Maida Hill West,[1] a spacious early Victorian house adjoining the Regent's Canal,[2] in the locality now known as 'Little Venice'. This move had doubtless been made in the interests of Constance's teaching and of her friendship with Isabel, for it meant that she was closer to Marylebone Road, where the school that she and Isabel were still jointly running was by now well established.

The Masefields were now also nearer to various friends – to the Strangs at St. John's Wood, for example, and the Rothensteins at Highgate. But for Masefield himself, with his heart in the wilds and on the oceans, social amenities counted for little. He plastered the walls of his study with charts and buried himself in his work; if sometimes he left his desk to gaze out of the window, he may have derived consolation from watching the coming and going of the canal barges: the Regent's Canal was then a main artery between the London docks and the Midlands. Nevertheless there was no forgetting that he was imprisoned in a great city, with its grime and stench and asphyxiating fogs. And round the corner lay the long stretches of Edgware Road to remind him of London's commercialism and tawdriness. Living thus cut off from the countryside and the sea – except for blessed interludes in spring and summer,

---

1 The street has since been renamed Maida Avenue.

2 In 1929 the name 'Regent's Canal' was dropped, and replaced by 'Grand Union Canal'. The Regent's Canal was in fact part of the latter (much more extensive) waterway.

chiefly in Ireland but now also in Cornwall[1] – he wilted like an
unwatered plant.

In 1909 however a new era began: the Masefields secured a
country foothold of their own. Jointly with Isabel they took a
small house, the Rectory Farm, in the village of Great Hampden
near Great Missenden. To Miss Flood Masefield described it as
'a lovely little farm in Buckinghamshire, high up on a chalk hill
surrounded by beechwoods and commonland, a very fresh,
pretty, but rather bare and cold country, like most chalk hills'.
Great Hampden, for the next few years, was a treasured retreat
for Masefield, and in holiday times a second home for Constance and Isabel, while for Judith (who was four at the time of
the move from Greenwich) life in the country was a new delight.
'Judykins'[2] was an enchanting child, with a great look of her
father, and colouring that was vivid and dark. In the diary of
one of her parents' friends – John Galsworthy – she is mentioned
with spontaneous admiration: 'On Sunday April 3 [1910]',
Galsworthy wrote, 'Lunched with the Rothensteins. Thence to
the Masefields for tea, where met Ada, who played with the
delicious Judith on the floor.'

Fatherhood meant a great deal to Masefield. 'Children make
life a different thing, to the man as well as to the woman,' he
wrote to Charles Ashbee, and to his brother Harry he re-
iterated this: 'Children are about the best things one gets out of
life, and they make all the difference in the world to marriage.'
The role of dedicated parent came naturally to him. To Janet
Ashbee (who had sought advice about her poetry) he wrote,
revealingly, 'A poem is like a little child; one ought to give it
all that one has.'

Judith herself, in retrospect, has testified to her intense
enjoyment of her father's company. Since her mother was so
often out, she spent most of her time with the family's devoted
maid, Nellie Martin, but her games with her father were what
she lived for. When she was tiny they had played at shops
together and she always remembered his hilarious impersona-

---

1 J.M.'s cherished links with Devonshire had had to be broken when Jack Yeats
decided to sell his house, and to move permanently to Ireland.

2 This was only one of the pet names that J.M. used for Judith when she was small:
others were 'Mouse', 'Kit', and 'Pusskins'.

tions of fussy customers – he was a brilliant mimic. And then, as she grew older, he built toys for her; a special favourite was a 'ship' consisting of a soapbox on wheels in which she could sit. He also taught her to read, and she used to sit on his knee in his study, after his morning's work, while he drew pictures in coloured ink of ships and horses and pirates, and told her thrilling adventure stories in serial form.

2

On 4 July 1910 Constance, at the age of forty-three, gave birth to a second child, a son. It must surely have been a time of great exultation for her husband, especially as little Lewis proved to be an infant of remarkable beauty. And one might have thought that it would also be a time when his writings would have reflected a new appreciation of Constance as wife and mother. But this was not so. One of the very few poems he wrote during the months that she was pregnant, a deeply melancholy meditation upon motherhood, and upon women in general, suggests that he had by now failed to find in Constance some of the qualities that he associated, at the deepest levels of his being, with the image of his own long-dead mother, whose initials, C.L.M., formed the poem's title.[1] It also suggests that he felt himself in some way to blame for this, and was suffering from an irrational sense of guilt.

> in the dark womb where I began
> My mother's life made me a man.
> Through all the months of human birth
> Her beauty fed my common earth.
> I cannot see, nor breathe, nor stir,
> But through the death of some of her.
>
> Down in the darkness of the grave
> She cannot see the life she gave.
> For all her love, she cannot tell
> Whether I use it ill or well.
> Nor knock at dusty doors to find
> Her beauty dusty in the mind.

1 'C.L.M.' was published in J.M.'s *Ballads and Poems* (1910).

If the grave's gates could be undone,
She would not know her little son,
I am so grown. If we should meet
She would pass by me in the street,
Unless my soul's face let her see
My sense of what she did for me.

What have I done to keep in mind
My debt to her and womankind?
What woman's happier life repays
Her for those months of wretched days?
For all my mouthless body leeched
Ere Birth's releasing hell was reached?

What have I done, or tried, or said
In thanks to that dear woman dead?
Men triumph over women still,
Men trample women's rights at will
And man's lust roves the world untamed.

*   *   *

O grave, keep shut lest I be shamed.

The gloom and pessimism of this poem, and Masefield's troubled, confused ruminations concerning womankind, should not however be taken to mean that his marriage was proving a failure. Rather it had settled down into its permanent pattern, with Constance ('My old darling' as he wrote to her) proving truly a helpmeet, the sort of dominant helpmeet, intellectual as well as practical, that he needed so essentially. After five years of married life 'Con' was more than ever the senior partner in their daily affairs, a sharer of his professional interests and also of his outdoor enthusiams: the spartan habits inculcated at Roedean stood her in good stead, and she happily roughed it on their holiday expeditions. She was also, he readily admitted, the foremost inspirer of his writings. 'She is my genius', he confided to a close friend, 'I am only a pen. Her pen at my best, I hope; but all my talent comes from her.' And yet it is evident that by now, in her husband's eyes, Constance was failing him in one important respect, though he may never have acknowledged this to himself. She was beginning to lose her looks, and the familiarity of marriage had come to mean that she was no longer his revered and enigmatic

'Lady', his romantic idealization of womanhood, the paragon of stately grace whom he had enthroned and worshipped during their engagement. And this, no doubt, partly accounts for the abnormal intensity of a relationship with another woman which began, and which also ended, within the period of his wife's second pregnancy. The woman in question was Elizabeth Robins, the expatriate American actress and author.

In order to understand why the infatuation took the course it did we must first of all remind ourselves that Masefield was at this time in a state of excruciating nervous tension from overwork. In February 1910 he himself admitted to Miss Robins that he was often so exhausted after a day of 'intense writing' that he was 'unable to talk sense, much less write it':

When I go out at the end of a day's work, I have been dying on the cross for eight hours, that the world may have a fairer soul, or something beautiful, at least, which otherwise it would not have. And I am dead for the day. My life . . . is burned out.

Such was his pitiful state when the passion for Miss Robins took possession of him.

Elizabeth Robins, who in the 1890s had established herself in the London literary world – she was a friend of Henry James and had made her name as a player of Ibsen heroines – was old enough to be Masefield's mother; she was a widow of nearly fifty (her actor husband, George Richmond Parks, had died many years earlier in America) when they first came into touch in November 1909, as a result of a fan letter that Masefield wrote after reading her play *Votes for Women*. But her bewitching charm and her vitality were ageless, her huge blue eyes had a hypnotic power, and the aura of mystery that surrounded her was, for most men, a compelling attraction. For Masefield she fulfilled to perfection his need for a woman would would overwhelm him by her loveliness and gentle ways, who would stand for the unattainable – a goddess to be revered – and who would also dominate him by her strength of will (Leonard Woolf once summed her up as 'gentle, soft, frail – and *iron*').

Miss Robins, on her side, accepted the adoration of the much younger man as she habitually accepted the adoration of her admirers, keeping him at arm's length, and maintaining her usual secretiveness. In response to his ardent letters (he was soon writing a minimum of two a day) she replied with a certain coolness and restraint, but also with maternal solicitude.

Your letters of yesterday make me anxious. What is this of watching all the night? It is not for that I have come into your life. Not for long waking and for fever. I am here for tranquillity and trust and peace. I want you strong and happy and armed to do your beautiful work.

Her own beautiful work too, for she had quickly realized that he could be useful. Eager to do some service he responded, as soon as he heard that she wanted to write an exposé of the white slave traffic, by volunteering to help her with the research, despite his own back-breaking load of commitments. 'I keep thinking of that noble book you plan,' he wrote to her after their first meeting. 'You must write the story, You will make it the most moving and the most noble thing. It was so beautiful to see your mind shaping it.' He was touched to the quick, he assured her, by her confidence: 'If I can be of any help, even the slightest . . . it would be very much to me. Or if my knowledge could help you, my knowledge of the wild beast in man. One only sees the good things through woman. Our hearts are stables for beasts and women bear the Christ there.'[1]

Miss Robins lived mostly in the country. She had a beautiful old house at Henfield in Sussex, and this was where Masefield first met her; he journeyed to Henfield and spent an enchanted afternoon there. But she often made trips to London, and a fortnight later she came to Maida Hill to meet Constance, bringing with her little presents for Judith. This openness did not last for long. Constance and John were in the habit of opening one another's mail, so the letters from Henfield were soon being discreetly sent to the Ladies' Athenaeum Club in Dover Street, addressed to John Masefield Esq., c/o Miss Elizabeth Robins. These letters came fairly often, but Miss

---

[1] Although J.M. did a certain amount of research on the prostitution laws in various countries, and wrote several reports for Miss Robins, the plans which they discussed for developing their ideas into a play (rather than a novel) never came to fruition. But Miss Robins later published a short novel, *My Little Sister* (1912), centring round the abduction and ruination of a young girl, and J.M. wrote a preface for a novel about prostitution in New York, *Daughters of Ishmael* by R.W. Kauffmann (1911).

Robins's side of the correspondence was a mere nothing compared to Masefield's. 'I wonder', he asked her in a letter penned late one evening, 'if anybody has written to you nine times in a day before this.'

In January their relationship took an unexpected turn. At one of their surreptitious meetings in London Miss Robins told him that long ago she had had a son who died in infancy; this confidence, and the fact that long ago he had lost his beloved mother, immediately drew them together, into an imaginary relationship of mother and son. With her encouragement he started calling her 'Mother', or 'Mütterlein', and to her he was now her 'little son', her 'grown-up son who had come home'. 'Your son brings you his first fruits, your first fruits,' he wrote on 20 January; here he was referring to the poem (quoted above) which he later entitled 'C.L.M.'. And not only this poem, but many of his letters – in fact most of them – showed the same obsession with thoughts of motherhood and of the embryo.

The 'second fruits' of Masefield's attachment was a speech in support of the movement for women's suffrage, in which Miss Robins was a leading figure. He delivered it at a Queen's Hall meeting in February 1910, and also published it as a pamphlet, *My Faith in Woman Suffrage*, but in spite of its title it hardly touched upon the political aspect of 'the cause'; instead it dwelt on the much wider question of woman's place in life in relation to man. Masefield claimed that he saw in the movement for the emancipation of women a first great step towards a real comradeship of human beings 'in an effort to perfect the world'.

Throughout February the clandestine rendezvous of 'mother' and 'son' continued, often now at the British Museum, and each post took letters full of rapturous filial yearning to Henfield. But by this time the enchantress had had enough. 'Oh dear! Why will he fantasticate like this; it spoils things . . . These Poets!' she scribbled on the corner of one of Masefield's outbursts. And in a letter to him at this time Miss Robins even expressed concern for his reason, telling him that she thought he must be 'delirious, poor beloved one'. From now on, gradually, and with consummate sensitivity to masculine psychology, she began to loosen the ties, to steer their strange liaison-of-the-imagination towards an ending. How cleverly she did this is clear from the response she evoked; for example on 25 February he wrote

Dear, your son wants to make you feel, if he can, that our intimacy is a thing to boast of. I want you to think very carefully, dear, before we meet again, of the course that would move you most, as the noblest possible, if you and I were the married of the three; and you were looking to me to do the noble thing.

Then in March she hinted that she might soon be going abroad. An attack of painful gastric trouble meant that she would probably have to spend several months taking a cure at a clinic near Dresden. She finally left England in mid-May. But already the end had come. On 2 May Masefield had written to her, utterly crestfallen, full of self-accusation, sadly submissive. 'Dear – You have closed your door. I think that I know that. I do not know why. Only I must have failed, somewhere . . . You have drawn the bolts. I won't come knocking.'

No wonder that the summer, and then the autumn and winter of 1910 passed for Masefield as a time of frustration and misery. After the months of living at a feverish pitch in the artificial light of a dream world, it was as though a supply of electric power had been suddenly, cruelly, cut off. The 'mother' to whom he had given his heart and who had seemed to reciprocate his devotion, had deserted him, had rejected him completely. Plunged from dizzy peaks into a black abyss, his writing – all of it in prose – reflected his anguish, for it was persistently negative in tone, dealing with failure, tragedy, horror, and death. *The Street of Today*, his third novel, which was published early in 1911, is a bitter, confused story of sexual frustrations; its main theme is the utter breakdown of the hero's marriage. He also worked on an adaptation of a Norwegian play, *The Witch*, concerning a sixteenth-century witch hunt in Bergen, a medley of violence, passion, and the occult.[1]

In the context of Masefield's life as a writer, the main importance of the Elizabeth Robins episode lies in its aftermath. During the period of desolation which he endured after she withdrew from his life his poetic impulse had no outlet. The

---

[1] J.M. was persuaded by Lillah McCarthy to undertake the writing of this English version of the play by H.Wiers-Jennsen. In February 1911 she produced the play at the Court Theatre, with herself in the title role.

secret turmoil, the chaos within him, was no soil from which it could spring. But eventually, after he had lived through his winter of the spirit, new creative life could once again be born in him. Almost a year after he lost his faithless 'mother' there came a great outburst of inspiration, and it took shape as *The Everlasting Mercy*, the long narrative poem which was to be a landmark in English literature as well as in his own life.

3

A vivid sequence of events immediately preceded the writing of *The Everlasting Mercy*, and long afterwards Masefield related it in moving detail. On a fine sunny day in the April of 1911, when he was alone in the country (we do not know where) he set off for a walk through some woodland. He was still full of bitterness and melancholy. But then, on the southern side of a hedge, he came upon the first primroses of the year – it had been a cold, snowy April – and as he gazed at them in delight he heard a man's voice within him which he did not know saying clearly, 'The spring is beginning.' In a daze of wonder, he felt convinced that he had received a supernatural message.

Some weeks later, at Great Hampden, the sequel to the message came. He had risen very early to accompany a friend who had to catch a train at a distant station. On their way down a lane 'in the freshness and brightness of the dew', they saw coming towards them, up a slope, in a field close by, a plough team of noble horses 'followed by the advancing breaking wave of red clay thrust aside by the share'. The ploughman was 'like Piers Plowman or Chaucer's plowman, a staid, elderly, honest and most kindly man', whom Masefield knew and respected. The beauty and nobility of this sight remained with him throughout the day, lifting him into a mood of entranced exultation.

That evening, after working hard and long he went out again, at dusk, and as he wandered through the beechwoods he felt in the presence of 'the incredible and the impossible'. At the upper edge of the wood there was a fence, or rather a line of old thorn trees; beyond it lay a stretch of common land 'most lovely in the tranquillity of the May evening'. The beauty of the scene and the excitement of his thoughts filled him with a kind of ecstasy, and as he burst through the thin hedge he said to himself, 'I will write a poem about a blackguard who becomes converted.' Instantly the opening lines of *The Everlasting Mercy* floated into his mind: the form and detail of the poem became visible: in an instant he perceived it all, the story of a country ruffian, a blasphemous, lecherous drunkard, a native of Ledbury, his own home town, who lurches into a wild berserk rampage, and then, when confronted by the stern reproaches of a Quaker 'mission lady', undergoes a sudden, revivalist conversion to Christian faith, and finally, in the joy of a spring morning, resolves to devote himself to honest work – as a ploughman. Masefield had a notepad with him, and before he reached the house the first lines were on paper.

> From '41 to '51
> I was my folk's contrary son;
> I bit my father's hand right through
> And broke my mother's heart in two.
> I sometimes go without my dinner
> Now that I know the times I've gi'n her.
>
> From '51 to '61
> I cut my teeth and took to fun.
> I learned what not to be afraid of
> And what stuff women's lips are made of;
> I learned with what a rosy feeling
> Good ale makes floors seem like the ceiling,
> And how the moon gives shiny light
> To lads as roll home singing by't.
> My blood did leap, my flesh did revel,
> Saul Kane was tokened to the devil.
>
> From '61 to '67
> I lived in disbelief of heaven.
> I drunk, I fought, I poached, I whored,
> I did despite unto the Lord,
> I cursed, t'would make a man look pale,
> And nineteen times I went to jail.
> > Now, friends, observe and look upon me,
> > Mark how the Lord took pity on me.

The voice that had said 'The spring is beginning' had spoken truth. And Masefield now knew that from henceforth he must be faithful to his true vocation as a poet: both by instinct and by aptitude he was a story-teller.

The publication of *The Everlasting Mercy*, which first appeared in the *English Review* in October 1911, and in book form a month later,[1] was a unique turning-point in Masefield's career, a breakthrough in his life as a writer into success and fame as a poet. In another, broader sense it was a breakthrough. The freshness, the crudity, the blasphemous violence of the story shattered the polite conventions of the Edwardian era. And although opinions vary as to whether Masefield should be regarded as one of the Georgian poets, a critic who personally witnessed the furore caused by *The Everlasting Mercy*, Frank Swinnerton, has not hesitated to call him the first of the Georgians, and to attribute to his first and most celebrated narrative poem a place of special importance in literary history. 'It was read, declaimed, interrupted and discussed with a sort of inflamed fever of controversy such as, in a case of poetry, I cannot in memory match,' Swinnerton wrote in his book *The Georgian Literary Scene*. Although attacked and parodied, Masefield, he maintains, was undoubtedly the first Georgian poet.

For he did something which at that time no other young poet could do – he made the general public read what he had written . . . His place in the Georgian panorama is very important indeed, historically. For, quite by himself, before Edward Marsh schemed with his fellow-enthusiasts to produce an anthology, he made new poetry a rage; and *The Everlasting Mercy* was the work that started all the excitement.

4

Did Masefield have some sort of premonition that *The Everlasting Mercy* was going to launch him on the way to lifelong celebrity? It is tempting to suppose so, for why otherwise, during the time between the poem's birth and its publication, should he have written the verses that he called 'Biography', in which he anticipated with bitter apprehension that one day his life would be analysed, interpreted, and put on record by means of

> That frost of fact by which our wisdom gives
> Correctly stated death to all that lives.

[1] Published by Sidgwick and Jackson.

He was only thirty-three at the time, but the perspective of
'Biography' is that of a lifetime; it is also a perspective which
he realized was at variance with that of biographers in general.

> When I am buried, all my thoughts and acts
> Will be reduced to lists of dates and facts,
> And long before this wandering flesh is rotten
> The dates which made me will be all forgotten . . .
> But men will call the golden hour of bliss
> 'About this time,' or 'shortly after this.' . . .
> They mark the height achieved, the main result,
> The power of freedom in the perished cult,
> The power of boredom in the dead man's deeds,
> Not the bright moments of the sprinkled seeds.

In 'Biography' Masefield showed his passionate conviction that
the 'bright moments' were the true landmarks in a man's life,
for they were the experiences which opened the way towards
the transcendent:

> . . . when men count
> Those hours of life that were a bursting fount,
> Sparkling the dusty heart with living springs,
> There seems a world, beyond our earthly things,
> Gated by golden moments, each bright time
> Opening to show the city white like lime,
> High-towered and many-peopled . . .

For Masefield as a poet, his thirty-fourth year can certainly
be likened to a 'bursting fount'. The great release of creativity
that resulted in *The Everlasting Mercy* in the spring of 1911
was by no means exhausted; during the ensuing summer
another long narrative of rural violence and tragedy *The
Widow in the Bye Street*, flowed on to paper.[1] And then in the
following spring came yet another poem in similar style,
Dauber, a tragedy of the sea which reflected the author's own
experiences under sail.[2]

---

1 Almost all J.M.'s poetry at this time was written at Great Hampden, but he
started *The Widow in the Bye Street*, in June 1911, when he was holidaying at Capel
Curig with a new acquaintance, Robert (later Sir Robert) Ross, the pioneer of
tropical medicine.

2 *Dauber* was J.M.'s first work to be published by William Heinemann Ltd., who
remained his chief English publishers for the remainder of his life.

Masefield's first three long narrative poems took him into a blaze of limelight, and fame brought its share of tributes and adulation. In November 1912, when he received the Edmond de Polignac prize,[1] J.M. Barrie described *The Everlasting Mercy* as 'incomparably the finest literature of the year'. Meanwhile an article in *Everyman* declared that the publication of the three long poems was 'certainly one of the literary events of the last twelve months', and another critic praised Masefield's 'rugged strength' and 'deep eye for beauty'. By 1913 he had become a public figure, caricatured by Max Beerbohm and invited to dine at Number 10 Downing Street, along with other literary lions, on the occasion of a birthday party in honour of the Prime Minister's daughter, Violet Asquith.[2] At the same time his poetry was selling extremely well; a 'Masefield boom' had come into being.

Celebrity did not go to his head. 'As for fame (save the mark)', he wrote to Jack Yeats,

I find no difference of any kind, but letters come enclosing no stamped envelope asking me to speak or lecture at the ends of the earth for nothing, and then ladies ask me to send poems to their charity bazaar[s] . . . for nothing, and bad poets ask me to write long introductions to their books for nothing.

To his brother Harry he wrote in the same vein:

The results of such fame as I precariously enjoy are queer. Today I received as a gift a beastly oil daub said to represent the *Conway*, and also a letter from a lady who says that she has 'always longed to have a friend who is a literary giant' and would I be the one.

In another letter to Harry (who was by this time a tea-planter in Ceylon) Masefield wrote after receiving the de Polignac award:

The prize was rather pleasant, but the worst of these things is that they make one so many enemies in a profession recruited from people who have not had the upbringing of men. It ought to be made

---

1 This prize of £100 was annually awarded by the Royal Society of Literature to the author of a work of pure literature.

2 Later Lady Violet Bonham Carter. At this party, which took place on 16 April 1913, the guests included Edward Marsh, Rupert Brooke, Shaw, Barrie, Gosse, and Augustine Birrell.

a penal offence for any man to write anything until he has knocked about a bit, and for any man to stay in Europe all his life. I am going to come out to the East one of these days I hope; one gets stagnant in these parvenu places like Europe.

One of the writers whose jealousy was roused by Masefield's success was Rupert Brooke. Edward Marsh, at the time when he was planning the first volume of *Georgian Poetry*, approached Masefield for a contribution, and Masefield, after some discussion, agreed that his unpublished poem 'Biography' should be included. And not only that; he obligingly offered to delay its publication elsewhere, and for this Marsh described him to Brooke as 'a perfect angel'. Yet Brooke, to judge from the condescending tone of his references to 'poor Mr. Masefield' and 'poor Jan', thoroughly despised Masefield himself as well as his writings. After alluding to his own verses which had been chosen for the anthology he wrote to Marsh, 'I get so excited, wanting to scrap those poems, and write you much better ones, that'd fairly boom the book and obliterate poor Jan – but I shan't.' The kind Masefield, however, was generous in his appreciation of the younger man's work, firstly of his poetry and then of his one-act play, the horror drama *Lithuania*. 'I hope that it will be produced and that you will go on writing plays,' Masefield wrote to Brooke, 'for you have such evident instinct for drama of a new and telling kind. Good luck to it and you.' He then added a piece of advice – speaking as one celebrity to another – which gives an amusing insight into his own attitude towards exploiters of literary fame. Brooke had asked whether he knew anything about a photographer called Murchison, who wanted to take some portraits of him; in his innocence Brooke had imagined that he might be liable for a fee. 'I know nothing of him,' Masefield wrote,

but I presume that he intends to sell copies of our portraits when he has done enough of them and when he can find buyers. I don't suppose that he expects to be offered money; if anyone ought to be offered money it is ourselves for the time spent and the dignity outraged, so be bloody bold and resolute and ask him for extra copies. I think I got nine out of him. Remember, that if you become as famous as we all expect of you, he will be able to make a lot of money out of your portrait.

Another writer whose attitude to Masefield was cool was J.C. Squire. Masefield's jogtrot metres and simplicity of style made him an irresistible target for parody, and Squire mocked him with venom. Nevertheless, as a later critic was to point out, one of the signs of good verse is that it can suffer parody and yet survive: 'Even after Mr. Squire had made us yell with amusement . . . we turn to Masefield's work and find it potent still.' The darts that Squire let fly were sometimes aimed at Masefield's style:

> Dogs barked, owls hooted, cockerels crew,
> As in my works they often do
> When flagging with my main design
> I pad with a descriptive line.

But some of his slyest digs were at the poet himself, as when he showed the erring sons and daughters of a poor widow trying to justify their crimes on grounds of altruism, claiming that they had been helping 'a poet up in London':

> Every crime that we commit
> He makes a poem out of it,
> And were we so unkind's to stop, he
> Would famish for congenial copy.

Yet not all the Masefield parodies were inspired by malice. Siegfried Sassoon later recounted how, in 1912, after he began amusing himself by scribbling a parody of *The Everlasting Mercy*, he suddenly realized that he was writing from real experience. He further claimed that this was the first sign of his being capable of writing as he did during the war:

After the first fifty lines or so, I dropped the pretence that I was improvising an exuberant skit. While continuing to burlesque Masefield for all I was worth, I was really feeling what I wrote – and doing it not only with abundant delight but a sense of descriptive energy quite unlike anything I had experienced before. Never before had I been able to imbue commonplace details with warmth of poetic emotion.

5

In 1912 a change came about in the pattern of Constance's life: she and Isabel decided to close their school in Marylebone Road.

Isabel now moved to Hampstead (to 31 Gayton Road) and there she started small morning classes for the children of artists, musicians, and writers, including Sturge Moore and Carl Dolmetsch. Soon the Masefields too pulled up their roots and took a Hampstead house, number 13 Well Walk, a tall, gaunt, Victorian Gothic house which had the distinction of adjoining the 'well' from which the street derived its name.[1] This meant that Constance and Isabel were still able to be together often, and that Judith, who was now eight years old, could attend Isabel's classes and make some congenial friends.

In Masefield's eyes the move was very much for the better; it was a step, even though a small one, in the direction of living altogether in the country. To Jack Yeats he wrote with glee,

Hampstead has a tube but no motor buses, so it is still very little known, and almost desolate after dark. I have walked on parts of the Heath after 8.00 p.m. and met no single soul in a whole hour and only heard one faint noise of kissing. The ponds are pretty good too and there is a brook and on windy days there are kite fliers.

At the end of the year he also wrote happily to his sister Ethel telling her that they were settled in, and liked the house, and were much healthier than at Maida Hill. 'One can walk out of London from here in about 25 minutes, and really get outside, into fairly clean country; and then the Heath is much bigger than we'd thought; really a big place.'

At Well Walk Masefield did a certain amount of writing, though he greatly preferred working at Great Hampden. By now he was concentrating mostly on drama, for by the end of 1912 a slackening had come in his poetic inspiration. Since *Nan* he had written only one play, *The Tragedy of Pompey the Great*, but the theatre was still one of his foremost interests, and some of the friends who meant most to him were playwrights – Granville-Barker, Galsworthy, Binyon. Granville-Barker, especially, had become his chief exemplar – the dominance of Yeats had by now waned. 'As you know, you are my father and my grandfather,' Masefield wrote to him in response to a letter of encouragement:

Your work is one of the things that I keep in front of me, to try to

1 The spring in question, with waters impregnated with salts of iron, had been the focus of the spa which in the eighteenth century made Hampstead a popular resort.

attain to. Your fine supple style that has a play and a glitter on it like a sword of the best temper, and the knowledge that the style comes from a mind of that temper instead of from (as with me) a treatment of the trite with extract of literature.

Not only Granville-Barker's writing, but also his revolutionary methods of staging, affected Masefield's style as a dramatist. After seeing his productions of *Twelfth Night* and *The Winter's Tale*, with their 'continuous performance' for a double or platform stage, Masefield knew that he must adopt a similar presentation for the play on which he embarked in 1913. This piece, *The Faithful*, was a venture into unfamiliar country; under the influence of Binyon he based it on a legendary episode in Japanese history, a tragic sequence of tyranny, vengeance, multiple murders, and suicides. He found the writing of it far from easy; to Granville-Barker he complained that it was 'like ploughing among roots'. But his discouragement did not deter him from further dramatic work. Early in the following year he completed a one-act play in verse, *Philip the King*, in which he showed how the defeat of the Armada appeared to Spanish eyes, and soon afterwards he began, laboriously, on another one-act verse play, *Good Friday*. Why, it may be asked, did Masefield choose a biblical theme? Did it represent some sort of spiritual development within him, some new attraction towards Christian belief? Although not impossible, this seems unlikely. The context of his choice was his persistent interest in the potentially dramatic, the interest that had led him, just previously, to pick upon an oriental legend as his theme.

While Masefield, at Hampstead, toiled away at his plays, much lively interest was aroused in the literary world by the death of Britain's Poet Laureate, Alfred Austin,[1] and there was, of course, much speculation about who would succeed him. J.C. Squire was one of those who wrote on the matter with relish. Kipling, as the most widely-read and popular of English poets, and William Watson, who 'could write loyal odes on his head', were the first two possibles he mentioned. 'But perhaps', he added, 'Mr. Asquith will try to think of somebody else':

Undoubtedly the poet of the hour is Mr. Masefield. It would be a very humourous stroke on the Prime Minister's part to offer the

[1] He died on 2 June 1913.

Laureateship to him. 'Mr. Masefield endeavouring to Chasten his Muse with a View to Celebrating the Nuptials of the Prince of Wales' would make a subject for a Max Beerbohm cartoon.

The broadside of irony misfired; it was taken as a serious forecast. Thus a rumour got about that Masefield was a leading possible, a rumour that reached even America. Writing to Edward Marsh, Rupert Brooke, who was then on his travels, reported that 'the chief topic which excites America is who (if anybody) is to be Poet Laureate. All the papers have immense articles, with pictures of Masefield and Noyes. They mention everybody as possible, except me and Wilfrid [Gibson].' But Masefield himself had no illusions about his chances of becoming Poet Laureate in 1913. When the gossip in due course reached his family he wrote to his brother Harry:

As to the Laureateship, about which you are so kind as to hope that I may be appointed, I haven't got a ghost of a chance, and never had. I cannot possibly be in the six most likely names. As far as one can see, the appointment lies between the following: Robert Bridges, Edmund Gosse, Henry Newbolt, Austin Dobson, Thomas Hardy and Sir [Arthur] Quiller Couch; but I am at once too young, too rebellious, and too coarse, to be in the running.

In the event, the choice fell upon the man whom Masefield had put first on his list, namely Robert Bridges. Seventeen years were to pass before Masefield himself – no longer so young, so rebellious, or so coarse – was to succeed in turn to the Laureateship.

PART III

War

Chapter Seven

SHOCK

Masefield's poem 'August, 1914', written in the first stunned anguish of realization that England was at war, sets the sombre stage for the varied parts that he was to play during the ensuing years, in England, France, the Mediterranean, and America. It was his only 'war poem' to be published, for although his wartime writings – at least his early wartime writings – included a certain amount of poetry, especially sonnets with a metaphysical flavour, most of his explicit reactions to the war are to be found in his prose works, and in letters written between 1914 and 1918. In these the emotions that welled up in him found outlet. In these he gave vent to outbursts of romantic patriotism and imprecations against the enemy, though by far the most dominant notes running through them are a sympathy with the common man and a profound compassion. Thus although Masefield is associated with only one war poem, and consequently is not bracketed by the critics with Brooke, Sassoon, Owen and the rest, he was still a war poet at heart throughout the years of conflict.

When 'August, 1914' was written John and Constance, with the two children, now aged ten and four, had just settled into a new country retreat. The Great Hampden arrangements had come to an end and they had abandoned their 'cottage' in the beechwoods for an ancient farmhouse in the Thames Valley near Wallingford. Lollingdon Farm, which lay immediately below Lollingdon Hill, at the edge of the Berkshire Downs, was eight centuries old, so Masefield claimed, and he boasted that it had 'a sort of moat' round it. There were many brooks nearby as well, which was pleasant after the dried-up Chilterns, and it was, to his joy, 'a good bird and flower place'. For the past few months, through the glorious summer of 1914, he and Constance had been rejoicing in the peace and beauty of their

new surroundings, and the slow rhythms of nature in a countryside that had been tilled for centuries. But perhaps their
greatest delight was the freedom of the open grassland up on
the Downs; 'one is said to be able to walk for forty miles on
grass, to Old Sarum gates', Masefield wrote to his brother
Harry. They loved sharing this joy with the friends who came
to visit them, Rupert Brooke for one. Shortly after returning to
England from his world tour he came to Lollingdon accompanied by his friend Violet Asquith, and 'the two days were full
of charm and friendship and happiness,' Constance wrote
afterwards in a diary which she kept intermittently at this time.
But as they all wandered over the Downs together, Masefield
aroused laughter when he said that 'the Austro-Serbian
business' might cause a European conflict in which Britain
would be involved. His young friends (Rupert and Violet were
both twenty-seven) – like the vast majority – had no inkling that
within a matter of months they and all their countrymen, as well
as millions of others, would be plunged into the abyss of war.

It was from those same chalk Downs, after the bombshell had
burst, that Masefield looked out over the valley of the Thames,
with its brooks and fields and quiet villages, and in the serenity
of dusk wrote his 'August, 1914':

> These homes, this valley spread below me here,
> The rooks, the tilted stacks, the beasts in pen,
> Have been the heartfelt things, past-speaking dear
> To unknown generations of dead men,
>
> Who, century after century, held these farms,
> And, looking out to watch the changing sky,
> Heard, as we hear, the rumours and alarms
> Of war at hand and danger pressing nigh.
>
> And knew, as we know, what the message meant
> The breaking off of ties, the loss of friends,
> Death, like a miser getting in his rent,
> And no new stones laid where the trackway ends.
>
> The harvest not yet won, the empty bin,
> The friendly horses taken from the stalls,
> The fallow on the hill not yet brought in,
> The cracks unplastered in the leaking walls.

Yet heard the news, and went discouraged home,
And brooded by the fire with heavy mind
With such dumb loving of the Berkshire loam
As breaks the dumb hearts of the English kind.

Then sadly rose and left the well-loved Downs,
And so by ship to sea, and knew no more
The fields of home, the byres, the market towns,
Nor the dear outline of the English shore,

But knew the misery of the soaking trench,
The freezing in the rigging, the despair
In the revolting second of the wrench
When the blind soul is flung upon the air,

And died (uncouthly, most) in foreign lands
For some idea but dimly understood
Of an English city never built by hands
Which love of England prompted and made good . . .

For Masefield himself it was not a matter of immediately
'taking ship to sea' (he was now thirty-six and too old for the
army). But almost at once the whole family had to leave
Lollingdon, for the house was temporarily requisitioned as a
billet for cavalry – 'their chargers drank at the moat. I saw
them there,' Masefield later wrote. So the autumn was spent
at Well Walk. But in the new year of 1915 the family was able
to return to Lollingdon, and during the next few months they
lived there very quietly, with a drastically reduced domestic
staff, while Masefield wrote poetry and pondered despairingly
over the future. 'He is uncertain whether he ought to take some
more active part,' Constance wrote in her diary. 'He has declared himself ready if he is wanted and that I think is his right
course.'

Wartime anxieties and problems brought husband and wife
into ever closer mutual dependence, and the diary shows their
deepening devotion. 'When we were saying how kind our
friends were to us,' Constance wrote, '[Jan] said "It's because
we love each other so, that people like us".' Doubtless it was a
relief to Masefield that at Lollingdon Isabel was no longer at
hand. She was still in Hampstead, trying to find war work,
and busy caring for children from the slums. And very probably
it was a relief to Constance too, for by now tensions had

developed in their friendship. 'Much as I love Isabel,' she had
written to John a little earlier, 'I get nothing from her that is
any comfort to the soul. She is awfully absorbed in herself and
her own point of view, and very little concerned with mine.'
Isabel did come to Lollingdon for one short visit at the beginning
of 1915 but it is mentioned only cursorily in the diary: 'When
she is here all occupations get shelved.'

There was a much more enthusiastic entry after Violet
Asquith had been to stay. Constance wrote that she felt very
much drawn to her, and she also sensed that Violet was
attracted to her and Jan, because they were living 'a simple,
arduous life'. She felt sure that in spite of Violet's great interest
in politics, many things in the life at Downing Street had no
meaning for her: 'I feel she wants to be real and earnest and
finds it difficult.' While she was with them Masefield read some
of his latest poetry aloud, and Constance was pleased that
Violet was moved by it. But there was also, of course, much war
talk, and Constance was surprised to find that Violet did not
seem to know much more than she did. And indeed some of the
inside opinions she reported were hardly convincing. She had
recently seen Sir John French, and apparently he had said he
would not be surprised if the Germans suddenly collapsed, for
'it was getting beyond the period for which they were fully
prepared'. The enemy, according to the Commander-in-Chief,
could not prepare themselves afresh as quickly as the Allies,
since they did not possess so many sources of supply. 'Well we
shall see,' Constance remarked sceptically. 'It is at the moment
very hard to imagine the Germans exhausted. They are concentrating in East Prussia and the Russians are again re-
treating.'

2

After their visitors left the Masefields reverted to their simple
round, and Constance's diary gives some fascinating glimpses
of 'Jan' both as family man and poet. While she herself was busy
with unaccustomed chores – she was trying to learn 'the ways
of hens' as well as 'all sorts of queer lore such as pruning' – Jan,
who was looking 'more like a nice farmer than ever' gave a hand
in many practical ways, such as constructing laying boxes for

the hen-house. He also walked miles across the squelching fields to Wallingford to shop for supplies, looked after a temperamental donkey called Joe which they had acquired as a steed for Lewis,[1] and kept Judith happy by sharing in her favourite games, especially with her teddy bears whom she called 'the Boys'.

His main activity however during this time of waiting was still his writing; chiefly he was putting into verse his deepest ruminations and spiritual gropings. The effect of the war upon his thinking, as upon that of so many at this time, was to bring him (in the percipient phrase of C.E. Montague) to 'hang unconsciously about the uncrossed threshold of religion'. Time and again he seemed to be reaching out towards the leap of faith; time and again he was somehow held back. Horror at the evil of war had intensified his yearnings for beauty, and most of the sonnets on the theme of beauty which were later published in *Lollingdon Downs and Other Poems, with Sonnets*, were written at this time. 'I envy Jan his work of course,' Constance remarked wistfully:

He goes out away in the mornings and afternoons with his working book in his shoplifter's pocket, and no matter how cold it is he sits and thinks, and sees the big world of his imagination, while he has all my world as well. I have bits of imaginative life too, but they are just fragments and his is a complete thing. Our world is very happy and busy, but everyone's heart is bigger than his own daily life.

Then on 7 February she wrote

Yesterday was my birthday. I was greatly surprised and moved to find that Jan had got a sonnet series for me, all quite new and undreamt of by me. It was wonderful having them, and they in themselves are most moving and beautiful. They are all questioning 'What am I?' and 'What is this Beauty behind? Is it in me?'

In the evenings Masefield shared his leisure with Constance; he did not usually write at the end of the day. And when it was

---

[1] Joe was not a success. On 4 February 1915 Constance wrote that the donkey seemed 'rather a devil. His mind and ours were working on different lines, and once he nipped Jan's hand to show him his disapproval.' Then on 27 February, after an expedition on the Downs, 'the donkey reverted to some wild ancestor and became quite frantic – tail up, teeth showing, four legs together. That is the end for us, we felt, Joe must go, so now we advertise a strong young donkey for sale.'

fine they often went out into the darkness, carrying a lantern, to wander up the hillside near the house. But on other evenings storm and wind kept them indoors:

It is very stormy and dark. This is one of the nights when a raid is expected. I feel sure Zeppelins won't get across, but ships may . . . Today's war news is bad, and it is difficult not to be afraid. The Turks have entered Russia . . . In the west the Germans have won some ground near Soissons. Oh for the war to end. No real peace of mind can come to one, while so much of the world is in pain.

The two also shared much of their reading, and they were now deep in Tolstoy. Masefield was also reading Spenser – when he could keep his eyes open.

Tonight he has fallen asleep in his chair reading the *Faërie Queene*. It is an easy book to fall asleep over . . . in spite of its lovely poetry. Jan is enjoying its fine stanzas and richness of picture . . . He seems rather tired and I do hope all his rough work in the stable and garden are not going to be too much.

This was only a week or so before the long vigil of un-certainty came to an end. On 18 February Constance wrote: 'Jan is to go out under the Red Cross.' This meant that he had accepted an opportunity to do the humble and strenuous work of an orderly at the British Red Cross hospital for French wounded which had been established at Arc-en-Barrois, a village in the Haute Marne not far from Chaumont, about sixty miles from the front. 'He was up in town all yesterday,' she continued matter-of-factly, 'saw the Secretary, accepted the work, tried on khaki tunics, breeches and caps, found his size, was inoculated and got back to dinner at 8.0.' Then at the remembrance of the previous evening she let out a cry of anguish: 'Oh dear, the pain is very acute . . . Lewis's queries break one's heart.' But her thoughts then turned to Jan himself, and to his urgent longing to offer himself for his country. Recovering herself she wrote, 'Jan is very quiet and resolute.'

3

Masefield's destination, the Château d'Arc-en-Barrois, was an imposing four-square castle, set among vast pine forests, which had been rebuilt as a hunting centre in the early nineteenth century by a rich sportsman with no taste and a penchant for grandeur. As a hospital it was roomy enough – there were more than a hundred beds for the *blessés*, who were brought in by the trainload, in the most unspeakable squalor and misery, from the Argonne area of the deadlocked front. But it was far from convenient, for there were no lifts, the stairs were winding, and the kitchens were underground.

Already before he reached Arc-en-Barrois Masefield had seen his 'first of war'; at Troyes his train passed a Red Cross train just in with the previous night's 'take'. There were a lot of wounded, so he wrote to Constance, as well as a lot of men on leave from the trenches, 'mud to the eyes, some still cheery and well, but most of them white, with a look of horror in their eyes, yet horror isn't quite the word, horror, terror and anxiety mixed'. This sight of suffering shook him, but no sooner had he set foot in the hospital than he had to face a much sharper ordeal. He was asked to help immediately with an amputation; a man's right arm had to be taken off at the shoulder (the man was a *cultivateur* from Brittany, 'brave and good and fine', with a wife and three young children). Masefield did his part 'all right', he told Constance, and got a compliment from the chief; he had been far too much moved by pity and interest to feel queer, even when he had to burn the arm afterwards in the heating furnace. Soon of course he became entirely accustomed to operations. Many of them were for the removal of bullets, and the men were usually under chloroform, though sometimes not. Ten days after his arrival he described a remarkable case which he had witnessed:

One man merely had a cocaine injection, and sat on the table being chaffed till the bullet dropped out of the hole they cut. It was a shrapnel bullet, as big as a small marble (the second we've had from him) and he was awfully pleased and proud with it; and especially pleased at a draught of brandy given him after the operation. Like all the other cases he ate a most hearty supper afterwards; a tumbler of wine, a tumbler of water, a pound of bread, three bowls of pea soup, a hunk of cheese, an orange, and a handful of biscuits.

The worst time for the hospital staff, Masefield said, was not during the operations, but when the men first arrived. It was terrible getting them washed and bandaged; they were like dazed mad animals for the first few days, raving of the last thing they heard: '*Mitrailleuse, tick, tick, tick – Mitrailleuse, tick, tick tick. En avant! En avant!*' But soon they realized more or less where they were, and after that the majority of them settled down happily – though of course some were not happy at all and were likely to die. 'The relief of being with us acts like magic on most of them,' Masefield observed, '[and] it is astounding to see what some of these *blessés* can eat. I suppose nature must be repaired.'

Wine as well as food was in plentiful supply, and one of the miscellaneous duties which fell to Masefield was to draw off twenty-eight bottles from the cask each day for the men's dinner. 'What our *blessés* would really like,' one of the volunteer doctors, Henry Tonks,[1] said to him, 'would be a nice good wound that would keep them in bed for three months and let them get drunk every day.' But alas, so Masefield wrote, most of the men got well sooner than that and went back to the front. 'Many of our men have been wounded twice. "It needs courage", they say, "to go back a third time".' There was a proverb 'No one comes back whole from the Argonne'.

For six weeks Masefield slaved away as an orderly with hardly a pause, except at the end of each day when, dropping with fatigue, he went off to the village, where he was billeted at the *Lion d'Or*. He did not relax with his colleagues in the evenings, for he had found that the hospital was seething with intrigue, and this decided him to avoid all off-duty friendships. Instead, in his icy little room, to the accompaniment of the distant roar of the guns, he wrote to Constance every evening without fail, pouring out heart and soul. To reassure her he insisted that the rough work suited him. 'I'm very well,' he wrote soon after his arrival,

the work is hard all through, and four times a day excessively hard, carrying wounded in and out and carrying meals up and down, but . . . whenever I look at these poor fellows my soul boils. Nothing else in the world matters but to stop this atrocious thing. Blood and intellect and life are simply nothing. Let them go like water to end this crime. You've no idea of it, you can't even guess the stink of it, from the bloody old reeking stretchers to the fragments hopping on

1 Later Slade Professor of Fine Art at the University of London.

crutches, and half heads, and a leg gone at the thigh, and young boys blinded and grey-headed old men with their backs broken. I never knew I loved men so much. They are a fine lot, a noble lot. I love them all.

'Don't worry about my being overworked', he emphasized afresh a few days later:

I'm broken in to it now; at first it was very hard. It's funny: I'm slight and slack-looking and not physically strong, but I can do the stretcher work better than any of the orderlies; perhaps I am younger, or perhaps it is that I learned to use my working muscles while they were strengthening their playing muscles.

Nevertheless Constance kept on pleading that he should give up and come home, and he continued to insist that he must stay. 'My dearest Con wife', he wrote, 'this is not a question of being "noble" or being "spared", it is a question of going through a little hardship to save the lives of beautiful human beings. I do more hard work than any orderly here . . . [but] I can do it, and I was never better in my life.'

The gratitude of the *blessés* was touching, he told her, and the helpers from the village, too, appreciated the activities of the British Red Cross in their midst, albeit with some reservations. Masefield sensed that their opinion was '*du bon cœur, pas du sens commun*'. He too had reservations about the hospital, or rather about the ways of most of the staff. 'I'm a bit vexed with a lot of the people here', he wrote,

because they are slack in their work, always knocking off for pipes (or asking leave for the afternoon if female) and generally not bucking to. It seems to me that I am feeling the pulse of my country here, and I'm trying to reconcile the slackness . . . with the excellence of the hospital . . . We are a queer race, I do maintain.

By the 'excellence' of the hospital he meant the work of the doctors and nurses, for the general standards of hygiene were far superior to those in most of the French hospitals. But the administration he regarded as very far from excellent: 'They have an impossible arrangement, a lady business-manager who thinks that she can control the medical staff, and a medical staff who claim to control the manager in the interests of the wounded. Endless rows, endless complaints.'

He took an especially critical, even jaundiced, view of the female staff: 'I like neither them nor their methods, but my job is mainly with men':

The really hard, trained nurse who knows her work is a fine soul, but we have a lot of catty young minxes who have never worked in their lives, and they have catty society ways of wheedling, when it is a question of carrying stinking blood in a bucket . . . [They] give me the feeling that they only come because there are no winter sports . . . They can't work and they bring hills of luggage.

'It is a fearful thing to let anyone grow up without the habit of industry,' he went on. 'We must see to it that Judith never gets like that.' After some weeks he reproached the 'lady probationers' for yet another fault, though in this case he admitted that they could be partly excused:

They pet the young good-looking patients and neglect the others, and so destroy both. This is a very human thing and I forgive it, having been like that myself; but I've learned now, here, that it is our duty to watch each human soul alike unceasingly and lovingly.

At Arc-en-Barrois there was, however, one woman whom Masefield excepted from his strictures, 'the only woman here [who] really works with us . . . without putting our backs up'. This was Jane de Glehn, the American wife of Wilfrid de Glehn, the British artist, who had accompanied her husband when he, like Masefield, had accepted work as an orderly. Masefield thought very highly of both husband and wife, and he told Constance that these two, as well as another orderly called Sibbley ('a rough kind of heavy worker'), and a fellow volunteer to whom he referred only as 'Bobby', were all of them 'quite first rate for this kind of work'.

He foresaw that the hospital would soon break up, not only because it was so inefficiently run but because, to judge from the amount of sepsis already in the wards, the flies in summer would make it 'a death house'. And in letter after letter he confided to Constance his ardent hopes that he might be able to co-operate with some of his like-minded colleagues in starting a new hospital for *blessés* run on better lines. 'In May some time,' he wrote, 'Tonks, Bobby, the de Glehns, and a rich doctor friend who has got a house in the Vosges, want to start an open air hospital . . . and they want me to come.' He knew that Constance would protest vehemently against such a renewed absence, and he himself pined to be back with her, but it was a question of priorities:

My beloved Con, the need of the French for hospitals is greater than I can say, and while I've a pair of arms these poor blinded bleeding stinking heroes seem to have the first call, in a time like this. Love and courage are the only things that matter . . . and their misery is greater than ours. It is hard to take a course, but the heaps of bloody rags in the night-train make our own loves and lives indulgences.

The idea of the Vosges hospital was still embryonic, but some of Masefield's views on it were very definite. He insisted, for one thing, that anyone they took on must be used to rough manual work. 'I'm afraid', he lamented, 'the instinct for work is not common.' He himself had an insatiable appetite for work, and at Arc-en-Barrois he took on many extra jobs, such as organizing fire precautions. He also made rope quoits, walking sticks, and crutches for the convalescents, and did a good deal of miscellaneous carpentry: one of his creations was a sabot stand for the entrance hall.

Wood is very cheap in this forest land, and there is a lovely big saw-mill just up the river, where they saw the wood for us and plane it smooth; and then in about an hour and a half I can tap up a four-leg table with a shelf underneath it complete.

4

But what about Masefield's instincts as a writer? Did he never long to stand back, to evaluate, to put his thoughts into verse? He answered these questions in one of his letters to Constance:

One must not say 'O, it is waste, your doing such work,' it is not waste; the real waste is war and spilt life and poor beautiful men bled dead for want of a man to hold them. I could not write, thinking of what goes on in those long slow filthy trains, full of mad-eyed whimpering men.

How remote from such desperate urgency was poor Constance in Berkshire, still living in a mental climate of detached and vaguely optimistic humanism, as she tried to dull her loneliness by toiling away in the Lollingdon garden: 'I daren't think of the pain of not having Jan,' she had earlier written in her diary. His faithful letter-writing was an immense consolation, but there was still the ache of not being able to discuss things with him face to face. 'I think a lot about the future,' she wrote. 'Will wars go on for ever, ever, ever? Not if mankind gets really more generous, less afraid.'

At this time Masefield had some harsh things to say about the 'literary men' who had been writing of war in England, and he did not hesitate to include himself in his censure. Constance had been reading a pamphlet entitled *The War and the Way Out* by Goldsworthy Lowes Dickinson, one of the earliest pointers towards the League of Nations. Although Dickinson was a pundit much respected in the liberal intellectual circle to which she and Isabel belonged, she herself had not found it entirely convincing. 'Goldie', she wrote in her diary, 'is awfully logical, but logic doesn't always work in human things as the French Revolution shows.' Masefield replied with a heated outburst:

Goldie and those other eunuchs with their messy points of view simply make me sick . . . God deliver me from talkers. To get this damned misery and crime at an end is the only thing . . .

We literary men have been very evil, writing about war. To fight is bad enough, but it has its manly side, but to let the mind dwell on it and peck its carrion and write of it is a devilish unmanly thing, and that's what we've been doing, ever since we had leisure, circa 1850.

He did realize, however, that those who had not had any first-hand war experience could not possibly understand the extraordinary impetus and elation engendered by it:

I don't think that people in England can realise what this is; I know they do not. Words cannot describe it, except as a crime and infamy, and a stinking filth, and out of it all comes nothing but a kind of rapture of courage to do anything to end it . . . It has made all the French here brother and sister to us. I never felt brotherhood before, for anybody, since I was a boy.[1]

During his time at Arc-en-Barrois, Masefield became more and more Francophile, as his contacts with the French and

[1] Presumably 'since I was a boy' refers to J.M.'s time in the *Conway*.

their way of life confirmed the knowledge of the country that he already had from its literature and art.

When I first heard sabots I felt that I had heard them all my life. I never realised before how curiously good French novels and stories are; ours very seldom come so close to the life; and I realise more and more what France has meant to modern civilisation.

He was also, naturally, becoming more and more Germano-phobe. 'I don't feel that I can ever think quietly of Germans again,' he exclaimed. 'They are guilty of this crime and folly and misery . . . One longs for these *sales Boches* and *Guillaume* to be driven like dogs out of this dear land they've harried.' Constance was always asking him how long he thought the war would last, and he told her that everyone guessed something different. Some said it would be over in six weeks, some in five months, but his own feeling was that it would not end till the following spring, 'in about a year from now; not before; they're too strong, and too well organised . . . France is not *épuisé* and Germany certainly is not, and the thing will go on and on.'

By April 1915 Masefield himself was certainly *épuisé*, and badly in need of leave. The thought of getting back to his family tugged continually at him. But he took care to warn Constance that when he first arrived they must keep at arm's length, for he was probably soaked with germs from septic wounds. He would have to begin with a strong carbolic bath, while all his clothes were washed in carbolic and then hung in the sun. 'I didn't know quite what day to expect him and hadn't prepared,' Constance later wrote in her diary. 'But one night when I slept I heard "Con" somehow in my dream, and I knew it was he. So down I rushed. He was very tired but how good it was to see him.' 'The days that followed were a little sad,' she went on. 'He had got this great new experience – the first independent one since we were married. But gradually his experience became mine to me.'

5

Back at Lollingdon, Masefield was still passionately obsessed with the plight of the *blessés*. The Arc-en-Barrois hospital was due to close shortly, as he had expected, and he now threw himself into efforts to implement his dream of a much better hospital for the French wounded. The scheme that Tonks and the de Glehns had proposed for a convalescent centre in the Vosges still seemed a possibility, but by this time a new, less ambitious, project had kindled Masefield's imagination. He envisaged a travelling field hospital 'to go close to the front, behind the Army of the Argonne, so as to give some of the badly hit men a chance of being treated at once'. He estimated that £3,500 would be needed to equip such a unit, and during the month of May 1915 – a month of disasters for the Allies, with defeats on both the western front and at Gallipoli, and also the sinking of the *Lusitania* – he wrote innumerable letters to friends, relations, acquaintances, and strangers appealing for assurances of support. Lady Ottoline Morrell, William Rothenstein, E.V. Lucas, an American lady, Miss Wheelwright, whom Masefield had never met, and his brother Harry, were among those who made a willing response.

Nothing however could actually begin unless the French authorities gave their sanction, and this they seemed loath to do. Having collected promises of sums totalling £3,000, Masefield imagined, with quite unrealistic optimism, that he would be able to go ahead within a month or so. But he had not reckoned with French bureaucracy. It was a tedious, frustrating wait. When Ethel asked him what supplies she could collect, in case the hospital for convalescents materialized, he wrote back to her

Very many thanks; but nothing can be done at present. Flannel pyjamas, roller bandages, felt slippers, crutches, penny whistles, musical boxes, gramophones, sunhats, handkerchiefs, bedsocks, are the things likely to be wanted, and these I'll be thankful for, but not till the fiat comes.

In the meantime he felt forced to anticipate that he might have to take the field hospital to a different front. 'We may be asked to go to the Dardanelles,' he explained to Harry, 'instead of to the Argonne, as the need may be greater there.'

At last, by mid-July, a new stage was reached in the negotiations with the French; Masefield was summoned to make a tour of the military hospitals in the west and south of France, 'to see what was wanted and what was not wanted'. This prospect filled him with dread. He had already heard, while still at Arc-en-Barrois, horrific accounts of the native hospitals. They were 'most fearful places', he had been told by one of the British doctors, 'made anyhow, either not warmed or not ventilated, never cleaned, and heaped with the dying and the dead and smelling of death and neglect'. 'I don't know what it is in . . . [the French] character which is so callous to suffering,' he had written at the time to Constance, much troubled by the contrast between the attitudes of the bureaucrats and those of the brave and lovable *blessés*. 'It is partly due to poverty of mind in a state department, and to unwise thrift, but mainly to some want in character. They have a disregard for others, and for life, which shocks us continually.'

Masefield's visit to the French hospitals, which lasted for about a fortnight in July 1916, and took him chiefly to the Tours area, was a grim and wearing experience. Towards the end of it he wrote to Constance that his head was swimming 'like an impressionist-futurist picture': '*Képis*, *sœurs*, salutes, doctors, wounds, beds, *sœurs*, bad jokes, bad French, *sœurs*, *salles*, sheets, sœurs, *salles*, *sales sœurs*, salutes, sheets, etc. etc.' But not all the hospitals were as squalid as he had expected: an 'annexe' he had seen was 'very beautiful and spotless', and one hospital was 'perfectly magnificent, said to be one of the two best in France, a very model of a place, with glass walls, quite amazingly fitted, and beautifully kept by White Ladies.' These however were the exceptions. In general he was shocked and saddened by what he saw. One vast hospital near Tours was filled mainly with cases of lunacy and idiocy and men whose minds had given way in the trenches. There he had seen 'a huge dark crowded ward, with the beds all jammed together and many men in them'. He had wondered that they should be kept so, and on asking was told that it was 'the cell of the malingerers, who pretended to be mad, so as not to go again to the trenches'. They were fed on bread and milk twice a day, and were kept in complete boredom till they had had enough.

Next day Masefield wrote home again. He was not going to the south of France. 'I know what the French want and do not want now . . . I have hated this job more than words can say; still, I have seen a little, and drawn a few conclusions.' Perhaps it was almost a relief when, shortly after the first anniversary of the outbreak of war, news came that the French authorities were not prepared to accept additional foreign units.

6

For Masefield the second year of the war was a time of even greater contrasts than the first. Again there were interludes of recuperation at Lollingdon and Hampstead, but from this calm background he set off on two intensely gruelling assignments, the first to the Middle East, the second across the Atlantic. In the late summer of 1915 he went for a short time to Gallipoli for the Red Cross, and then in the early months of 1916 he visited the United States on a lecture tour which was also an intelligence mission.

Gallipoli . . . Although in the history of the First World War the name is synonymous with failure, at the end of July 1915 it meant a challenge, a supreme challenge, at least to those who believed that the campaign might still be reinfused with sufficient life to open up the way to Constantinople. And it was at this point, in this mood, that Masefield, quite unexpectedly, became personally involved. An opportunity had arisen that fired his heart. The British Red Cross Society in London had received an urgent appeal to send out reinforcements for the motor boat ambulance service which carried English and French wounded from the battle areas to the sixty-mile distant base at Mudros Bay on the island of Lemnos. A picket boat and barges were asked for as well as two motor launches to carry men and stores. Funds had to be raised, suitable craft had to be found and equipped, and some-one was needed to lead the expedition. Masefield himself was invited to take charge, and at once he wrote to the friends and acquaintances – some forty in number – who had earlier responded with promises of financial help for his projected hospital in France. Within about a week he had collected enough money to purchase a 32 hp twin-screw motor boat (the *Agnes*) and two smaller launches, as well as a barge (which was to be named *John and Ada* after the Galsworthys, and fitted out as a transport for wounded). On 13 August he wrote trium-phantly to his brother Harry, 'I am starting this morning for the Dardanelles.' How ironic that this high-spirited departure should have coincided with the final annihilation of Allied hopes on the Gallipoli peninsula, the débâcle that followed after the Anzac and Suvla Bay landings. Yet because of the strict censorship Masefield can have known nothing of this at the time.

The passage from England to Lemnos via Gibraltar took Masefield several weeks in his small craft; by 4 September he had reached Malta, but after that he ran into heavy weather. No details of the journey have survived, and we know very little about the short time, probably only a week or so, that he spent at Mudros amid the stench, the flies, and the sickness, in an atmosphere of bewilderment, misery, and demoralization, before he returned home in a transport by way of Alexandria. Yet the heartbreak that he must have suffered can be well imagined, for the inadequacy of the hospital services was beyond belief. At the same time he must have rejoiced to feel that his own expedition had been unquestionably worthwhile. Writing later to his brother Harry, he summed up his experiences: 'Gallipoli was a crowded and disappointing time, and I got dysentery there, which lost me about a stone . . . I was at Anzac with the Australians, and had in a brief time a full experience of war: lice, fleas, dysentery, shells, bombs, shrapnel, sniping and a chase by submarine.'

By mid-October Masefield was again in England, weak and ill after his dysentery, and he was, of course, immediately confronted by the question 'What next?' No new opportunities in France had come up, and it seemed that he must look in some quite different direction. Already in the spring, after his return from Arc-en-Barrois, he had been approached – as from another universe – by a New York firm, the J.B. Pond Lyceum Bureau, well known as organizers of lecture tours, with a pressing invitation to come over in the following January. His writings were by now popular in America, and they wanted to present him as one of the special attractions of the 1915–1916 season, along with Dr. Grenfell of Labrador, Helen Keller, and Granville-Barker. At that point Masefield had replied that he could not possibly commit himself; he was hoping to return to France. Furthermore he assumed that such a tour would be essentially a peace-time enterprise, and he believed that the war might well continue for a year or more. But he did go so far as to suggest some topics on which, if he came later, he would be prepared to speak; these were 'one or two poets, say Chaucer and Shakespeare', 'the drama generally', 'The Spirit of France', 'The War' (as it had struck him from what he had seen of it), and his 'last visit to the U.S.'.

That had been in May 1915. Now, after five months, and after the collapse of his hopes for starting a hospital in France, he saw things differently. He had now come to realize that a lecture tour of the United States *in wartime* could be an excellent means of serving the Allied cause. For it would provide innumerable chances of observing American opinion, and also for presenting the war news from a British angle (the Germans had long been pushing their propaganda in the United States). His eyes were opened to all this by Sir Gilbert Parker, the versatile Canadian author and politician who during the early years of the war was one of the leading figures at 'Wellington House', the secret propaganda and intelligence department which had been brought into being by C.F.G. Masterman, then head of the National Health Insurance Commission (the Commission's offices in Buckingham Gate provided cover for the bureau's work).

By November the Pond Bureau had sent out a brochure announcing 'The first American tour of John Masefield, the Sailor Poet, in Lectures of Literary Interest'. And Masefield's American publishers, the Macmillan Company, were advertising the eight books of his which were currently in print. Meantime at Hampstead Masefield spent the final months of 1915 preparing his lectures: 'Jan read me his Chaucer lecture,' Constance wrote in her diary. 'It's a splendidly concise, clear simple statement. He has brooded over Chaucer and his work till I feel he has really understood his imagination and interpreted it.'

7

Although when Masefield first returned from Gallipoli he had joined Constance at Lollingdon, they soon moved back to Well Walk. 'It is rather beautiful to be near one's friends again,' Constance wrote in her diary, 'and to leave the ducks and hens alone a bit.' She also felt that London was a better place to live in during wartime than 'at other whiles'. 'One thing, I like the mystery that comes with the dark, and I like the greater quiet and simplicity of it.' But some nights were far from quiet. Constance put on record her impressions of an air raid which took place on the very evening of their return to London.

The night we came up there was a Zeppelin raid. I was at Isabel's at 9.30 when suddenly 'bang' went the guns. In an instant I was in the street running with head down to get home to the children, rather awe-struck at my first experience of war. The sky was lit up with searchlights and bright bursts from the shells, but the enemy was four miles off in the Strand. My body trembled under me but in my mind I didn't seem frightened. Fear is largely physical. Some-things happens in one's body when there is a great noise, or an unusual light, and it has nothing to do with being a coward.

When I got in my dear Jan was calmly writing a list of groceries that I had forgotten to send. He was not going to bother as he couldn't do anything, and I felt how absolutely right he was. I filled the bath and turned off the gas and by that time the sounds were distancing . . . The children slept through it all which was a great mercy.

The threat was there, night after night. A day or two later, one of the Masefields' acquaintances, Lady Henry Somer-set,[1] came to tell them a distressing story. 'Her little flat in Gray's Inn Square, a delightful little home she had made, has been all smashed by a bomb.' When Lady Henry visited them she was accompanied by a friend, an old clergyman called Father Russell,[2] whom they had previously met with her, 'an Anglican priest of great beauty and refinement'. Constance's further comments on Father Russell are revealing. Apparently she, and Masefield too, had felt 'a sort of influence from his intense spiritual life'. 'I wish', she remarked wistfully, 'there were more like him and then one might believe in the Church.'[3]

---

[1] A leader of the Women's Temperance Movement, who had resided for many years at Eastnor Castle near Ledbury.

[2] The Revd. E.F.Russell, for nearly fifty years a curate at St. Alban's Church, Holborn.

[3] Constance and J.M. were both emphatically anti-clerical. J.M. repeatedly de-clined to be a godparent, and neither Judith nor Lewis was baptized in infancy (though in adolescence they chose for themselves to be baptized and confirmed).

Constance wrote frankly in her diary about her beliefs, and also about those of her friends. By now she had, so it seems, lost confidence in the pacifist philosophizing that had earlier satisfied her; certainly her thinking as regards the war was growing closer to her husband's, although she was still groping intellectually. After Lowes Dickinson lunched with them on 3 November she wrote, 'Goldie is very wobbly in his mind':

He hates German ideas, but feels we ought to be very slow to condemn Germany, that it is hard to prove she meant war, that we do just as bad things, etc. I believe that in a sense it's all true, but men don't seem able to help fighting, and we with right in our hearts feel we must fight Germany because of Belgium, and the harder we fight the sooner it will be over. War is never reasonable in its beginnings but there comes a sort of inevitability as it goes on and nations get drawn in, like the characters in a tragedy, who are involved in the hero's fall.

Another attitude which Constance shared with John was impatience with those who paid lip-service to the war effort but continued to live a life of extravagance. The Asquiths for instance. At the end of November, when Violet Asquith was married to Raymond Bonham Carter, the Masefields attended the wedding service ('such a gloomy dark ceremony') but they did not go on to the reception afterwards:

We didn't much want to, but we heard she had a gorgeous vulgar set of presents. Her father gave her a diamond tiara, yet next day he admonished working men not to give presents to their wives and daughters, but to think of England's need. I never can quite forgive people for systematic extravagance. I never can forgive them for taking the labour of others as a matter of course. I don't mind if they sit quite loosely to it ... Motors and beautiful dresses are good to have sometimes, but let me always thank God for them and be ready to go without.

Constance and John far preferred their own way of life, which according to the standards of the day was a very simple one. 'We make the beds and clean the boots and live humbly with our old grumbler Annie, and our dear little nurse Bessie.' And when, occasionally, they emerged from their seclusion for some social engagement, the world of celebrities seemed irksomely

John Masefield – 'Jack' to his family – at the
age of about three.

Edward Masefield   Caroline Masefield

'Aunt Kate', Mrs. William Masefield   J. M.'s godmother, Miss Hanford Flood

Masefield's father and mother, and two women who influenced his youth.

Masefield as a *Conway* cadet with his sister Norah at the
Priory, Ledbury. He won the telescope as an essay prize.

In the school-ship H.M.S. *Conway* the boys studied mostly nautical subjects. Lieut. A. T. Miller, R.N. (left) was the ship's captain in Masefield's time.

The *Gilcruix* was the White Star ship in which Masefield
served as an apprentice during a voyage from Cardiff to
Iquique – round Cape Horn – in 1894.

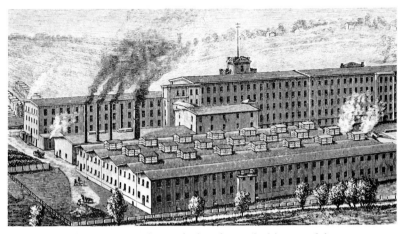

In America, between 1895 and 1897, he worked in one of the carpet
mills of Alexander Smith & Sons at Yonkers, New York.

Masefield aged nineteen, at the time of his return
to England from America.

Masefield in his early twenties when his poetry was first published.

Constance Crommelin (later Mrs. John Masefield) and
Isabel Fry (right) were schoolmistresses in the 1890s.

Masefield and his wife
after nine years of
marriage. The portrait
of Masefield is by
William Strang.

Several times during the First
World War Masefield served in
France, while his family lived
mostly at Lollingdon in the Thames
Valley. From left to right:
Constance Masefield, Judith, Lewis,
and a nurse.

Florence Lamont

Elizabeth Robins

Two American women whose friendship meant much to Masefield.

The Masefield family
in the 1920s.

Masefield's enthusiasm for producing amateur theatricals at Boars Hill in the 1920s inspired this cartoon in *Punch*.

As Poet Laureate Masefield became a public figure. At Boars
Hill (above) he posed for photographers with his daughter Judith, and at
Hereford with his wife, after receiving the freedom of the City.

In 1935 Masefield attended a Dublin dinner to celebrate
the seventieth birthday of W. B. Yeats (right).

In old age, at his home near Abingdon, Masefield
often wrote poetry out of doors.

superficial. 'We lunched at the Asquiths on Wednesday,' Constance wrote on 13 November. 'A very desultory entertainment'. She had sat next to the Prime Minister, and 'we were mild as mild'.

We discoursed about colours of uniforms and Lord Kitchener's figure and other trifles, and I thought how much more we had to talk about at our little table, where we can speak at times burning words. The great don't seem very great. The great man is the man who has imagination.

Chapter Eight

NEW WORLD

_____

I

When Masefield arrived in New York on 12 January 1916 the harbour, which he had last seen in the blazing summer of 1897, was foul with floe ice, and the ships moved through it 'as though they were breaking all the glass in the world'. Returning after almost twenty years was a strange experience. The shabby old waterfront had vanished away – in its place were efficient modern installations – and the city itself had exploded in size. This was his first sight of the new skyscrapers – the Singer Building, Woolworth Building, and Metropolitan Tower in Madison Square – and they staggered him with their 'amazing beauty'. At the same time he was horrified by the pace of New York life. By evening he was dropping with fatigue after a non-stop day of meetings and press interviews, but before turning in he summed up his impressions for Constance, in the first of the many letters he wrote to her during his tour:

New York is a colossal place; rather terrifying. I am glad you are not loose in such streets in the glare and the whirl, nor indoors in the stuffiness. Its devilish vastness, ingenuity and speed are overwhelming. It is a mechanical triumph, and I suppose the glitter catches moths, but it seems a heartless fearful city. It really daunts one. It is like meeting a splendid devil. I am limp from it.

'I am thrilled by your letters,' Constance wrote back to him. 'I gather that it is being a sort of fierce electric fun. Rather like being a wonderful mechanical toy in an electric workshop.' She was missing him desperately (especially as Judith had just left home for boarding-school for the first time) yet she rejoiced that the tour was being a success, and in her diary she wrote, 'He is being much feted and run after in America, and a little flattery will be a rest and a treat just now.'

The flattery was not turning Masefield's head in the least.

He was taking immense trouble to fulfil his obligations and to be nice to everyone, but he viewed what was happening to him, and the people he was meeting, with cool detachment and realism. 'They are as kind as we are,' he wrote to Constance, 'their hospitality is biblical, but they don't produce such fine individuals; they live in company and grow up with communal minds.' One of the things that struck him most was the apparent utter change – since the 1890s – in the general attitudes in New York and the East.

I find them so strangely earnest that I hardly recognise the race. Everywhere there is a deep love of poetry and an almost religious eagerness to hear and talk about it. A few people want autographs of course, but, behind all that, [there is] a deep seriousness, though sometimes the depth is not articulate and is cloudy with words.[1]

Masefield criticized the Americans but he did not despise them; indeed he sincerely felt that Britain needed America as an ally, not only in immediate wartime terms: 'They are a great-hearted people . . . And I am deeply impressed with the need of linking such a race to ourselves, now, while the iron is hot. So far, nearly everybody is hotly pro-Ally, but one has to be careful, the Boche taint goes deep.' In more formal language, he expanded upon American attitudes to the war in one of his first reports to Sir Gilbert Parker. Everywhere among the cultivated Americans he had met, he said, he had found a fear of being despised for not having gone to war. Everywhere, too, there was a determination to be prepared for a war in the future, and an uneasy suspicion that there would soon be acute trouble with the strongly organized German population.

Soon he would be in the Middle West, in the thick of the 'Boche' areas, but for the first fortnight of the tour he was based in New York, with an intensive programme of lectures in and around the city, as well as up and down the East Coast. The engagement which he considered the most important, and which he greatly enjoyed, was at Yale. 'The spirit of the young men is very much that of Oxford,' he told Constance,

1 Here it must be remembered that when J.M. was previously in America he was a raw, humble youth, living among tough manual workers, with no chance to come into touch with the well educated.

and their freshness and affection is irresistible, so I did not lecture, but read from my poems and had a jolly afternoon . . . I find the young men enthusiastic about poetry, and all the old arrogance seems changed to a kind of humble self questioning and doubt.

Back in New York he found this same seriousness in a young woman whose work was then in journalism but whose heart was in poetry – she was soon to become a Masefield disciple. 'I had a talk with a young poet, Louise [Townsend] Nicholl, an earnest soul, whose verse is not bad.' This last remark was quite a concession on Masefield's part, for his opinion of American poetry was not high. 'Of course we write them simply off the map in every kind of writing,' he had declared to Constance in one of his earliest letters.

The first press cuttings he sent back to her had also given her an adverse impression. 'What a people for thinking well of themselves,' she exclaimed, 'I'm amazed at the tone of the American papers. Evidently they think you have come to study *their* literature. And who on earth is Masters?' Edgar Lee Masters, the Chicago poet, was much in the limelight at the time. 'When I landed,' Masefield explained, 'I found all America seething with interest about his book *The Spoon River Anthology*,[1] and of course the first thing they wanted to know from me was "Is Masters really any good as a poet?".' After reading the book Masefield said that he could not regard Masters as a good poet; there was 'nothing deep enough behind it to atone for it or make it human'. To Constance he wrote that the book was a great advance 'on anything they had had for years, but even that is not saying much':

I will bring it home, and you'll be quite interested to see American parochialism, and you will feel Masters behind it to be a nice-minded man, who very nearly does something big. They have a phrase about him and me which is quoted everywhere. 'He is not so good a poet as Masefield but he has more sense.'[2]

[1] J.M. told Constance that *The Spoon River Anthology* was 'a very good idea'.
   The man takes all the gravestones in a country churchyard and makes a little poem about the essential life of each corpse, man, woman and child, and in doing this constructs a kind of picture of the village history. It is a rather good picture of the rather thin and varnishy life in an American town, adultery without passion, murder without lust, robbery without greed, all the ghastly event.
[2] Later in the tour, in Chicago, J.M. met Masters. He described him to Constance (14 February 1916) as 'solid, earnest, sincere, and a little like a Puritanical Belloc'.

During the first two weeks of his tour Masefield became
accustomed to being whirled hither and thither; he lectured
in Boston, Bridgeport, and Stamford, and went twice to Philadelphia (a place that he took to). He also spoke at several
women's colleges, Vassar, Wellesley, and Bryn Mawr; Wellesley
especially pleased him: 'Nearly all the professors were Quakers,
and there was a gentleness and beauty of mind about them all.'
By this time Masefield was gathering confidence as a public
speaker. 'It is still too early', he wrote to Constance, 'but the
agency tells me that I am being a success. I think I have succeeded with the press, and know that I have done so with Yale
and New York, where the audiences were splendid. I am glad
to say that I am not in the least being done, but am getting
practically top prices.'[1] Yet although this suggests that he now
felt at ease on the platform, he did not in the least appear so.
In fact right up until the end of his tour he seemed a nervous
speaker. We know this from a very candid description of 'Poet
Masefield' written by a reporter who attended one of his New
York lectures:

Poet Masefield has a puzzled brow, a small close-bitten mustache,
a boyish bang, and the tiredest eyes that ever looked out of a human
countenance. He read his lecture . . . [and] his high-pitched voice
and deliberate delivery and monotonous rising inflections made it
all seem a little like going to church . . .

Mr. Masefield went through his apparently sternly appointed
task with firmness and precision. He kept the hand that was not
needed to turn the leaves of his manuscript safely behind him –
where it could fiddle all it pleased. He teetered rhythmically back-
ward and forward, from one foot to the other, as if to help him keep
going. He 'swallowed' hard. And when he had finished his lecture
he stopped.

Then he read some of his poems with the same meaningless and
monotonous delivery and with the same Church of England service
inflections . . . Then he stopped again and looked around apologetic-
ally as if to say 'Well, that's all'. He made several stiff little bows.

What a cruel portrayal! Yet at the end of it the sharp-eyed
New York reporter suddenly dropped his critical manner, and
exclaimed, as from the heart, 'One could have wept aloud with
gratitude that in this day of shallowness and pose there could

[1] Usually a minimum of $150 per lecture.

be anything so honest and genuine – and a great poet, too – as John Masefield. One adored him!'

It is very clear that before leaving New York, to set off westwards on the second stage of his tour, Masefield had won many hearts. 'Evidently the Americans like and trust you,' Constance wrote. 'You have the power of making friends wherever you go.' This had always been so; for instance when he had been an unknown boy in New York twenty years earlier. And one great joy of his return to the city was that he was able to see once again several of the Americans who had helped him in those far-off days. Mrs. MacLachlan, in whose home he had lodged at Yonkers, came to one of the New York lectures with her son Howard; Mr. East, the Yonkers bookseller, was also there, with a representative from the Alexander Smith carpet factory. At another lecture, in Brooklyn, Masefield's erstwhile companion Billy Booth was waiting to see him. But perhaps the most cordial of all the reunions was with Luke O'Connor, whose down-town saloon was flourishing more than ever, and who had been thrilled to learn of his former employee's success as a writer.[1]

2

The main objective of Masefield's tour, as far as his reports for Wellington House were concerned, was his expedition into the German-dominated areas of the Middle West, and in the last week of January he set off for Chicago, with engagements *en route* at Pittsburgh and Cincinnati. Already at Cincinnati he found 'lots of Boche', but the war seemed 'curiously distant and put away'. 'It is not of vital moment to people here,' he wrote

---

[1] In 1904 when W.B. Yeats visited New York, he called on O'Connor (at J.M.'s urging) and told him about the success of *Salt-Water Ballads*. This spurred O'Connor to write a letter to J.M. as follows:

Mr. Masefield

Mr. Yeats has been here and tells me that you are getting along very well. I am very glad to hear this, I hope if you will ever come to N.Y. you will come in and see me. I have enlarged the place very much. I have now four bartenders and five waiters.

Mr. Yeats tells me that you are making quite a name as a writer and that you expect to write books. There is one book that I suggest that you write. It is a badly needed book, especially here in New York . . . I am sure it would have a big sale and give you a considerable amount of fame. The book I suggest is the Complete Bartenders' Guide.

to Constance, 'except as it affects trade and the coming presidential election. Wilson is much criticised and disliked, and there seems a strong likelihood of [Theodore] Roosevelt being re-elected.'[1] Here and there in his letters to Constance he remarked thus on the political situation, but for the most part they are diary letters, overflowing with personal impressions.

Time and again he was struck by the contrast with the America he had known twenty years before. 'The land has changed beyond all recognition and belief; its wealth and opportunity are indescribable . . . Prices are fearfully high and I suppose expenses average 8 or 9 dollars a day . . . but I have ceased to wonder.' Manners, too, had changed:

Little girls here, who used to be such little terrors, now are mild as doves and drop little quaint curtsies to America's distinguished guest. Little boys, whose like I once saw dicing, smoking cigarettes and reading the *Licensed Victuallers' Gazette* . . . now explain electric accumulators . . . to the visitor from sleepy Europe.

Another thing he noticed especially was that life in America was 'a very social matter':

Everybody knows everybody else, and one is profoundly struck by the absence of walls, hedges and fences between the houses; few bother about gardens and everybody seems to be glad to see his neighbour, so hedges aren't made, nor barriers between men and men.

His first reaction to Chicago was that it was 'a sort of mixture of London and Birkenhead', but he had no time to look around before being taken under the wing of a lady who habitually acted as guardian angel to visiting celebrities, Mrs. William Vaughn Moody, a widow whose poet-dramatist husband had taught English at the University of Chicago. He was disconcerted to find that her house was full of strange foreign protégés, but he much enjoyed the stimulating company of his hostess; he assured Constance that he had been 'held spellbound' by the 'most profound wisdom' with which she discoursed on Shakespeare. She also talked of much else, and he

---

[1] The 'strong likelihood' was Middle-Western wishful thinking. In November 1916 Woodrow Wilson, who had been at the White House since 1912, was re-elected to the Presidency.

learnt that she knew Rabindranath Tagore and William Rothenstein, ran a candy factory in Chicago and a provision business in London, had a flat in New York and a farm in the wilds, and 'a tent or something' in the desert.

For Masefield, Mrs. Moody was Chicago's only delight. The great ruthless, heartless, commercial city – 'Hog Butcher for the World' – repelled and disgusted him. He was not deceived by the veneer of culture:

It is a terrible city . . . Truly for dingy grubby dirty don't care ruination this town would take some beating. I never saw any place so truly stamped with the legend 'This is what you come to if you sell your soul to the devil'. Pentonville is joyous to Chicago, Manchester is a paradise to it, Wapping, Whitechapel and Deptford are smiling gardens to it, Mudros even. I never saw a town so hopeless nor so sad. Endless miles of degenerate mind, with more cars than in any city in the world.

The Chicago audiences before whom he had to speak also filled him with loathing. The bookings that his agency had arranged did not include any lectures at the University, and he found the townspeople 'hard, repellent and flippant'. So it was indeed a relief when he set off for the South for a few days, leaving behind him the fetid stench of the stockyards and the glue factories.

He was bound for Tennessee, with stops at Indianapolis and St. Louis, and it was going to be his first sight of the South, though it could only be a brief one, for after lecturing in Memphis and Nashville he had to dash back to Chicago for further engagements. But although so rushed, this trip proved to be an invigorating tonic. Masefield had long been addicted to Mark Twain, and he was stirred to the depths by the sight of the Mississippi, then in mighty flood. He also fell head over heels in love with the South, especially with Memphis. 'I don't know why one goes to Italy when there is a place like Memphis on the globe,' he wrote to Constance.

I came from Chicago dead beat, and Indianapolis made me worse, and at St. Louis I nearly gave up, but directly I reached the river and the cotton and the floods and saw all the negroes going about, and the mules everywhere . . . it did me more good than a week's rest.

He went on to paint a colourful picture of the people, the place, and the river.

I can't describe it, as it is all flavour, but it is a wonderful living town, full of negroes who ride about on mules, and all the whites fly about in cars, and then there are dogs, and dirty negro shanties, and the houses look exactly as if they chewed tobacco, all very lean and knowing, and rather hard in the mouth, and then I expect you could get killed for five cents almost anywhere there, and little negro boys and girls go around on roller skates, and whenever two negresses pass you, you see that one has a green turban, and purple skirt and an orange parcel, and the other a scarlet parcel, a green skirt and a black turban, and the men wear purple and bright blue, and spit through their teeth *à merveille*, and just as you think it is all worth ten of the best, you see the river, in bigger flood than has ever been known. It is a mile and a half across and changes its bed nightly and licks up the dry land and flings islands down, and great trees go wallowing by.

'This,' he assured Constance, 'apart from the lovely welcome everywhere, is the one thing I wish you could have seen.'

He was still in euphoric mood after leaving Memphis, and rejoiced as he gazed out from the train over the endless plains of western Tennessee.

Open windows, O joy, and draughts down one's neck, just as at home, and a country immeasurably wild and lonely and beautiful, cruised and poised over by great eagles, and often flooded, and often like the beginning of the world, but lovely, lovely, lovely . . . There was a kind of tree, like a cross between a silver birch and a beech, and below it a kind of thorn with a pure scarlet berry, and below that a small evergreen cane; miles and miles and miles of it.

After Nashville, where he lunched with six college professors and had tea with an Anglophile lady whose forbears had fought for the South, returning to Chicago was like being slung into a stinking dungeon. And speaking again before its people, who seemed harsher and more repulsive than ever after the slow, courteous Southerners, was a nightmarish ordeal. It was not however one of his own audiences, but a gathering of another kind that roused him to a real frenzy of hatred against the Chicagoans. He had heard that there was to be a Paderewski concert in aid of Polish charities, and as the date happened to coincide with one of his rare free days he decided to go. From the moment he arrived he was appalled. The audience of 4,000 rushed into the concert hall 'as though they were going to wreck the building':

I never saw an audience enter a building more like a mob, with so complete a want of order, quiet decorum and consideration. After some unlovely hustling and barging we got into our places, and presently a mob came upon the stage, and jammed the stage full, again without any order, except that they all wore red rosettes, and presently this mob sang the Polish anthem . . . Then Paderewski came on and made a speech which was on the whole a very good and tactful appeal. He spoke for half an hour, and then went off to rest, as he was to play Chopin later on to us.

But then came a performance in a very different key, which Masefield found totally repellent. As soon as Paderewski had left, an eminent banker came on to the stage, with a draughtsman and an enormous blackboard. Money and promises of money were then received, and the draughtsman kept chalking and rechalking the total received, while the banker shouted aloud the amount of each gift or promise.

It was a very good way to get a big subscription, but . . . what a revelation it was of the commercial mind. This was what they really liked, to hear of a sum of money growing bigger under their eyes, and the way they cheered the word dollars, and the sort of loving roll the banker gave the word in his mouth,

'Mrs. James P. Lewvinski, one hundred dollars'

was beyond belief oily with Mammon. That was the music the audience came for.

After an hour or so he could stand it no longer, and he came away without hearing a note of Chopin. 'No music could have had any taste after the money grubbing.'

A Chicago experience which tried him in a different way was an engagement to speak before 'the enemy'. He had to lecture to 'a sort of limited club' in a private house, 'all very rich and fashionable', where about half his audience were either Germans or Americans of German birth. He dreaded the prospect but when the time came he carried it off well. 'I felt myself probed and tested by a lot of subtle minds', he told Constance afterwards,

so I put my ears back and was cheerful and made myself agreeable, and a word seemed to go about that I wasn't going to say *Gott*

Strafe Wilhelm, and it was as nice a house as man could have to speak with, and I found myself talking with Baums and -Heimers and -Eisslers, just as though they were civilized human beings.

Before the evening was out, however, his newly cordial feelings were put to the test.

A lot of queer food was thrust upon us, done up in green jelly and in transparent green sugar, and a wicked old Boche who was as clever as the devil (and as cunning a liar) told me of der privilege to hear so great a poet, whom he had so oft times read, though I knew from his wicked eye that he'd never read a word of me and never would.

'But I can always jolly that kind of knave along.'

Yet another trial he had to endure during his Chicago stay was of a kind with which he was already sadly familiar: he had to speak before a women's club. 'Oh God, you don't know how awful these women can be afterwards,' he wrote to Constance:

Hundreds of parochial matrons throng round to press your hand while you long for a good knobby club to clump them on the head with. Yesterday it was worse than I have ever known it, for there was a tea, and such a squash that one could not move, and one most fearful elderly spinster who was mad, and laughed in a padded cell kind of way, came up time and time again literally almost to embrace me . . . My God it was a fearful time.

Nevertheless he had to admit that sometimes the matrons were 'picturesque'. There had been one 'fearful hag' at Pittsburgh, for instance, who kept saying 'Pittsburgh extends to Mr. Masefield a spiritual embrace,' and who had also made the memorable remark, 'I would like to have you meet my husband; say he's an elegant man. I could trust him with Venus, and he weighs 195 pounds and he's in love only with me.' Looking back afterwards this seemed funny, but poor Masefield had to remember that he was due to return to Pittsburgh later, 'and she'll be there again, the hag, when I go back there, unless God gives her influenza'.

3

During the latter part of Masefield's three weeks based at Chicago his engagements took him to Grand Rapids, Milwaukee, La Crosse, and Beloit, as well as to Minneapolis where he was entertained by the President of the University of Minnesota, Dr. Vincent, and his wife. This Minneapolis visit was specially enjoyable for a sleigh ride with Mrs. Vincent on the morning after the lecture:

We careered along the banks of the Mississippi, which is here but little broader than the Thames at Richmond, and frozen partly, and in a deep sort of combe. We were in Hiawatha's country . . . It was a bright spring day with the genial temperature of zero instead of the 20 below of the day before [and] the drive did me good. I get no air in this beastly life of barnstorming.

Minneapolis was a refreshing change, too, after the atmosphere of anxiety he had encountered in the intensely German Milwaukee. He told Sir Gilbert Parker that the supporters of the Allies there were almost afraid to speak of the war, lest what they said should be reported to the Boche; 'they might, and very likely would be, made to suffer for it'. They were really afraid of being blown up or set fire to.

Back again in Chicago Masefield clung to the fact that he had only a day or two more there. By this time he felt he was really getting to know the city, although he still seems to have become acquainted only with its commercial side. It revolted him more and more, but in one letter to Constance he made a faint try to be dispassionate: 'Chicago is still very much what New York used to be. New York is now, in the main, a marvellous, erect, and noble city, and I suppose Chicago will be the same in twenty years.' 'But', he added, 'till then I'll hope to avoid it.' At last, on 14 February, he left Chicago for good, and as he sat in the train, 'bowling along through the sunny prairie, where the cows eat dead cornstalks in temperatures of about zero', he gave thanks in a sort of ecstasy. 'Oh my dear, the joy. I'm out of Chicago. I've left Chicago, Chicago is behind me. I may never have to go back to Chicago.'

I never saw the sights of Chicago. I never saw the 700 hogs killed in an hour, nor the 10,000 cows butchered in a day, nor the men brooming the blood into the pans and having their fingers sliced off into the sausage-meat, and no time to stop to pick them out, so perhaps I ought not to judge the place. I never saw its art; I saw its soul though . . . and as the train goes south I sing 'I'm going away from Chicago. I'm going away from Chicago. I may perhaps never be in Chicago again'. My God, I did hate the place; in spite of people's kindness.

Even with Chicago behind him, however, Masefield was still in the Middle West, and he now had to face St. Louis – 'as fierce a town of commerce' as Chicago itself, and also as full of Germans (among whom, so he heard, 'feeling was high'). On his arrival he was seized on, as usual, by a crowd of reporters, and as usual they invaded his room. Masefield generally got on well with the press, but there were of course exceptions, such as the 'hard-mouthed terror of a female' at Milwaukee, who had begun by saying 'Now Mr. Masefield, I want a good long story from you with plenty of pep,' and worse, far worse, the team of 'four slimy female reporters' at Grand Rapids, 'all dirty and evil looking, like retired whores'. Their dodge had been that three of them should question him while the fourth hid behind his back and took notes. But a mirror had betrayed their ruse, and he had refused to co-operate. Once or twice, elsewhere, reporters had called to him through the bathroom keyhole to ask for interviews, but in St. Louis, he said, 'they weren't quite so bad as that'.

He described St. Louis as 'a big noisy smoky city . . . the third biggest town in America, and it stretches for miles and miles in a sprawling wasteful haphazard dirty way. It is dim and smoky here, not black and foul like Chicago.' Yet the haze full of floating smuts, the roar of the factories, and the 'absence of civic sense', prompted him to put into words his deeply pessimistic thoughts about industrial towns in general, and about the Americans who lived in them.

I never felt it much before, but since I've been in these big commercial cities I have said to myself almost all day long 'What shall it profit a man?' and a kind of pitying wonder takes me, and I ask myself what in God's name do these people get by it? They keep chaste and temperate and rise early and slave like factory hands all to make a city as like hell as it may be, and they die young and their children have no love for them; their children despise poppa for not living longer and making more dollars; and momma takes to Christian Science and flounces out of the room at the mention of death. It is a land all false teeth and spectacles, the most tragical hollowness I know, the elaborate shell of a coffin, without the humanity of a corpse inside.

Almost equally gloomy thoughts came to him, again in St. Louis, after being taken round an immense shoe factory, which was said to make fifteen million pairs of shoes a year. There he saw the raw hide going in at one end and the finished boot coming out at the other, 'after being bedevilled in a hundred machines by a hundred weary men and women'. It left him feeling 'O God, is it not better to go barefoot, than to degrade all these thousands'. But he added a remark to Constance that must have made her smile: 'I saw one monstrous pair of boots size 16 (men's) and was told that it was made to order, and that sometimes they had orders for 19's, so never you talk to me of my big feet again. The negroes here have truly monstrous feet, and they are the people who buy these canoes.'

After St. Louis Masefield's programme took him back through Ohio, and although its towns seemed less abhorrent than the great industrial cities, they were still Middle Western. 'I don't know why I hate this Middle West so much, but I do. It has a raw feel of east wind always, and it is dirty and flat and very haphazard.' The Middle Westerners too came in for violent abuse; they seemed to him, so he declared, 'carnal, hard, rough, overbearing, false, crude, bumptious, empty, flat as their prairie land, and inflated as their natural gas'. But there were a few exceptions. In Columbus he met a doctor, 'a very nice friendly fellow', whose name, strangely enough, proved to be the same as his own. Apparently Dr. Masefield had been in Columbus for many years as a general practitioner and he had never been to England, yet, to their mutual delight, he knew a lot about the regions of the English countryside whence the Masefield family had sprung.

In the small town of Oberlin, too, Masefield had a pleasant encounter, this time with some young people who touched him by their naïve seriousness. They were the sort, he said, to whom Ibsen would seem frivolous. After the lecture (in a gigantic chapel 'which was the very devil to speak in') he invited a few of them to go with him to a little restaurant nearby 'for a dish of soup and a grapefruit'. This cost him ten cents a head, and 'seemed to give them a kind of morbid joy':

I daresay they repented bitterly for the levity of it during the night, for I never saw students so mild and good. The boys did not smoke, and the girls only ate ice cream twice a week, they said, and evidently they felt most frightful rakes at eating tomato soup with a poet at 10 p.m.

Next morning, at the station, he found that his guests of the previous evening – who apparently regarded him as 'a highly popular but Byronic sort of figure, a regular satanic sort of fellow, who went the pace' – had brought their parents with them to give him a send-off. The last he saw of them was a little crowd standing in the snow, waving hats and handkerchiefs. One of the girls had given him a box of home-made sweets and told him to eat them at once as otherwise they would get sticky.

The gentle friendly innocence of youth is very touching . . . This land makes one love the young. I never realised before how wise youth is . . . Generally speaking I find no really good audiences except among the highly cultivated and the very young. Youth never asks fool questions nor bothers one, nor says any silly idiocy like 'poetry ought not to be sad', nor asks me for autographs, nor drives one mad with half-baked praise.

4

Ever since boyhood Masefield's spirit had been stirred by the sight of water – the sea in all its moods, the brooks at Lollingdon, the meandering River Thames. And now in America, after having seen the Mississippi in flood he set out to see Niagara. As the train took him, in icy weather, towards the Canadian frontier, it was as though he were a pilgrim approaching a holy place. In such a mood, it is not surprising that the account of his impressions that he set down for Constance was obviously written under the influence of deep emotion.

The fall itself is not easy to describe. It is rather clear, greenish water, and it is quite quiet, not very deep, just before the fall, and it rises and goes over the lip almost like metal, and then seems to see what it is doing, and seems to try to get back, and ceases to be water, or anything like water, or anything on earth, but something rather white and devilish and astonished, and one could watch it all day for ever, not with awe, perhaps, but with a kind of kinship with it. The air is so mist-soaked that everything near, roads, gorge and rails, is caked and heaped with hard, white ice.

The gorge, he estimated, was something like two hundred feet deep, and

> this vast bulk of water topples into it and comes up again in a mist much higher than the fall and floats around everywhere, not like mist so much as escaping steam, and in among it are great noble gannety sea-eagles, drowsing and drifting and cruising, and underneath a vast glacier bulk of ice, with rifts of bedevilled water, and a whirlpool going round and round, churning up ice and trees and chunks of things which might be bodies, and slowly freezing, so that the ice there has big irregular curves in it.

After gazing at this for a good while Masefield tore himself away and went on to another place, below the fall, where he could view the rapids.

> Whatever the falls may be in dignity and majesty, the rapids are in savagery and hellish force. I never saw such water . . . It is not water changed to something else, as at the falls, but it is water that has become a devil. Before it goes down the fall, it is like the star of the morning, like Lucifer, so pure and green and bright, and at the rapids it is really re-emerging after the fall, the very devil of hell. It comes along with a sort of blind sweeping romp, and then as it sweeps, a great big belly of a wave will rise up from underneath, right in its path, and the first wave will go over it just as if they were playing leap-frog, and then they both shout 'Hooray, hooray!' and go on with the romp together in the biggest game of all hell.
>
> What makes it specially fearful is the dead wan colour and the thick slush of ice on the top, which makes it almost semi-solid, and to see a semi-solid acting like this makes you marvel. Sometimes you see a big heap of water thrust its snout out of the rush and swim back and bite some big wave coming at it and burst it all to bits, and then it jumps aloft and laughs and smashes itself on a rock with a kind of devilish glee, as one who says, 'Well, I killed my enemy, anyway, first'. I could have watched the place for hours and days and months.

At Niagara Masefield was a spectator, separated by protective railings from nature's fury; but soon afterwards he had to take part, unexpectedly, in a personal battle with the elements. He had to fulfil a lecture engagement in upstate New York, at Hamilton College in Clinton near Utica, and for once his agency's organization broke down. Usually he was met at the station, but this time his guide had been given a wrong hour, so he had to fend for himself. He found a taxi-man – 'a fine fellow, of burly Red Indian appearance' – who was however loath to take him to Clinton, insisting that the road was impassably blocked with snow drifts. But Masefield persuaded him to try, and off they went, in twenty degrees of frost. After the first two miles they came to a country track, with a foot of snow on top of it.

Of course one foot of snow is not much, but on a rough road it so easily drifts into 18 inches or more, and it was just like being in the *Agnes* in Mudros Bay. I sat, cheering on the driver, through the window, and at each swerve and drop and skid, I would say, 'Say, you got her out of that in great shape', or 'Say, you are some driver; I guess you know your job'. And he would grin back and say 'I got plenty of power. I guess I'll bring her through if anybody can'. And then he would take a cavort that would throw her half across the road, and then dance back and stagger and half stop.

The frozen country all around was a sort of open downland or tableland, 'very white and big and featureless', and then presently they came to 'a horrid place where a smoke of snow drift was flying steadily, noiselessly, and continually, just like smoke upon water' over the road. All the air was dim with this smoke of fine snow and they realized that here they were up against it, and they ran right into it and stuck. Clambering out they prospected, but there was no sort of house anywhere near, no hope of borrowing shovels, so they climbed into the car again and the driver backed a bit, and then charged. They ran deep into the drift and stuck again, then backed again, charged again, and this time they forced the wretched car through and over, and ploughed up and down beyond, and finally wallowed clear. After that the road was only 'bad in bits' till they reached Clinton, 'a little town built about a brook in a valley'. But just beyond the brook was a precipitous hill, and there they really stuck. The college was at the top of the hill, so they got out and walked, or rather battled their way, in the teeth of a howling wind. Thus Masefield arrived in time for his lecture on English Poetry – but how was he going to get back? He had to be in New York next day. Fortunately his driver was ready to wait for him, the return trip to Utica was 'a romp', and they reached the station just in time for the New York train.

From New York, during the final weeks of his tour, Masefield returned twice to Boston. After the earlier of these two visits he told Constance that he liked Boston for the 'almost pure English being spoken, and the houses so like English ones inside and out, and people drinking china tea and reading *Punch*'. He also found the Bostonians very courteous; he noticed that some of them, in speaking about the war, referred to the English side as 'we', and he thought that perhaps this was just their good manners. Elsewhere in New England he found a good deal of anti-British feeling, although the Boche were causing anger and heart-burning by appropriating goods sent out to the Belgians; one lady assured him that long after sending out some woollen underclothes she had received a letter from a German soldier who said: 'Dear Madam, This is to thank you for your esteemed drawers. You will be interested to hear I was wearing them when I received the Iron Cross.'

Masefield enjoyed Boston, but the time he spent there was clouded by the fact that he had not been invited to speak at Harvard. He sensed that there were complex reasons for this: 'I wish I knew the truth of all the Harvard intrigues.' He had also been hoping for an invitation to Princeton, where Alfred Noyes was in residence as a visiting lecturer. But here too he was disappointed. An invitation did eventually come, but so late that it was 'almost an insult'. The programme for his remaining days was indeed crammed (the peak fixture was a vast banquet at the Hotel Astor on 15 March, a 'Poets' Dinner' at which he was to be a speaker and guest of honour) and only once or twice was he able to escape from his public. One welcome interlude was 'a rove in the Park, in glorious clear frosty weather', and another was a call on his publisher, George Brett of Macmillan, with whom he had a long and helpful talk about business – to Constance he afterwards wrote 'he has been really good to me during my stay'.

5

In one of Masefield's letters written shortly before he sailed for home he endeavoured to stand back and ask himself what he really thought of America.

I suppose that in the big eastern cities, New York, Boston, and of course in Yale, I have felt in the presence of the English mind set free, and going to be immense and generous and beautiful beyond all modern idea. Then outside that (which has been happy and inspiring) there is a crudeness and a baldness and a self-satisfied mechanical achievement which is the very devil in Hell, and some of those ghastly mushroom makeshift towns, like Chicago, which I shall always regard as hell on earth, and Pittsburgh, which is where the devil was born, and those rough middle west cities like Columbus, are among the beastliest places I've ever seen. Mudros is a gentleman to any of them.

He also asked himself whether his tour had been a success. He was not sure. He now realized that the mass of Americans did not care two straws for literary criticism of any kind; if he had known this in advance he would have laid very different plans. What they loved was good poetry as long as it was cheerful – 'they will listen to cheerful readings for hours'. So he could generally 'pull through' by reading some of his poems, as he had done, with such success, at Yale. In some towns he had felt that he failed, owing to a bad throat or a bad hall or a bad lecture, and then once or twice there had been a bad audience; but several times he knew he had done well. Sometimes he felt that people had liked him personally; 'among the young I seem to have had a strange effect quite unsuspected by me.' Louise Townsend Nicholl, whom he now described as 'an enormously strong sort of poetess here', and who, he felt, represented '*les jeunes*' in New York, had told him of this, 'so if I have won "*les jeunes*" all is well'.

Not all of Masefield's final appearances in New York were distasteful to him. There was one in particular which he not only enjoyed, but which was the occasion of a personal encounter that was destined to lead on to a lifelong friendship. On 28 February he had to give an afternoon talk on the subject of 'The Tragic Drama' at the Aeolian Hall, under the auspices of the New York branch of the Drama League of America, and for once he tasted 'the pleasure of speaking', because of the hall's excellent acoustics. 'It was a good audience,' he told Constance, 'but the hall was perfectly divine, the best I have ever had or shall have, a glorious place in which even a whisper carried.' After his lecture he was mobbed, as usual, by the press 'five or six deep'. 'Some Yonkers people' also crowded round, as well as 'three or four souls who wanted either consolation or autographs'. And it was at this point that the chief of his agency, Mr. J.B. Pond Jr., introduced him to Mrs. Thomas W. Lamont.

Florence Corliss Lamont, dark, smiling, dynamic, and then aged forty-four, was the wife of a leading figure in the great international banking house of J.P. Morgan. The Lamonts, as Masefield was soon to learn, moved in a circle of diplomats, politicians, and literary and academic celebrities, and their lives overflowed with every kind of material advantage. Yet despite all this – or perhaps because of it – Mrs. Lamont proved to be one of the souls who wanted consolation. 'A lady took me to my hotel,' was how Masefield put it to Constance,

asking me all the way in her car how to get to Christ, for that was what troubled her night and day, that she could not find Christ, and she felt that I had found him. I've long since ceased to be staggered by people here, so I told her what I could remember of Quakerism and the ways of Christian Recollection.

Mrs. Lamont lost no time in following up this first meeting, and within a few days Masefield was again writing to Constance:

Last week I told you of a lady who asked me how to find Christ. I now know her household and most of her friends, and have been able to see one very new queer side of America, the side of overwhelming business ability and wealth. Her husband is a very very nice fellow, one of Morgan's allies I suppose, and wealthy beyond all computation.

As she says, she has everything her soul can possibly desire, love, children, wealth, wit, beauty, friends, great practical ability, energy that makes one sick, and a restlessness that would wear out a diamond, and no inner peace, nor any suggestion nor any possibility of ever finding any. She is a nice-minded woman, and he is really a fine fellow, directing vast concerns all over the world, and coming home quietly to play with his babes, who are very dear little children.

I don't know what to say to such souls: it seems as though peace were not for those who live here. The drive of the fever in the air is too great, and they whirl on, and wear out, in some blind feverish delirium which they call their 'hope' or their 'uplift'.

A further word on Masefield's budding friendship with Florence Lamont and her family, and on the newly sympathetic attitude towards America that stemmed from it, was not however written in his own hand. Some months after his return to England Constance wrote in her diary, 'Henceforth the thoughts and desires of those fine Americans whom he liked will make a new company in our minds. He was very happy there.'

Chapter Nine

IN PRAISE OF HEROES

I

Masefield's first American lecture tour had unexpected results that determined the course of his life for the next three years. Before it his war service had been practical rather than intellectual: after it he was to serve primarily as a writer, a recorder of the heroism of others. On his return from America in March 1916 he submitted a formal report to the Foreign Office, in which he stressed that during his tour he had been persistently questioned (by hecklers who had obviously been under the influence of enemy propaganda) about the failure of the Dardanelles campaign. Might he not write an article which would dispose of the enemy's lies?

Soon he was starting on a book, not an article, but it proved to be no mere conventional apologia. Masefield's *Gallipoli* is an intensely romantic book. He even went so far as to claim that the Dardanelles campaign could be regarded as 'the second grand event of the war; the first was Belgium's answer to the German Ultimatum'. He compared the spirit of the British and Dominion troops to that of Charlemagne's army at Roncevaux, the Frankish army which according to the *Chanson de Roland* battled to the death against Saracen hordes in a Pyrenean ravine, abandoned by the Emperor who might have sent troops to their aid. Each chapter was headed with a quotation from the French epic, and the parallels were indeed striking. Especially, in the figure of the tragic Roland, blowing his great horn so as to burst his lungs, in desperate hopes of securing reinforcements, Masefield saw a forerunner of Sir Ian Hamilton.

In order to write the book he was given access to brigade and battalion diaries (he worked sometimes at Lollingdon, sometimes in London), but inevitably, because of censorship, *Gallipoli* was only a partial account. There was no choice but to leave much unsaid. To William Rothenstein Masefield wrote,

'Someday, perhaps fairly soon, the truth about that affair will be known, and then some measure of justice will be done.' 'The fact is we shan't know the real truth . . . until the Turks tell their own story at the end of the war': such was the dispassionate opinion expressed by Sir Ian Hamilton himself, in a letter to Masefield written after he had read the *Gallipoli* manuscript. Masefield had by now become friends with 'Ian'. He also idolized him as a hero, and made no secret of it, for he dedicated *Gallipoli* to 'General Sir Ian Hamilton, G.C.B., D.S.O.' and the men under his command, 'with deepest admiration and respect'.

A few weeks after *Gallipoli* was published it was selling 'like wildfire'. The bewildered anger that had been seething in Britain over the whole episode was evidently mollified by Masefield's romanticism. And to his own friends the book seemed a triumph. H.W. Nevinson called it 'a brilliant poetic sketch', and Edward Marsh 'the supreme *Gallipoli*' (with the added comment to Constance, 'That is war service if you like').

2

Masefield was thirty-eight when he wrote *Gallipoli* – not yet middle-aged – but the strain of wartime was wearing him down. Physically he was in a poor state; in the summer of 1916 a scratch on his left arm turned septic and for a long time would not heal. Nevertheless by the end of August he set off again, this time back to France, on a new non-combatant assignment. 'A very delicate mission' had been proposed to him by Sir Gilbert Parker: he was to collect material for a report for the American press on America's contribution to the Allied war effort in the matter of relief organizations (field ambulances, hospitals, and other charitable work).

This mission appealed to him because it promised to coincide with a cause that was now close to his heart, the promotion of Anglo-American friendship. Ever since his lecture tour, and since meeting Florence Lamont, he had been dreaming of trying to cultivate transatlantic relations. In a small way he was already doing so by corresponding steadily with her, but he hoped to do very much more. To his brother Harry he wrote that he would like to work up 'a big scheme for bringing

England and the U.S. into closer touch and getting them to understand each other'. 'It is pretty hopeless trying to get a government of lawyers and civil servants to do things; they've no imagination and no feelings; it will have to be done by people like ourselves.'

Masefield was pleased to be in France again, and from his base in Paris, the Hôtel Meurice, he wrote to Constance that his one regret was that his French was so slow and bad: 'it is dreadful to have an accent as gross as a Boche's'. During his first week he made repeated visits to the American hospital at Neuilly, which he said had been made into 'a very beautiful thing', and as for the medical work there he was especially struck by the 'face making', 'really an adaptation of dentistry to surgery'. But even in his earliest letters from Paris there is a note of disappointment. 'I don't find the people very forthcoming,' he wrote after one of his days at Neuilly. 'They are all very busy, and they have with very few exceptions never heard of me, so this is uphill work.' It was also uphill work trying to arrange other visits. 'I do not find the Americans as helpful as I could wish. They seem not centrally organized, but working in independent, unrelated groups, and it is difficult to get into touch.'

One of the independent groups with which he did however get into touch at an early stage was the American Ambulance Field Service, and at their Passy headquarters he was heartened to find the atmosphere very 'jolly, bachelory, and free and easy'. Soon it was arranged that he should accompany one of their Sections (a fleet of twenty motor ambulances) to the Verdun area, where things were now quieting down, 'though by no means quiet'. For ten days he had what he called a wonderful time, 'living in motorcars, flying from post to post, often all day long', while from far away he could hear the big guns on both sides – they sounded like blasting in a quarry. He was often up all night as well, for the ambulance men did most of their work after dark, but this sort of life suited him. 'Being in the air night and day for a week has done me good,' he wrote at the end of it.

To Constance he described some of the horrors – the mutilated corpses, the dead horses, the rats. And as to Verdun itself, which he visited twice, he wrote that it was 'like a town sick

of the plague, or some city after the sack, or what Pompeii was'.
But the surrounding desolation was what shocked him most:

> The hills outside, a sort of ring of low downland . . . were once
> covered with trees, and green and pleasant. Now they are ploughed
> with shells, pockmarked with shells, lepered with shells, on a sort of
> livid and earthy scab of shell holes which looks like a disease. They
> look like sick hills, and all the blasted splintered rampikes of the
> trees stick up like bristles.

Back in Paris Masefield received, to his dismay, a long new
list of 'places run by Americans', including twenty-nine hospitals and sixty-eight 'other works': convalescent homes,
schools, refuges, canteens, etc. They were mostly in and near
Paris but some were as far off as Limoges and Aix-les-Bains, so
he had to make a number of long train journeys, some of which
proved to be in vain, as the list was out of date. In addition he
had to visit various French hospitals to see how the American
system for distributing supplies was working. Of these the
hospitals served by the Sisters of Mercy seemed to him by far
the best, and the Sisters themselves, with their courtesy and
gentle radiance, inspired in him a reverence akin to awe. They
were 'beautiful human souls', he told Constance, 'with that
best sort of politeness that comes with holiness.'

As his stay in France drew to a close, and Masefield thought
back over the American establishments he had seen, he concluded that the best work was being done in the hospitals
where new methods were being tried out. The 'face-making'
at Neuilly seemed miraculous, and there was also some notable
work in the treatment of surface burns, by means of a preparation called Ambrene which stopped pain at once and then
formed a new skin. But in his report he did not want to discuss
medical matters; he wanted to write about heroism. And as the
weeks had gone by he had been disturbed to find that there was
so little he could regard as heroic in America's overall contribution to Allied relief. By October, at the end of a month in
France, disillusion was turning to scorn (a scorn which he found
was shared by the Americans living in France, who 'had no
language fierce enough for their own country'). 'I am beginning
to open my eyes,' he wrote to Constance on 4 October. 'What a
row I shall have with Gilbert Parker!'

When I get back, I shall tell [him] . . . that the Americans have really done very little. A lot of generous young men have served in the Ambulance [Field Service], and the hospitals are very well done, and a lot of bold and brave young souls have come to serve in the French and English armies, but apart from that, at present my feeling is that the nation at large has done nothing.

The individuals (always rather numerous) who live in France, did their best, and started a lot of things, and ran them as best they could, and then had to stop them.

As in the case of *Gallipoli*, however, Masefield found a way of escape from failed hopes and harsh truths. There were in France a few American heroes to whom he could in all honesty give praise. In due course the fruits of his researches took shape as an article entitled 'The Harvest of the Night', which was published in the May 1917 issue of *Harper's Monthly Magazine*. It was a vivid and moving account of a night's work with a Field Service Section of the American Ambulance near Verdun, and it ended with a heartfelt tribute to the American drivers:

These drivers (there are now, and have been, some hundreds of them) are men of high education. They are the very pick and flower of American life. Two of them have died and many of them have been maimed for France, and all live a life of danger and risk death nightly. To this company of splendid and gentle and chivalrous Americans be all thanks and greetings from the friends and allies of sacred France.

3

Gallipoli had been published soon after Masefield came to France, and the enthusiasm it aroused in Britain had spread quickly across the Channel. As a result, while he was still in Paris he found himself a literary lion, invited to dine by ambassadors and 'spangled staff officers'. Some of this he found very tedious, and after a dinner at the American Embassy he told Constance that his buttons were probably the brightest things there. At certain other gatherings, however, some of his fellow guests were congenial and interesting, and he made special mention of a young diplomat, Eric Phipps from the

British Embassy in Madrid – 'an amusing, clever, well informed man'. His petite wife, too, was 'rather amusing', and Masefield noticed with approval the head-dress she was wearing, 'a sort of black hat' (it must have been very striking, for he seldom commented on women's clothes).

But by far the most important personage he met during the final stage of his stay in Paris was not merely a fellow guest at a party. On 9 October he was summoned to the presence of the mysterious Lord Esher, confidant of royalty and secret counsellor to prime ministers, who was then head of British Military Intelligence in France;[1] there he learnt that as a result of the success of *Gallipoli* a pressing invitation had come for him from the British Commander-in-Chief, Sir Douglas Haig. 'Lord Esher,' Masefield wrote to Constance,

who is a friend of Ian's and of Haig's and of most of the Staff . . . said that I am wanted on the Somme, to write the Chronicle of the big attack from the very beginning. If I will go there next week, and look round, I shall have every facility, shall be allowed to see everything, and shall then be able to decide about it. He said that he and Haig are very eager for me to do it, that if necessary an honorary Commission shall be given to me, that a car shall be at my disposal, and a guide and maps and everything else.

It was an opportunity, a challenge, that excited and attracted him, but Masefield hesitated. 'There is loneliness for you in it, my poor dearie,' he wrote. 'Think it over'. Poor Constance! But the letter she wrote back, and the reply she gave, are striking evidence of her wifely devotion and moral stature.

My darling darling old Jan,
    You must do this Somme business . . . The fine thing is for you to use your brain to win the war . . . Don't think *about* me, my dear, think of me, and let us love and help each other to be brave, and that's all the happiness we can have till Hell is over. Hell is hell to such a degree of fierceness that sometimes tears of agony seem to blind out everything. But I know you ought to do this. You'll have some weeks with me first, won't you? . . .

[1] At the time, the reason for his being in Paris was a well-guarded secret; even the British Ambassador is said to have asked several visitors from the Foreign Office, 'What is that fellow Esher doing here?'

I long for you as I have never longed before. Each absence is worse than the last. But of course my darling old Jan I'm awfully proud of you, and feel honoured by my husband's honour . . . Nothing else is worth talking of, I can think of nothing but you and this work.

Three days later the die had been cast. Masefield had again seen Lord Esher, and he was to start for the Somme, for a preliminary visit, almost at once.

On 17 October Masefield's ears were for the first time deafened by the Somme cannonade, and for the first time he set eyes on the battlefield. To Constance he wrote that he could not convey even a dim conception of it.

Imagine any thirteen miles by nine miles known to you . . . then imagine in all that expanse no single tree left intact, but either dismembered or cut off short, and burnt quite black . . . No single house is left . . . No man can tell where villages were. Then imagine that in all that expanse there is no patch of ground that has not got its shell hole. To say that the ground is 'ploughed up' with shells is to talk like a child. It is gouged and blasted and bedevilled with pox of war, and at every step you are on the wreck of war . . . with defilement and corpses and hands and feet and old burnt uniforms and tattered leather all flung about and dug in and dug out again, like nothing else on God's earth.

There was steady rain for sixteen hours on the first day of his visit; at the end of it he tried to describe the mud. But, he wrote, 'to call it mud would be misleading'.

It was not like any mud I've ever seen. It was a kind of stagnant river, too thick to flow, yet too wet to stand, and it had a kind of a glisten or shine on it like reddish cheese, but it was not solid at all and you left no tracks in it, they all closed over, and you went in over your boots at every step and sometimes up to your calves. Down below it there was a solid footing, and as you went slopping along the army went slopping along by your side, and splashed you from head to foot.

Yet looking back afterwards to those three days, the memory that stood out most in Masefield's mind was not the horror or the mud. On his second day, a beautifully fine, clear, cold day, he received an invitation, or rather a summons, to lunch with Sir Douglas Haig. He polished himself till he shone but unfortunately the car which was to take him to Haig's head-quarters got stuck in the mud, so he arrived forty minutes late and covered with filth. So he could be with Sir Douglas for only a few minutes, but what he saw made an indelible impression. The Commander-in-Chief, he told Constance, was 'a rather tall man, with grey hair, a moustache, and a delicate fine resolved face and a manner at once gentle and eager'. 'I don't know what it is in such men,' he went on, 'it is partly a very fine delicate gentleness and generosity, and then partly a pervading power and partly a height of resolve. He made me understand Sidney and Fairfax and Falkland and all those others, Moore and the rest . . . No enemy could stand against such a man. He took away my breath.' After this there was no doubt that the invitation to write 'a chronicle of the big attack' was a command to be obeyed with all devotion and to the uttermost.

4

'It is incredible that after producing such a masterpiece as *Gallipoli* his unique gifts should have been wasted.' So, after the war, wrote Neville Lytton[1] – artist, Francophile, aristocrat turned Bohemian – whose admiration for Masefield's narrative poems was such that he called him 'a second Homer'. In early 1917 Lytton was a major attached to the General Staff Head-quarters in France, with special responsibility for the French war correspondents, and when Masefield returned to the Somme at the end of February, a humble and somewhat bewildered honorary second lieutenant without pay, eager to make a start on the research for his new book, Lytton met him by chance and thenceforth helped and befriended him. But he was amazed when he heard that the book was to be confined to the Battle of the Somme, which was by now virtually over. If only, he felt, this great poet could have been attached to the armies that would soon be going into the heat of new battles, and given a free hand! Then perhaps there might be another long narrative poem of the calibre of *The Everlasting Mercy* or *Dauber*. In Lytton's view, a commissioned book on the Battle

---

[1] The Hon. Neville Lytton (1879–1951). He became 3rd Earl of Lytton in 1947.

of the Somme savoured of official history, and was doomed to failure.

Masefield himself, however, saw things in a different light. He regarded the assignment he had received from Esher and Haig as a supreme opportunity. He believed that the Somme battle was 'the biggest thing' that England had ever been engaged in, that it must be 'a possession of the English mind for ever' and that he himself was privileged to be its chronicler. As to his plans for work, he intended to become as familiar as possible with the topography of the battlefield – this was an essential beginning – and he also hoped to talk with men who had taken part in the fighting. Then when he returned to England he would combine all this with the factual material contained in the brigade and battalion diaries.

Soon after Lytton met Masefield he asked to have him attached to his mission. The request was granted, and Masefield found himself surrounded by French correspondents to whom at first he was a great puzzle. As Lytton later wrote,

They could not understand his shy, unassuming manners. '*Mais voyons, c'est une jeune fille*', they said, until gradually they found out that he knew considerably more about most things, including French literature, than themselves, and that his remarks, uttered with a voice no louder than that of a mouse in a cheese, were full of point and wit.

On one of Masefield's earliest expeditions to the battlefield he was accompanied by Lytton and a French correspondent. That evening, as usual, he related his impressions to Constance:

We set out . . . to go out beyond Beaumont Hamel, to see the ground of the battle of the Ancre . . . It is roll upon roll of rather gentle downland . . . but mile after mile of it, wherever you look, is blown into holes, mostly very big deep holes, half full of water, and running into each other, and without any grass, but all raw and filthy, and littered with bits of man and bits of weapons and old ragged sand-bags, helmets, skulls, barbed wire, boots with feet in them, bombs, shells . . . till it looked like an ash heap put as a dressing on a kind of putrid pox that was cankering the whole earth. You can perhaps imagine what walking on such mud means. There is no skin nor grass nor twig nor shrub nor building nor anything left alive upon it. It is bedevilled mud, with a few broken bricks where the village stood, and a swill of mud where the road was, and we wandered in that kind of land for hours and hours.

Masefield toiled on in France until mid-May, quartered sometimes at Albert and sometimes farther from the front at Amiens, which meant 'working the lorries'. Week after week, and usually alone, he walked at least twice over every part of the Somme battlefield where British troops had been engaged. To many parts, those which specially moved him (Delville Wood, High Wood, Pozières, Mouquet Farm, Thiepval, and the Hawthorn Ridge) he returned more times than he could remember. And in the meantime, he did not question the offhand treatment he got from the staff officers who were supposed to look after him, although the privileges enjoyed by some of the war artists did occasionally rile him. In writing to Constance he referred to Muirhead Bone as 'that d——d Scotch etcher' though for Orpen he had kinder words after he had been given a lift in the artist's 'noble rich car'. During this difficult time the friendship of the strong, flamboyant, sympathetic Neville Lytton meant a great deal to Masefield. He described him to Constance as 'a most winning attractive person' and added, 'It is wonderful to be in this accursed kind of life with one of one's own kind.'

Letter-writing was, as always, one of his chief consolations; he wrote not only to Constance and not always in terms of compassion. In a letter to Hugh Walpole, written at the time of the Allied offensive at Arras,[1] he expressed himself in the impersonal language of the military observer, which indicates that he was by now capable of a newly hardened attitude towards human suffering and the carnage of war – he could not have written thus from Arc-en-Barrois:

All the prisoners speak of the awful fire and how terrible a time it has been for them. It was a full week before they held up their heads after they were taken. I never saw men so broken . . .

We had rather a score a few days ago. We dropped a bomb on a main ammunition dump, and blew it up, with nearly 2,000 men and a whole village.

[1] Walpole was then in Petrograd, where he had been put in charge of an Anglo-Russian information bureau.

Nevertheless the poet was always there. A few days before Masefield returned to England (by which time the German withdrawal to the Hindenburg Line had been completed) he wrote at some length to Agnes Fry, one of Isabel's sisters with whom he shared an interest in botany and a love of flowers and wild life. When he first came out, he said, the battlefield had been 'one vast blasted moor of mud', but now that the enemy had moved back the field was deserted

and most of the shell holes have dried up, and the grass has come, and is even shyly creeping into the burnt and awful places, Thiepval and Beaumont Hamel, and the black stumps of trees put out each a leaf or two. I never saw so many dandelions; and there is a tall plant, like a cabbage run wild, with bright pale yellow flowers, the colour of a yellow poppy, it was too pretty to pick or I would have sent you some . . . In one old trench, near Pozières, I found the nest of a wild hen, with five eggs in it. There are larks and partridges everywhere, and I have even seen two hares.

Now that the mud was dry, he said, the place was no longer awful-looking. 'It has a kind of mystery and strangeness and suggestion about it.'

Here on this field there are perhaps seventeen or eighteen largish villages without inhabitants. Each village is utterly ruined and smashed and flung about and gouged into great holes, without any living soul within a mile of it, and when you go into these places and find yourself the only person there, in the midst of the desolation, with perhaps some tulips or currant bushes, green or in flower, in some ruined garden beside you, and some bent Christ in the church flung sideways by a shell, you get a feeling, not of horror, but almost of romance, as though any strange thing might happen or be discovered, and as though there were a kind of soul in it, trying to speak.

5

When Masefield went to France in 1917 he had with him a small leather-covered notebook, and in it, along with miscellaneous jottings, he wrote a number of poems. One of these is an intimate expression of his feelings about himself and his family; it has no title but he might well have called it 'Autobiography'.

At this time the tone of his letters home was usually detached, even optimistic, but in this notebook poem he set down the despair of his secret heart. To read it is like catching a glimpse of his 'private' face, the face which as he grew older always bore, when in repose, an expression of sadness and melancholy.

> I was a little child
> Laughing so merry
> At the blue wind flower
> And the black berry
> I was a little boy
> With a mind eager
> Going with a friend in joy
> At the goal's leaguer
> I was a lad with thoughts
> of hot devotion
> A ship bound for all parts
> On every ocean
> I was a man, with life
> With purpose gathered,
> With my found mate, my wife
> With children fathered
> I had no dream, but this
> To grow in power
> To see my children's bliss
> Push shoot and flower.
> Then this began, this crime
> This hell of evil
> This bloody smear on Time
> Done by a devil
> And all began again
> No more, oh never
> Love, beauty, power of brain,
> Peace like a river.
> But in the mind a hell
> Of terror, waiting
> For the blind thrusting shell
> To have his mating
> Now in the mud a rag
> A skull bone clinging.
> By the clear brook the flag
> is gold i' the springing
> In the green garden gay

My wee son's planting
the scarlet wind flowers sway
to the wind's flaunting
No joy to them, those three
In the spring's glory
There is no joy in the bee,
No lift in the story.

Masefield was devoted to both his children. His letters to
Constance always included endearments for both 'Jude' and
'Timcat' as well as for her, and he was continually sending them
picture postcards. Lewis, who was now nearly seven, a curly-
haired, round-faced, attractive little boy, had a little boy's
enthusiasm for the mechanical (the postcards from France were
often of aeroplanes and motorcars) though at this time his
chief interest was in quite another direction. To the puzzlement
of his parents the make-believe games that he played with his
family of toys, 'the bunnies', centred round liturgy and ritual,
for he insisted that he wanted to be a priest. Constance adored
her little son but this craze exasperated her, and she was less
patient than his father. 'Lew talks ceaselessly of you, rather to
my discredit', she wrote, '"Father is never cross with me, you
sometimes *are* a *little* cross, Mother".'[1]

Judith, by this time a thirteen-year-old schoolgirl, preferred
real rabbits to toys, and kept several as pets; animals were soon
to be one of her chief delights. In a snapshot of her clutching
to her bosom a rabbit called Tommy she looks really blissful,
although with her father away this was not an easy time for her
at home; she and her mother did not get on. Constance, although she tried to understand her daughter, often failed, and
she lamented that 'Jude' was 'a strange inward creature, hating
compulsion'. Masefield, in reply, insisted that it was no good
using anything with Jude but 'mild and loving joking'. 'You
can coax her into being a saint, but that is the only way.'

In Judith's life a difficult problem had arisen. Since the
school where she was a boarder, St. Felix's at Southwold, was

1 In one of Constance's letters to J.M. she mentioned that she could hear the *Te
Deum* being chanted, in another that Lewis and the bunnies had 'daily, even bi-
daily Communion', and in another that the bunnies were now taking it in turns to
preach, and that 'Furball' was a bishop. Finally she reported that Tim and the
Buns had all become R.Cs.

on the Suffolk coast, it was frequently exposed to Zeppelin raids. Both her parents worried very much about this though for a time they made light of the risk and let her stay on. 'Our Judith is at school on the east coast,' Constance had written to Edward Marsh in the autumn of 1916, 'and is getting quite inured to Zeppelin raids, and sleeping on cellar floors. Jan and I try to argue that two thirds of England is as dangerous.' 'No one can make a safe decision in war time,' was Masefield's own summing-up. 'Even Lollingdon is not safe.' In the spring of 1917, however, at the time when America came into the war, and when it seemed likely that the east coast would be shelled, they decided that although Judith herself was most unwilling to leave, she simply must be moved; they would send her for the summer term to the 'farm school' that Isabel had started near Aylesbury at Mayortorne Manor. Judith was much distressed, and in the Easter holidays she poured out her misery to her father. He replied with wonderful tenderness:

I am so very sad to hear of you being unhappy in your holidays. My dear, we do try to give you a happy time, and I want you not to go to St. Felix for a bit because I am afraid you may be shelled there, and though I know you are very brave and would not be frightened, still, you might be hurt.

I promise you, darling Jude, you shall go back just as soon as the danger is over, and until then try not to be unhappy at home. You see, this war makes us all unhappy and unable to be where we would like. I would like to be at home and Mother would like to be in London, and we would all like to be together in Ireland, but we can't have all these things because of the war. Cheer up, my sweet, the war may not last very much longer.

1917 was a time of uprootings for all the Masefield family. John and Constance had decided, before he left for France, that because of the Zeppelin raids they must try to let Well Walk, and that Lollingdon, too, must be abandoned, though for a different reason. Much as they loved their moated manor house, it was 'damp as a bog' especially now that the roof was leaking, and Lewis's health was suffering, while Constance found the isolation depressing. At the end of April she supervised a complicated move (which was delayed at the last minute because of unseasonable snowstorms) to a stolid red-brick house called Hill Crest, on Boars Hill outside Oxford, which she described variously as 'ugly' and 'a rather dear little villa'.[1] It was certainly a good deal smaller than Lollingdon, but a cottage went with it, and the situation was enchanting, for as its name indicated it was set at a vantage point on the wooded hill, with a superb view southward towards the Berkshire Downs, and also a view towards Oxford. 'The air is delightful,' she wrote, 'and though we haven't the dear walk up Lollingdon Hill we have very pure fresh air, and a jolly scent of gorse and bracken.'

Boars Hill was already well populated, though it was not yet the colony of celebrities that it became after the war. Gilbert Murray did not settle there until 1919; Lillah Mc-Carthy two years later. Sir Arthur Evans, it is true, had already taken root on 'the hill', and Robert Bridges had built a house there, but the neighbours who hastened to give Constance a welcome were all strangers. 'Many people have called today,' she wrote soon after their arrival. 'All Boars Hill I should say, offering to lend a hand to settle us in. I'm liking the hill. Lew looks better already . . . [and] the maids have nothing to complain about. The kitchen is quite good.' But a fortnight later she was having second thoughts. The people on the hill were a kind set, she said, but she had not found any great intelligence among them.

6

By June 1917 Masefield was back in England, 'sunburnt brown' and well, still in khaki, and keen to start as soon as possible on his history of the Somme battle. He was pleased with the new house but he did not pause to explore Oxford – 'all these things must wait for the peace'. Instead he plunged into a preface for his book, a study of the battlefield itself. Meanwhile in London he tried to arrange for access to the brigade and battalion diaries which he needed, but to his dismay and deep disappointment he was told that he could not be allowed to make use of them. In the complicated bureaucracy of Whitehall

---

[1] The house has now been renamed Masefield House.

Haig's sponsorship counted for nothing. Thus the original plan for the book had to be abandoned, and Masefield then decided to present his preface as a short book (128 pages) which he entitled *The Old Front Line*. He tried to justify its very limited theme by claiming that 'perhaps some who had lost friends in the battle might care to know something of the landscape in which the battle was fought', but gradually the truth came out. When *The Old Front Line* was published in December 1917 it was criticized for its brevity. 'I must apologize for the book's shortness,' Masefield wrote to one of his theatrical friends, Miss Horniman. 'It was simply the preface to my book on the Somme fighting, which has been laid aside . . . I hope to finish the book someday, and then it will not be such short measure.'

But this hope, too, was destined to remain unfulfilled. Later on, after the war was over, Masefield did bring out another book, *The Battle of the Somme*, which traced the course of the actual fighting. But it was even shorter than *The Old Front Line* (96 pages) and in a foreword he gave the sorry reasons for this. After being denied access to the official records, he had set himself to write as full an account as he could from what he himself had seen and heard. But before the book was anything more than a sketch he was 'turned to other work, of another kind, many miles from Europe and the war'. Nevertheless he consoled himself by dedicating this second book, as he had the first, to the man whose comradeship had transformed his time on the Somme battlefield, namely Neville Lytton.

The new work to which Masefield was summoned was a second American lecture tour. In the interests of British propaganda, at the beginning of 1918, he set off on a four-month tour (again organized by the J.B. Pond Lyceum Bureau) which was to take him to the West Coast and the South-West as well as to the East and the Middle West. The first part of his time in America was not a success; he felt that his 'set-piece' lectures were not being liked, and he was also uneasy about the commercial basis of the tour. Since Britain and America were now allies, he felt he ought to have been attached to some non-commercial organization which would have booked halls and given him publicity, but would then have allowed him to give his talks free of charge. He longed to speak at the camps where the multitudes of young Americans, the 'draftees' who would soon be fighting in Europe, were in military training. Much to his relief it did in fact prove possible to arrange a further programme on these lines.

In April he was in New York for his final engagements in Pond's programme, and after that quite a new kind of 'tour' began. From May until August, under the auspices of the Y.M.C.A., he dashed hither and thither to the Army camps of the West, South, and South-West, often speaking impromptu, with great success, to vast audiences of enlisted men in the open air. At Fort Monroe, where he spoke before five hundred negro soldiers, they afterwards showed their appreciation by singing and dancing for him.

Neville Lytton maintained that Masefield's 1918 American tour was a waste of his talent as a poet. But it was not a waste in other ways. One of its worthwhile results on a personal level was a breakthrough in his manner of public speaking. He now knew that he possessed the ability to move an audience by speaking directly to their hearts from his own. Another result was that it gave him chances to get to know the Lamonts better, and his affection and respect for both of them had deepened. Furthermore an important event, or rather two events, took place during the latter part of the tour: Masefield was given recognition by the American academic world. In June both Yale and Harvard conferred on him honorary Doctorates of Letters.

In England again by mid-August, he was attached to the Ministry of Information in London, which enabled him to continue 'talking to soldiers' – in other words to give talks and lectures to the American troops. It was, in a sense, a continuation of his American tour, for he was continually on the move from camp to camp. 'Jan had to be away lecturing', Constance wrote in her diary when she described the family's peace celebrations, which took place in the garden at Hill Crest a week after the Armistice.

We had our own bonfire. We burnt the former laurel hedge in the middle of the potato patch. It was splendid. We chose the night of the full moon, a gorgeous night and a gorgeous fire. Everyone loved its warmth and brilliance, but Judith had influenza in her and next day she sickened . . . The influenza was raging everywhere . . . The thought of all the illness and death struck a chill.

On Armistice Day Masefield had been in London, and he wrote to Constance that it was 'a joyous thing to see the Strand filled with yelling, cheering, flag-waving and singing soldiers, suddenly released from the bloody business'. 'Now', he reflected, 'we have peace, thank God, and may know no more war as long as we live.'

PART IV

In Fruition

Chapter Ten

BOARS HILL

I

Masefield was always a countryman at heart. Ever since boyhood he had been pining to strike root again in real country. But not until he was forty, when he was reunited with his family at Boars Hill in 1919, did he feel that he was settling down at last into the English countryside. It was not of course real country like Ledbury: Hill Crest was only four miles from Oxford and there were neighbouring houses close at hand. But the Masefields' woodland garden, to which they soon added a field, made their house seem 'quite remote and in nature', and their closeness to the heaths, woods, valleys, and downs of rural Berkshire[1] linked them with rural people, rural ways, rural pursuits. Masefield would have been delighted to hear a comment made by a young friend of Gilbert Murray's[2] who met him briefly when he was pottering in the Hill Crest garden; Masefield, he said, looked much more like a farmer than a poet.

The years that the family spent at Boars Hill were happy ones for them all. Masefield became a 'country gentleman' and an owner-driver of a motor car (a small – and temperamental – Overland called 'Black Nag'),[3] Constance was soon a keen gardener, Judith a fanatical horse-lover, and Lewis, during his school holidays,[4] an explorer by bicycle of 'wild Berkshire downland' and also a lover of birds. Yet although he enjoyed looking after the bees, the goats, the poultry, at one time a pig, and Judith's horse when she was away, Masefield was

---

[1] Boars Hill itself (since the revision of county boundaries) is now in Oxfordshire.

[2] Henry Smith, brother of Jean Smith (one of Gilbert Murray's secretaries).

[3] 'Black Nag' was often in trouble. J.M.'s pocket-diary for 1922 includes such entries as 'B.N. a devil', 'B.N. blows her fuse', 'Have B.N. greased. We jolt home in terror.'

[4] Lewis went to Durnford School in 1920, to Lynam's School (now the Dragon School) in Oxford in 1921, and to Rugby in 1924.

always primarily a writer, and during the 1920s – despite engagements and holidays that took him to Ireland, Scotland, the Midlands, the Isle of Wight, and as far afield as the Middle East and America – he spent most of his time in his attic study or 'out in his shack amidst the gorse'.[1] As a result, throughout the 1920s Masefield produced a steady flow of diverse writings that included plays, novels, essays, articles, lectures, speeches, and a story for children, *The Midnight Folk*, which was to become a classic. And besides all this he was – to his joy – writing poetry again.[2] The first blossoming of this new poetic impulse was a trio of long narrative poems, the first of which, in 1919, was *Reynard the Fox*. The zest and fresh vigour with which he wrote this tale of a great chase, seen through the eyes of the fleeing animal, were echoed in the jaunty rhymes that he jotted into his pocket-diary whenever he posted to his publishers the various parts of the manuscript. On 10 May he wrote triumphantly 'I post the second half of Fox' –

> Now blessings on the whole two parts
> May those who thwart it burst their hearts
> And may God make me a better poet
> And give me time and place to show it.

But why did Masefield chose to write with such enthusiasm about a fox-hunt, when his compassionate nature must surely have restrained him? He was not in the least a 'fox-hunting man'.[3] Yet in the old days at Ledbury, where the hunt had been an integral part of local life, he had often followed the hounds. Hunting was in his blood. 'The bright colour and swift excitement of the hunt', 'the thrill of the horn' and 'the cry of the hounds', awakened memories that were 'hidden in

---

1 This 'outdoor study' was burnt down on 2 May 1928 after sparks from a bonfire set alight an adjoining gorse bush, but the Masefields, with help from servants and neighbours, were able to remove all books and manuscripts before the fire took hold.

2 During the 1920s J.M.'s writings were extremely popular. His *Collected Poems* sold some 80,000 copies in the Heinemann 1923 edition, and his novels of adventure, *Sard Harker* (1924) and *Odtaa* (1926) almost as many. (The title *Odtaa* represents the phrase 'One damn thing after another'.)

3 Although it is understandable that an American visitor, Thomas C. Chubb, should have assumed that he was, from the clutter of riding boots and crops in the hall at Hill Crest. J.M. often wore riding boots, but most of the impedimenta in the hall were Judith's.

the marrow' (while he was writing *Reynard* he sought opportunities to recapture this fervour and went several times
by bicycle to Berkshire meets). But on a more rational level,
when questioned about his motives, he claimed that hunting
was the sport which brought all ranks of society together on
terms of equality and good fellowship. He confessed that he was
saddened by the sombre fact that this fellowship involved the
torment and possible death of an animal, and he wished that
this were not so, but huntsmen had told him that hounds would
not hunt unless they killed their fox fairly often. 'I am not and
never have been a fox-hunter,' he wrote to St. John Ervine,[1]
'but it is *the* passion of English country people, and into it they
put the beauty and the fervour which the English put into all
things when deeply roused.'

Masefield's next long poem, *Right Royal*, was a drama of
the steeplechase, in which he developed the idea of the subtle
relationship between horse and rider, and as in *Reynard the
Fox* he wrote not only of an animal under great stress, but of
the people who thronged to take part in the excitement, in this
case the vast, mixed racing crowd. 'I hope the poem will be
great like *Reynard*,' Constance wrote in her diary in March 1920.
'He has the gift of making the commonest human crowd seem
rather significant and tragic . . . He could never be vulgar even
if he tried, though he can write of people as vulgar as you like.'

After *Right Royal*, in *King Cole* (which has been called
a fairy-tale for grown-ups) Masefield dwelt once more, in poetic
narrative, upon 'the excitement and beauty of moving horses',
for the story centred round a travelling circus. But in this poem
an underlying spiritual theme was dominant. King Cole, a
legendary figure, was shown as 'a spiritual force wandering the
world helping those in need' because, so Masefield explained
in an introduction to the poem, he believed that 'the spirits of
good people live thus after their lives on earth'.

2

In the afternoons at Hill Crest, when visitors were received to
tea, Constance was firmly in charge, and although her husband

---

[1] Irish dramatist and novelist (1883–1971).

far preferred to remain in his shabbiest clothes, busying himself out of doors, or rigging model ships (his favourite indoor hobby), he had to tidy himself up for these occasions. Constance herself, now in her fifties, wore extraordinary shapeless garments and strange hats, which made her look quite uncouth. A candid description of Mr. and Mrs. Masefield at this period was later given by the distinguished Italian scholar Mario Praz, who visited Boars Hill in 1923. He had been eager to meet a poet whose work he much admired, and had evidently expected Masefield to be a gracious aesthete who would impart memorable wisdom to an attentive audience. Instead he found himself in the presence of

a rather wooden-looking little man, dressed a little like a porter on a Sunday, with short nut-brown trousers above his ankles and an impossible collar, who stuck his head forward like someone about to take a dive – and with a lock of hair falling down his forehead as if he had just come out of the water.

And then there was Mrs. Masefield, 'a woman with a little pancake on top of a bun of hair', who talked all the time and answered all the questions, while her husband nodded his head up and down 'in the manner of a papier mâché donkey, and said something or other, it is true, but that something might have been said by anybody'. A much more sympathetic impression of Masefield as he was in the 1920s has been given by a man who saw him more frequently than Praz, Professor Kenneth Muir, who was then an Oxford undergraduate:

There was often a sadness in his face, and in his voice, but this seemed to be due to his brooding on the human tragedy rather than on any personal disappointment . . . He had a genuine selflessness, an extraordinary modesty . . . Not everyone who met him admired him, but many loved him.

Although celebrities from abroad, like Praz and the American poet Vachel Lindsay,[1] and friends like Florence Lamont (who from 1919 came quite often to England) visited Hill Crest every now and then, most of the Masefields' social life was now

---

1 When Vachel Lindsay (1874–1931) visited Oxford in 1920 the Masefields gave an at-home for him.

local. There were people nearby such as Lillah McCarthy[1] and the Bridges'[2] whom they had known for years, and newly acquired friends included a family named Pearce (Mrs. 'Peggy' Pearce was a warmhearted and hospitable American) and most notably Gilbert Murray and his family. Yatscombe, the Murrays' house, which in the 1920s was the main centre of intellectual life on Boars Hill, was not far from Hill Crest, and Masefield and Murray had plenty of opportunities to get to know one another. Masefield had long admired and respected the older man, both for his popularization of Greek drama, and also for his leadership as a Liberal thinker. Although never personally involved in politics, Masefield reckoned himself a Liberal, and he regarded Murray as 'the very soul of cultivated Liberalism'.

The presence of congenial friends nearby was certainly a joy, but other acquaintances were less congenial, and Constance became very conscious of her responsibilities as a poet's wife in the matter of protecting her husband's privacy. Among some of the neighbours she acquired a reputation for aloofness, even for disagreeable severity, though she was not in fact averse to social intercourse, and was welcoming when visitors came to Hill Crest at the appointed times. The most popular of these times was Sunday afternoon, when undergraduates flocked out to Boars Hill on their bicycles. Both John and Constance liked befriending the young, and men who were then up at Oxford, and who later cherished memories of the Masefields' kindness, included Julian Huxley, Wilfrid Blunt, Eric Gillett, and Corliss Lamont.[3]

Oxford in the immediate post-war years was not at all its normal self, for many of the undergraduates were young men just back from the war, some of them, like Robert Graves, suffering from the effects of shell-shock. Graves, who came up

---

1 Lillah McCarthy (1875–1960) came to live on Boars Hill just after her second marriage in 1921 to Professor Frederick Keeble (he was knighted in 1922). Her divorce from Harley Granville-Barker in 1918 had much distressed the Masefields.

2 Constance was very fond of Robert Bridges' daughter Margaret. At Lollingdon she had written in her diary (18 January 1915), 'Margaret Bridges walked over from Yattendon. She is so straight and strong and clever. I like her more than any girl I know.'

3 The Lamonts' second son, Corliss, after graduating from Harvard, came to Oxford in 1924 to study at New College for a year.

in the autumn of 1919 to read English, lived for about a year and a half in the Masefields' cottage, along with his feminist young wife Nancy and their baby girl. Constance in her diary was scathing about Graves and described him as 'a tender-hearted, rather vain, very domestic creature. Sometimes . . . a little garrulous . . . He tells me more than he ought about his domestic life.' As for Nancy, she had 'not got enough adventure in her to be a poet's wife':

Nancy is a strange shy boyish girl, very clever with her fingers and quick in brain. Affectionate too, but spoilt in a sort of artistic way, ready to find fault with anyone else's work. I quite like her, but I wish she weren't so mulish. For some reason she insists on calling herself Miss Nancy Nicholson.

The young couple's unconventional ways roused a protest even from Masefield himself. After six months he wrote a note to Graves stipulating that he and his 'charming family' should not come to Hill Crest except between 4.15 p.m. and 5.15 p.m. on weekdays, or between 4.00 p.m. and 6.00 p.m. on Sundays, and the note ended with a further mild reproof: 'We attach an old fashioned importance to our visitors entering by the front door.' But whatever the embarrassments of Graves as a neighbour, Masefield thought very highly of him as a poet. 'I myself back Robert Graves as the most likely young man now in literature over here,' he wrote to Louise Townsend Nicholl:

He has mirth, and I don't believe that people grow very far without mirth . . . The other war men, so far, seem to me to be remarkable less in themselves than in the accident of their experience. The strange thing happened to them, and the thing gives them for the moment something of its intensity.

Graves was not the only young writer living on Boars Hill at this time; Constance's diary contains typically forthright remarks about several of them. Robert Nichols, she decided, was 'as mad as a hatter'. 'Some days he is pouring out sonnets to the memory of Aurelia – a very sordid amour apparently. Other days he is pregnant with a religious drama "the greatest religious drama ever written".' With Edward Liveing[1] she was more in sympathy; he had 'a jolly simple way with him . . .

1 J.M. had written an introduction for Liveing's book *Attack: An Infantry Subaltern's Impressions of July 1st 1916* (Heinemann, 1918).

He is much more of a person than either Graves or Nichols. He takes one as a person, the others take one as a listener.'

Such were some of the friends and acquaintances with whom the Masefields came into touch during their time at Boars Hill. It cannot be said that they in themselves formed a 'circle', for the orientation of almost all of them was towards Oxford. Yet at the same time Boars Hill was in an anomalous position *vis-à-vis* the University. Some of the residents, such as Gilbert Murray and Sir Frederick Keeble, were currently professors; and senior members of the University, not only undergraduates, often visited their friends on the hill. Masefield's Oxford friends included Sir Walter Raleigh and the Provost of Worcester College, Professor Charles Daniel, whom he regarded as 'the most perfect type of scholar'. Yet Boars Hill was never really part of intellectual Oxford; an unspoken barrier existed between the citadel of learning and the Berkshire highlands.

This situation suited Masefield very well. He would never have wanted to be drawn into the academic world, though he liked to resort to the Bodleian occasionally, and enjoyed walking through the 'collegy streets', where 'one is seldom out of the smell of venerable libraries, all old calf and thought'. Nor would the dons have wanted to adopt him as one of themselves; by their standards he was uneducated. Masefield was well aware that the Oxford scholars looked down on him, and with characteristic humility he accepted their attitude as very reasonable. Later, when he wrote affectionately of Oxford as 'a gray town for Learning excellent . . . A Sovran City of Civility', he admitted frankly that he himself did not really belong to her.

> A vagrant, I, not rightfully her own,
> Who draw from her not Learning, having none . . .

Nevertheless in 1922 Oxford University paid tribute to Masefield's achievements as a poet by making him an Honorary Doctor of Literature,[1] and at the Encaenia he was introduced as a neighbour in whom Oxford delighted, an inhabitant of 'that Helicon of Boars Hill, so hallowed by poetic associations'.

---

[1] Other honorary degrees received by J.M. during the 1920s were from Aberdeen University (1922), Glasgow University (1923), and Manchester University (1923).

He was also hailed as 'a realistic poet of nature, who shrank
from no theme in the interest of truth, and did not disdain the
use of unconventional methods of expression, but whose realism
was always guided by an artistic sense'. Masefield must surely
have been gratified by this recognition, but he could not take
academic Oxford as seriously as it took itself. After the Encaenia
he and the other Honorary Doctors were entertained at a lunch
which did not finish until mid-afternoon, and alongside this
date in Masefield's pocket-diary appears the following couplet:

> With squeaky wit the light improper verse
> Falls on the heavy lunch and makes it worse.

3

In the course of the 1920s Masefield's name came to be associated with Boars Hill chiefly because of his untiring efforts to
produce drama there, especially plays in verse; the speaking of
poetry 'with the living voice' was a cause that he had very
deeply at heart. And these amateur theatricals were an
intensely absorbing hobby not only for him, but for Constance
and also for Judith. Masefield himself was primarily the
producer, while Constance looked after the tickets and seating
arrangements, and Judith was wardrobe mistress and maker of
properties. She was also, now, a passionately enthusiastic
actress. In her late teens she had striking looks – flashing eyes
and dark swinging hair[1] – and encouraged and coached by a
keen semi-professional actress, Penelope Wheeler (a friend of
the Gilbert Murrays), she threw herself into her parts with
verve.

The idea of building up a company of amateurs to perform
worthwhile plays was nothing new for Masefield; it had first
kindled his imagination long ago when he saw *The New Inn* at
Chipping Campden, but what was new was his own involve-
ment. Another new factor was a serious motive which he shared
with Constance; just after the war they had both, like many
others, felt the urge to create a better England, and it seemed

---

1 L.A.G. Strong, in *Green Memory* (1961), p. 238, mentions admiring Judith's eyes
and hair when he met her at Garsington in the early 1920s. (Although the
Masefields were acquainted with Lady Ottoline Morrell, they were never in her
circle.)

to them that any effort 'designed to brighten and gladden the national leisure', on however modest a scale, was a step in this direction. The venture that the Masefields initiated certainly began on a modest scale. At the outset, in 1919, their productions did not take place at Boars Hill itself, for the village had no suitable hall. But in the neighbouring village of Wootton there was a recreation room with a small stage, and Masefield seized upon the chance to make use of it, in the hope of attracting not only the Boars Hill gentry but the Wootton villagers, who in the days before television (indeed before radio) were likely to welcome any local entertainment. Like Gilbert Murray and his followers, Masefield believed in the popularization of the best in drama: 'The simple souls everywhere will accept the great work ... Euripides and Shakespeare,' he wrote to Laurence Binyon, 'it is the half-baked who want the half-boiled!'

By the autumn of 1919 highbrow plays were being performed at Wootton, with various neighbours taking part. In December, after plays by Yeats and Anatole France had been staged, Masefield wrote to a friend, 'It was a successful evening and I think they liked it. Jude was very good as the Wife in Yeats's *Pot of Broth*.' During the next eighteen months half a dozen more plays were put on, including the *Hippolytus* of Euripides, and to Masefield's satisfaction the verse plays proved the most popular.

Then in 1922 a theatrical company called the Hill Players was formed.[1] The plan was to invite experienced amateur actors and actresses to take leading parts, and to recruit the rest of the players locally, many of them from amongst the villagers.[2] The Hill Players' first production, *King Lear*, on 6 April 1922, did not go according to plan. The Shakespearian actor who had promised to take the part of Lear cried off at the last minute, so poor Masefield, abandoning his usual job as

[1] Penelope Wheeler was President, and the Vice-Presidents were John Galsworthy, John Drinkwater, Lillah McCarthy and Thomas W. Lamont. J.M. was General Director, Constance Treasurer–Secretary, and Judith Properties Director.

[2] In the earliest days at Wootton, undergraduates had taken part in the Masefield productions, but by 1922 the University authorities had enforced a rule that they must not participate in theatricals outside the University. This meant that J.M. was hard put to it to find enough men.

prompter, played the part himself, book in hand and wearing a long red gown and a hook-on beard which came badly adrift. Yet this fiasco only spurred the company to bolder efforts, and they were soon tackling *Macbeth*. The Masefields' fearless enthusiasm was infectious and the players followed their lead.

But it was no easy matter to harmonize a team consisting of yokels speaking broad Berkshire and intellectuals with Oxford accents. 'There is a lot of class feeling,' Masefield wrote some-what naïvely to one of his actor friends in London, Leon Quartermaine: 'The poor are shy of the rich, and the rich shy of the poor. They don't seem eager to work together. It is shy-ness, not unkindness. One thing, however, they love the big and beautiful thing.' As to the village audience, one of the visiting amateur actors, Basil Maine, later asserted that its 'wayward verdicts' were 'a delight', but unfortunately such verdicts could only serve to expose an unbridgeable cultural gap. Before long Masefield's hopes for sharing the classics with the uneducated began to wither. Perhaps it was just as well that in 1924, thanks to the generosity of the Lamonts, a small theatre which became known as the 'Music Room' was built next door to Hill Crest,[1] and thus the need for the Wootton recreation room came to an end.[2]

For seven years after the opening of the Music Room (a beautiful little theatre with excellent acoustics and a stage on two levels) there was an almost continuous sequence of produc-tions, including *Hamlet*, Binyon's *Boadicea*, R.C. Trevelyan's *Meleager*, Yeats's *Deirdre*, and two pieces by Masefield himself, the verse play *Tristan and Isolt* and the prose play *The Trial of Jesus*. Masefield continued to concentrate on the producing, giving special attention to diction. 'His chief care was for the rhythm and music of words,' so Basil Maine remembered, 'and over a refractory player he would take great trouble, trusting that the fellow was not entirely tone-deaf . . . The play, he believed (and many of us with him) could be brought to pass not so much by scenic realism as by live speech.'

---

1 After the Masefields left Boars Hill the Music Room was converted into a house which is now known as Masefield Cottage.

2 Some of the early productions had been performed in other nearby villages, and in 1923 J.M.'s verse play *A King's Daughter* was presented by the Hill Players at the Oxford Playhouse.

4

Considering the vast amount of time and effort that Masefield devoted to his dramatic productions at Boars Hill, it seems amazing that he was able to launch and manage another project – this time in Oxford itself – which was equally or even more demanding. Between 1923 and 1929 he was the leading organizer of the annual verse-speaking contests known as the Oxford Recitations.

The purpose of these contests was to discover good speakers of verse and to encourage 'the beautiful speaking of poetry'. They represented a major step forward in a movement which had already been afoot for some years in Britain,[1] a movement aimed at rescuing poetry from the stranglehold of the elocutionist, who resorted to mannered gestures and mime instead of identifying with the poet. Since 1912 verse-reading competitions with poets as judges had been held, and it was at one of these, at Edinburgh in 1922, that Masefield – who had been invited to adjudicate – conceived the idea that he must stage similar contests. The melodious intonations of some of the Scottish competitors, especially those of a Glasgow girl, Jean Downs, made him hold his breath, with the thought 'Oh, if only Yeats could hear this.' 'I had heard no speech so beautiful,' he later wrote. 'I could not sleep for three nights.' Immediately on returning to Boars Hill he and Constance, with the encouragement of Gilbert Murray and other University friends, began to make plans for the Oxford Recitations.

It was not merely a question of this or that accent; Masefield did not trouble himself with the problems that were soon to torment the newly-formed B.B.C. His concern was with a deeper issue. He was becoming more and more obsessed with the belief that poetry, like poetic drama, should be communicated by the living voice and not by the printed page. The printing press was largely to blame, so he believed, for the estrangement between the poet and his audience. Poetry was one of the delights which should be conveyed directly from person to person, from heart to heart. The poet should not be 'a man apart, with long hair and a velvet jacket, endeavouring

1 Led by Elsie Fogerty, who since 1906 had been Principal of the Central School of Speech Training and Dramatic Art at the Albert Hall.

to be unlike his audience', but rather a man 'who shares with his fellows what his vision catches'. Enchantment was the main function of poetry, and this enchantment always had to come from the excitement of the poet. Equally if others were to interpret the poet's excitement, they must sink themselves in his message and not remain outside it.

With these inspiring convictions and aims before him Masefield threw himself into the back-breaking work involved in organizing the first of the Oxford Recitations, and it took place in the Examination Schools, under University auspices, on 24 and 25 July 1923. The entry was impressive, indeed overwhelming – more than five hundred competitors took part – and there was also a formidable array of judges and patrons.[1] But the preliminary rounds were a sorry revelation of the low standards that were generally accepted at the time: 'some ranted, some acted, some flung themselves prostrate or struck attitudes'. Nevertheless in the midst of the tumult and the drawling there was some exquisite speech, and at the finals – evening gatherings of the Oxford élite, resplendent in evening dress (Masefield himself appeared in a white dinner jacket) – the audience discovered that listening to poetry could be an intense pleasure.

Judging the contests, on the other hand, was often not so pleasurable. During the ensuing years Masefield was responsible for approaching likely judges, and those who agreed to come (including Walter de la Mare, Harold Monro, and H.W. Nevinson) undertook a task which often taxed their endurance. Bernard Shaw, when invited to adjudicate, declined, explaining that the competitive spirit was abhorrent to him. He did not object to contests such as the Recitations if someone else judged them, but he himself could never reduce any sort of artistic performance to examination marks. This same feeling eventually overcame Masefield himself. In 1928 he began to think that the character of the Recitations must be changed; they must be developed as festivals rather than contests. This

---

1 The adjudicators of the nine classes – for narrative poetry, reflective poetry, dramatic poetry, etc. – were Sir Herbert Warren (President of Magdalen), Gilbert Murray, George Gordon (then Professor of English), Laurence Binyon, and J.M.

would, however, entail a break with the University, which would be regrettable (so he wrote to Laurence Binyon) because 'association with the University stands for a very great deal with many of the competitors as well as with ourselves'. Yet he was convinced that a fresh start must be made; the meetings must be on a smaller scale, and they must be held in a place 'not tainted with mental strain and gloomy scholastic examinations'.

Thus the Oxford Recitations came to an end in 1929.[1] They had undoubtedly served a useful purpose in exposing and gradually eliminating the artificial methods of verse-speaking that had previously been taken for granted, but this raising of standards was not all: people had begun to learn how to listen, an appreciative audience had been made. The Oxford Recitations had proved that 'beautiful speech' was not only possible but popular.

5

The enthusiasm for drama that fired Masefield during the 1920s was not confined to his work as an amateur producer; he himself wrote quite a number of plays. One of them, *Melloney Holtspur*, which was produced in London in 1922, was a fantasy concerned with psychic influences, but all the others (except for one, *Tristan and Isolt*) were interpretations – or rather reinterpretations – of biblical subjects: *A King's Daughter* (the story of Jezebel), *The Trial of Jesus*, *Easter*, and *The Coming of*

[1] During the next three years J.M. followed up the Recitations by holding small verse-speaking festivals in the Music Room. Planned on entirely new lines, they were designed to bring poets and their interpreters into much closer partnership, since he and several others wrote work especially for performance by their favourite speakers. J.M.'s *Minnie Maylow's Story and other Tales and Scenes* (1931) is a collection of such poems and verse plays. In this book, after J.M.'s usual dedication 'To my Wife', there is a second dedication: 'I thank the beautiful speakers [15 names are then listed including Betty Bartholomew, Rose Bruford, Nevill Coghill, Judith Masefield, and Penelope Wheeler] who, in the speaking of these tales and scenes, have deeply delighted me.'

One of the verse-speaking festivals at the Music Room was in honour of W.B. Yeats: it took place on 5 November 1930, the thirtieth anniversary of J.M.'s first meeting with him. Yeats, by then living at Rapallo, was visiting England at the time, and he came to Boars Hill for the occasion.

Christ, which was performed in Canterbury Cathedral in 1928.[1] As in the case of *Good Friday* a decade earlier the question arises: why did Masefield turn for his themes to the Bible, and especially to the Gospels? And this leads inevitably to the further question of whether his religious plays represented an expression of Christian faith.

When *The Trial of Jesus* was first produced in London one of the critics spoke his mind (in the *Morning Post*) about the author's evident *lack* of faith. The play, he wrote,

has not the emotional acceptance of Oberammergau or of the old miracle-plays. One is never made to feel that Mr. Masefield is aflame with a sense of personal salvation . . . On the contrary, he seems to be always evading any definite confession . . . We finish on an interrogation mark . . . In short, beyond hinting a doubt, Mr. Masefield does not seem to have anything to tell the world about the divinity of Christ – a Passion play's necessary theme.

Nevertheless in the plays that Masefield wrote in the 1920s, as well as in some of his other writings and in certain remarks, there is evidence that when he was in his mid-forties, with youth behind him, he was in fact groping, probably often unconsciously, towards Christian belief. At the beginning of the 1920s he steeped himself in Dante: 'I read Dante's *Divine Comedy* again and again', he later wrote, 'till the lack of such liberty, such law, such beauty, in myself (as in the world) became unbearable. What could be done to remedy such a lack?' What dould be done? By temperament a mystic, with a mysticism constantly veering towards the psychic, he was at the same time too independent in his thought, too confident in the sufficiency of man's intellect, to accept the Christian absolutes with humble trust. Furthermore, although his philosophy of life was theistic, it was utterly eclectic.

And yet, when in 1924 he delivered an Oxford lecture on 'Shakespeare and Spiritual Life',[2] he seemed to be reaching,

1 On the initiative of Dr. G.K.A. Bell, then Dean of Canterbury, *The Coming of Christ* was performed in the cathedral on 28 and 29 May 1928; this was the first time that a play had been staged in an English cathedral since the Middle Ages. The music was by Gustav Holst, and the costumes and production by Charles Ricketts, producer of Shaw's *Saint Joan*. More than 6,000 people witnessed the performances.

2 The Romanes Lecture delivered on 4 June 1924.

time and again, towards Christian truths.[1] And in 1925 he made a remark to Corliss Lamont (who noted it down immediately afterwards) which revealed a nostalgia for what he called 'the old religion'. After reading aloud one of his earlier poems (the sonnet which speaks of 'the skeleton of a religion lost', and 'our soul's foundation stones')[2] he reflected that he himself had once had 'a deep religion', that he had then become agnostic, and that finally, looking back, he thought that perhaps he believed in the old religion after all.

[1] For example he voiced dissent from Shakespeare's expression 'Mercy itself'. He would not accept that mercy was a 'thing'. Instead, so he declared, he saw 'a great and lovely figure, beyond all sex, throned somewhere and crowned, to whom the sharp prayer might pierce'.

[2] Sonnet XLII in *Lollingdon Downs, and Other Poems, with Sonnets* (1917).

Chapter Eleven

POET LAUREATE

I

'I am not a ready writer and can write verse only rarely in moments of deep feeling. As this may perhaps be a disqualification I feel that it should be declared to you at once.' Thus Masefield, by now in his fifty-second year, wrote to Ramsay MacDonald on 30 April 1930, in reply to a letter from the Prime Minister offering to submit his name to King George V as a successor to the recently deceased Poet Laureate, Robert Bridges. Ramsay MacDonald, though at the time in the midst of overwhelming national problems, in particular soaring unemployment, replied at once with a personal letter of encouragement, telling Masefield that if the spirit moved him he could write 'odes and such things' on high occasions, but if it did not he could keep quiet. A week later the Lord Chamberlain's Office announced that the King had appointed Mr. John Masefield Poet Laureate in Ordinary to His Majesty.[1]

But how far were MacDonald's reassurances justified? Certainly the Laureate was no longer required, as in the distant past, to write two odes a year in praise of the Monarch, to be set to music by the Master of the King's Music and sung in the Royal Chapels. Although he was still a paid officer of the court, ranking between the Gentleman Usher of the Black Rod and the Marine Painter, since the time of Victoria he had supposedly been free to write or be silent according to his inspiration. Nevertheless an unwritten moral obligation remained, and the Laureate was undoubtedly expected to produce some appropriate verses whenever a notable occasion of royal rejoicing or mourning occurred, as well as at other moments of national emotion.

---

[1] J.M. was the sixteenth in the line of Royal Laureates (which included Southey, Wordsworth, and Tennyson) since Dryden had been appointed by Charles II in 1668.

After the death of Bridges there had naturally been much speculation about his successor. To some Kipling seemed the obvious choice, despite his great age. Yeats, Housman, de la Mare, Drinkwater, Binyon, and Newbolt also had their supporters. But the appointment of Masefield, who was still at the peak of his popularity on both sides of the Atlantic, and who was also reputed to be King George's favourite poet, was greeted as an inspired choice on the part of Ramsay Mac-Donald. It was good, too, that England's first Labour Prime Minister should have chosen a poet famed for his affinity with the common man, a poet who had never attended a university, who had toiled at menial jobs in his youth, who could 'touch to beauty the plain speech of everyday life', and who had furthermore pledged himself, at the very outset of his career as a writer (in his poem 'A Consecration') to devote himself to the cause of 'the man with too weighty a burden, too weary a load'.[1]

At the time of the appointment there were the usual protests that the Laureateship was obsolete, an archaism which ought to be abolished. But conservative opinion was well in the majority: the *New York Times*, teasing but serious, spoke out firmly in favour of retaining the post: 'The office itself has a beautiful absurdity . . . But it is the peculiar wisdom of the English to value the absurd whenever it is also harmless.' Yet such facetiousness ignored the fact that there is much more, or *can* be much more, to the Laureateship than the writing of eulogies and dirges. If the incumbent so wishes, if he has the initiative and the will, he can do much to promote the interests of his fellow poets and of English poetry. Besides this he provides a focal point; he symbolizes England's recognition of poetry and poets as worthy of honour, and this is realized, even though

---

[1] After J.M.'s appointment to the Laureateship this poem caused him a certain amount of embarrassment, for in it he had shown (as well as sympathy for the oppressed) antagonism towards those in high places, even towards royalty. He had declared that he was *not* going to write of

> The princes and prelates with periwigged charioteers
> Riding triumphantly laurelled to lap the fat of the years

nor of

> The be-medalled Commander, beloved of the throne,
> Riding cock-horse to parade when the bugles are blown.

very vaguely, by the general public. Vaguely indeed . . .
Masefield, as Laureate, once received a letter from a London
examiner in speech and drama, who told him that a candidate
in a convent school, who had recited a poem of his, when asked
who Masefield was replied 'the Pope Laureate'. Masefield
wrote back, 'I was delighted with your story, which I can,
luckily, just cap. In some little boys' school . . . in a general
knowledge paper, one little victim put me down as the Patron
Saint of England.'

2

On 10 May 1930 the press swooped down on Boars Hill, or
rather jolted up the potholed road from Oxford, and at Hill
Crest they encountered the new Poet Laureate who, so they
noted, had grey hair, red cheeks and an athletic figure, as well
as shyness, simplicity, and gentleness. For the photographers
Masefield posed by the sundial and then in the field. Constance
kept out of sight, nor was there any sign of Lewis (by this time a
Balliol undergraduate) but Judith, the pony, and the donkey
all came in for a share of the limelight. There was also of course
a bombardment of questions, both now and during the ensuing
weeks. Yes, the Laureate admitted, his appointment was
certainly the culminating point of his career; no, he had no
interest in his own poetry once it was written.

While I am writing my poems I rejoice in the task. It is the work
that is being done that appeals to me. But when it is finished I have
no further interest in it. I never read it again, and the correction of
proofs is a bore to me . . . I take no pride in my work in the sense
of keeping it in my mind and thinking about it. When it is done it
is done.

Had he any strong preferences about the subject of his writings?
No, though he did enjoy writing about the country. What was
his next book? He had just finished the story of a great sailing
ship, the *Wanderer*. 'Do you write out of doors?' he was asked.
'Always, whenever I can,' he replied, 'until the rain makes the
ink run, or the frost freezes it on my pen.' Yes, he had got a
typewriter, but he did not like using it. 'You know,' he mused,
'writing always seems such a clumsy way of getting thoughts

down; a pity we can't just rest our fingers on the table and allow the words to run out.'

Letters of congratulation were soon pouring in. A poet whose work Masefield had much admired in his youth, A.E. Housman, wrote from Cambridge,

My purpose in writing is not chiefly to congratulate you that the King has made the choice which I should have made myself, but rather to warn you, if you need the warning, that you will now become the target for a great deal of spite, and to exhort you not to worry about it.

He ended with a good-humoured dig at Masefield's Oxford connections: 'In sporting circles here they are asking the question: if Boars Hill get it three times, do they keep it?' From Rapallo Yeats wrote 'I think the government has done well and that you will touch hearts nobody else could have touched . . . Your work will now take its proper rank and those poems you read and sang to me in Woburn Buildings will be recognized for the classics that they are.' This letter must have moved Masefield, for although he was no longer closely in touch with Yeats he still revered him. To Jack Yeats he wrote: 'I feel that *he* ought to have had the laurels, and none would have rejoiced more than I had they been given to him.'

For Masefield's brothers and sisters, indeed for all his relatives, the Laureateship was naturally a cause of jubilation and pride, and his home town Ledbury basked in the glory of its illustrious son.[1] His home county, too, jumped briefly into the news when Masefield made his first public utterance as Laureate at Hereford. On 23 October 1930 he became a freeman of the City of Hereford, and his speech on that occasion is significant for what it shows of his frame of mind at the time. He evidently accepted, in all seriousness, that he must now speak out for England – not the commercialized England of John Bull, waving the Union Jack as a trademark, nor the false Utopian England that many identified with 'progress', but the Christian England whose patron was St. George, the England of King

---

[1] Liverpool, too, celebrated J.M.'s connection with the city (through his time as a *Conway* cadet).

Arthur and his knights, of Chaucer and Langland and Shakespeare, the England of the undivided faith, whose churches
had been living shrines.

In retrospect the speech may seem a wallow in nostalgia, but
at the time it made a stir in the national press for its heartfelt
message. Masefield spoke of his burning hope that in the future
there might be a revival of the life lived close to the soil. He also
spoke of the beauty of nature, and of what he called 'the real
world', the world which is not seen or heard or touched by the
senses. 'I am linked to this county by subtle ties, deeper than I
can explain,' he asserted. 'They are ties of beauty . . . Whenever I think of the bounty and beauty of God, I think of parts
of this county':

I know no land more full of bounty and beauty than this red land,
so good for corn and hops and roses. I am glad to have lived in a
country where nearly every one lived on and by the land, singing as
they carried the harvest home, and taking such pride in the horses,
and in the great cattle, and in the cider trees. It will be a happy day
for England when she realises that those things and the men who
care for them are the real wealth of a land: the beauty and the bounty
of earth being the shadow of Heaven.

Formerly, when men lived in the beauty and bounty of Earth,
the reality of Heaven was very near; every brook and grove and hill
was holy, and men out of their beauty and bounty built shrines so
lovely that the spirits which inhabit Heaven came down and dwelt
in them and were companions to men and women, and men
listened to divine speech. All up and down this county are those
lovely shrines.

He also spoke on a more personal note:

I passed my childhood looking out on these red ploughlands and
woodland and pasture and lovely brooks, knowing that Paradise
is just behind them. I have passed long years thinking on them,
hoping that by the miracle of poetry the thought of them would get
me into Paradise, so that I might tell people of Paradise, in the words
learned there, and that people would then know and be happy. I
haven't done that of course or begun to, but . . . I have tried.

The theme of the need for a return to simple country life
recurred often in Masefield's pronouncements at this time.

Sometimes it led him to indulge in naïve prophecies, as when he opened a new library at Ledbury. In the next generation, he said, when motor cars were no longer a novelty, men would return to those things which were an inspiration to their fathers. He had been less optimistic when interviewed for a *Daily Herald* series on the subject 'What are we here for?' 'The only hope for civilisation,' he concluded, 'is a return to simpler things. And what hope is there for that?'

3

Masefield was Poet Laureate for thirty-seven years, from 1930 until his death in 1967, a longer span than that of any of his predecessors except Tennyson. And throughout this time, during which three successive monarchs were on the throne (and Edward VIII came and went) he was exceedingly conscientious about producing verses to commemorate royal occasions. Punctually on the day, one of his 'dutiful little odes' appeared in a place of prominence in *The Times*, bidding its readers to remember 'our beloved monarch' or 'our gracious queen'.[1]

These so-called obligatory verses have often been damned as banal by Masefield's critics. Even one of his most faithful admirers, Professor Fraser Drew, has said that although they are often nobly conceived and gracefully executed, they generally bear, like most occasional verse, 'the unmistakable stamp of the duty done and the deadline met'. Professor Drew has also pointed out that very few of the poems Masefield wrote in exercise of his official position have been reprinted in subsequent volumes of his verse: 'It may be that he did not consider them worthy of inclusion among the poems that he wished preserved.'

Nevertheless from the biographical angle there is much to be learnt from the Laureate verse. Although sometimes trite it is never superficial, and it is evidently sincere. When George V died in 1936, for instance, Masefield wrote:

---

[1] J.M. did not take publication for granted. After his death *The Times* revealed that with each manuscript he sent a stamped addressed envelope so that it could be returned if not acceptable.

> This man was King in England's direst need;
> In the black battle years, after hope was gone,
> His courage was a flag men rallied on,
> His steadfast spirit showed him King indeed . . .
>
> No king of all our many has been proved
> By times so savage to the thrones of kings
> Or won more simple triumph over Fate:
> He was most royal among royal things.
> Most thoughtful for the meanest in his state,
> The best, the gentlest, and the most beloved.

And then a year later, for the coronation of George VI, he composed 'A Prayer for the King's Reign':

> O God, the Ruler over earth and sea,
> Grant us Thy guidance in the reign to be:
> Grant that Our King may make this ancient land
> A realm of brothers, working mind and hand
> To make the life of man a fairer thing:
> God, grant this living glory to the King . . .

But Masefield did not confine himself to royal occasions, and his output as Laureate was indeed remarkable. Needless to say there were times when he was pressed to compose verses to order, and in such circumstances he could hardly be expected to give of his best. Yet every now and then he was stirred to take up his pen by events of historical or topical importance and sometimes duty clearly coincided with pleasure, as when he wrote with boyish enthusiasm on the launching of the 'giant Cunarder', the 534, later known as the *Queen Mary*.

> I long to see you leaping to the urge
> Of the great engines, rolling as you go,
> Parting the seas in sunder in a surge
> Treading a trackway like a mile of snow,
> With all the wester streaming from your hull
> And all gear twanging shrilly as you race,
> And effortless above your stern a gull
> Leaning up on the blast and keeping pace.
>
> May shipwreck and collision, fog and fire
> Rock, shoal, and other evils of the sea
> Be kept from you and may the heart's desire
> Of those who speed your launching come to be.

Masefield's personal relations with the royal family were in the main extremely formal; usually he communicated with them indirectly through court officials. But sometimes he composed a short, deeply respectful letter to the monarch himself, ending 'Your Majesty's most obliged and devoted humble servant', and occasionally he met the King and his family face to face (as when he presented a model of H.M.S. *Conway* to George V – it was the work of the ship's carpenter assisted by the cadets). He evidently enjoyed these meetings, and perhaps something of the lovable graciousness of royalty imparted itself to him, for when he was an old man those who met him nearly always commented afterwards on his kindness and 'old world courtesy'. In one of his letters to Miss Flood, written during the 1930s, he mentioned a happy stay at Windsor Castle (probably shortly before the coronation of George VI). 'The main impression made upon me', he wrote, 'was of a quite extraordinary charm and kindness, which came down from above and permeated everywhere, so that like Gerard Hopkins "I remember a house where all were kind".' Windsor itself had also delighted him: 'I had not known that the Windsor Park was so beautiful; it is indeed a noble site.' And within the castle,

the pictures, which I had not seen, were of the greatest interest and beauty, most of them brought together by George the Fourth; a big room full of choice Van Dycks; a room full of Rubens, including a most lovely landscape; and some wonderful Louis Quinze and Seize furniture, bought from time to time by George the Fourth's chef, who was sent over to buy it when it was unfashionable in France.

One further memory of Windsor was a personal one: 'It was strange to sleep in a castle with a sentry on the gravel walk below, on guard all night long.'

4

During the 1930s Masefield was the recipient of many honours, the most distinguished of which was the Order of Merit awarded to him in George V's Jubilee Birthday Honours in 1935. Cambridge University gave him an honorary degree of Doctor of Letters in 1931 and he also received honorary degrees from the Universities of Liverpool and St. Andrews (1930) and the University of Wales (1932). In the United States, he was elected to membership of the American Academy of Arts and Letters in 1930. At the same time he showed himself willing to undertake a number of responsibilities in the cause of literature and of writers; in 1937 he became President of the Society of Authors, a position of dignity which had been held by Tennyson, Meredith, Hardy, and Barrie.

Soon after becoming Laureate Masefield was struck by the realization that no public encouragement, other than the Laureateship itself, was given to any British writer of verse. So he put forward the idea that a royal award should be made periodically for the best recent book of verse by a young British poet. As a result it was announced in November 1933 that Royal Medals for Poetry would be awarded each year for a first or second published volume of verse, or to a poet still under the age of thirty-five. Masefield, as Poet Laureate, was chairman of the Awards Committee, and throughout the remainder of his life he took an immense amount of trouble in seeking out possible recipients. Often he found the work discouraging. 'I have read through about seventy volumes this time,' he told Laurence Binyon in 1936, 'and at night I lie awake thinking of the obscure geniuses who will one day flame in the heaven, whose books were either not in the seventy, by some unhappy chance, or worse still, were in the seventy, and were damned by my blindness.'

Some of Masefield's letters in this connection throw interesting light upon his opinions of the younger poets. To Laurence Whistler, who at twenty-three was the first recipient of the Gold Medal in 1935 (for his second book of verse, *Four Walls*) he wrote that he was 'enchanted by the grace and newness' of his work and by its 'astonishing dewy beauty'. As for Auden, he told one of the members of the Awards Committee, Professor I.A.Richards,[1] that he considered him to be 'a man of genius . . . a dynamic person', and he wrote to Laurence Binyon that he thought highly of Christopher Hassall: 'When he does get out of his overcoats and swaddling bands he gets into a state

---

[1] The other members of the original Awards Committee were Gilbert Murray, Walter de la Mare, and Laurence Binyon.

of illumination.' On Andrew Young he wrote, 'His verse is very true and right, but it is poetry *aux petits pois*', and he had considerable reservations about Dylan Thomas. In 1937, when *The Dog Beneath the Skin* was being considered for an award, Masefield wrote to Binyon,

There are three or four poems in the book which are very fine. The rest is the result of one of two things, wilfulness or impotence. Up to a point, I enjoy working on a difficult poem, but beyond that point I feel that the poet has not done his part of the task. I shall watch Mr. Thomas with great care, but I could not vote for the present volume.

Masefield had always been spontaneously willing to help other poets, and not only the poets but the amateurs, the mere beginners, even the children who sometimes sent him their little rhymes. One might have expected, however, that after his appointment to the Laureateship he would have had to withdraw somewhat from the would-be poets, since the Laureate is a defenceless target for the missives of earnest beginners (Tennyson in his day complained that 'two hundred million poets of Great Britain' deluged him daily with poems). Yet Masefield, although he sometimes groaned about the stacks of letters, still sought out ways of encouraging the inexperienced, and of bringing new talent to light. As basic principles, he liked to repeat the three 'guides to literature' which had often helped him in his own youth, 'Bold Design, Constant Practice, and Frequent Mistakes'. He also recommended, again and again, the pruning of adjectives. But even his direct criticisms were always made with a charming diffidence. 'You must not mind my giving advice often given to me by my elders long since,' he wrote to one lady who sought his counsel:

They used to say to me 'You say this in fifty words. When you say it in ten, it will be a poem'. Or 'Leave out all the adjectives and adverbs for a year, and then note how much more vivid the work has become', etc. etc. I never believed them of course, but 'Now I'm two and twenty: And O 'tis true, 'tis true'. Please you must forgive my passing on these comments and suggestions. Writing is so much a matter of using few words. Read your poems aloud to people. You will not hold them with adjectives.

All the best of good wishes to you; and remember how the little boys infuriated Elisha. 'He said, if you call me names, I'll call a bear and he'll eat you; and they did and he did and it did'. You see. No adjective, but a real effect.

Chapter Twelve

AUTUMNAL

I

While Masefield the Poet Laureate played his part as a public figure with dedication and dignity, his home life was undergoing major changes. In 1932 Constance, who was by now in her late sixties, became gravely ill. She had been suffering increasingly from deafness and mental lapses, and it proved that she had developed a brain tumour. An operation was performed successfully in London, but she might well have died; afterwards she wrote that she had 'paused on the line between life and death'.

This sudden rupture of life at Hill Crest showed Masefield how completely he depended on his wife. There was no question of continuing the Music Room productions without her active help. It would probably be best to move away from Boars Hill; in any case he had been feeling that he himself had had enough of amateur theatricals, and besides, disturbing changes were taking place in the vicinity.[1] Not only were new houses going up but an aerodrome was being constructed.

In April 1933 the Masefields left Hill Crest (though the house was not disposed of till some years later). Accompanied by their domestic staff – Tom Heavens the gardener-handyman and his wife Alma, and Julia Smith the housemaid, who acted as personal maid to Constance in her convalescence – they moved to a Cotswold manor house belonging to Earl Bathurst, Pinbury Park, which Masefield had been able to take at a nominal rent. The beautiful old house, set in the solitude of an upland valley – long ago it had been a nunnery – with its smooth lawns, herbaceous borders, and yew hedges, was

---

[1] As early as 1929 J.M. had written to Laurence Binyon 'It is no longer pleasant country here, but thrusting suburb. After another four or five years, if we live so long, we shall probably go.'

obviously a place where Constance could recuperate in peace, and where Masefield himself might well find inspiration.

We can picture life at Pinbury in the years just before the Second World War from the memories and letters of friends and relatives. Games were always being played: croquet and bowls were Masefield's outdoor favourites, while various parlour games, as well as chess, draughts, and backgammon, were *de rigueur* indoors. If children were about, Masefield shared in their fun; his niece Prudence,[1] one of his brother Harry's daughters, who came to Pinbury as a little girl, tells of wonderful games of 'rescue hide and seek' in which Uncle John took part. When Masefield was enjoying himself 'his impish smile lit up his face and his blue eyes shone': this is how Professor Nevill Coghill likes to remember him in the Pinbury days. He says, however, that Masefield's more usual expression was a lugubrious one: 'he normally had a very sad look'. Coghill was then a young don at Oxford, and he often came over to Pinbury in connection with a venture that he helped to launch in the late 1930s, an annual festival of the arts known as the Oxford Diversions.[2] Another friend who enjoyed coming to Pinbury was Laurence Whistler, and he remembers especially Masefield's courtesy and kindness: 'If a young man interrupted him he would pause, to listen to the younger man.' To his own family, too, Masefield was super-polite: Nevill Coghill recalls that he always passed the butter to Mrs. Masefield before anyone else had the chance to.

Constance, on the other hand, after her operation, and as she reached her seventies, seemed to visitors more than ever forbidding. She still wore extraordinary clothes – 'gorgeous rags', they have been called – and she spoke in a slurred, rasping voice, with her eyes half closed. A Gloucestershire friend, Diana Awdry, one of the few people in the neighbourhood with whom Masefield found an affinity, has summed up Mrs. Masefield as 'remote'.[3] The acuteness of Constance's mind, which had

1 Now Mrs. John Barker.

2 J.M. encouraged and supported this venture, but it had a short life due to the onset of war.

3 Diana Awdry, later Mrs. Bernard Oldridge, had met J.M. in the 1920s when she was an undergraduate at Oxford. During the mid-1930s, beginning in 1933, the two were constantly in touch in connection with a scheme for helping young

formerly given her the mastery of any conversation, was now something of an embarrassment, and her remarks could be disconcerting. She would turn suddenly to one of the guests and fire off some startling question, apropos of nothing, such as 'I do think beauty is the most important thing in life, don't you?' And since her deafness was now getting worse, the poor guest had to shout a reply.

And what of Judith and Lewis? Judith was now in her early thirties and Lewis in his mid-twenties, and they still spent a good deal of time at home, a fact which led Constance to assume, with a pang of disappointment, that they had decided to remain single. From Pinbury she wrote to a friend who was making ready for a family wedding: 'My two haven't married as you know . . . I think that the present day aversion to doing the obvious thing is a little unnatural, and I like a good old-fashioned wedding.'[1] Judith, in fact, pined for a full-time stage career but her health prevented this – she was afflicted by chronic asthma. She was able to take part occasionally in theatrical projects in Oxford, but at Pinbury she was often ill.

Lewis, since he came down from Balliol, had been living in London where he had devoted friends; several of his contemporaries have testified to his charm (as well as to his enigmatic character), though he had a very 'direct' way of speaking, and like his mother he could be formidable and forbidding, especially when references were made to his father's celebrity. For a time he worked in a publisher's office; he then wrote a novel, *Cross Double Cross* (1936), meantime relying mainly on his mother's generosity for financial support. He liked to be 'independent', and when he came home, although he was affectionate enough to his mother, he seldom concerned himself with the family's guests. Smoking incessantly, he spent his time reading or amusing himself with the cats (he was very fond of animals) or else playing the piano, sometimes classical music

unemployed vagrants. Under the auspices of the Anglican Franciscans, Dick Whittington's family home at Pauntley in Gloucestershire was taken over and organized as a place of rehabilitation. J.M. worked hard to raise funds for this cause by giving poetry readings throughout Gloucestershire.

1 This last remark shows how entirely Constance's views on church weddings had changed since her own youth (see p. 83 above).

and sometimes jazz – as a pianist he was almost up to professional standards. His father loved him dearly, though not so demonstratively as his mother. 'My son comes home for weekends,' Masefield wrote to Janet Ashbee from Pinbury in 1938. 'He lives in London and is writing another novel.' He then added proudly 'He is very musical, plays well, and is something of a musical scholar; he is a thoughtful young man, who will make his mark.'

2

The winters at Pinbury were bleak; the ancient house was chill and damp from autumn onwards and the great log fires were hopelessly inadequate as a means of heating. When frosts were sharp the pipes froze and when heavy snow came the house was isolated. 'Deep deep the drift / What tons to shift' Masefield jotted in his pocket-diary on one specially bitter day. The severity of the Pinbury winters was doubtless the main reason why he travelled a good deal during the 1930s, and the longer journeys that he made with Constance, to America in 1933 (this trip included a month in Arizona), to Australia in 1934,[1] and to the West Indies and California in 1935, were obviously planned with sunshine in view. Masefield also made quite a number of other trips abroad during the 1930s, for speaking engagements. Before the move to Pinbury, in 1931, he had been to Greece and Turkey, giving a lecture on English Poetry at Athens University and speaking at Robert College in Constantinople. Later, in 1936, he made a brief visit to America to deliver a commemorative ode at Harvard's tercentenary celebrations, and no sooner was he back than he went off on a lecture tour of Finland, Norway, and Sweden.

Early in 1938 he and Constance went abroad for an unusual holiday. Accompanied by Judith, and for part of the time by Lewis, they spent three weeks at Monte Carlo. This may seem out of character, but there was a compelling reason for the visit. When in London during the past few years Masefield had become passionately addicted to ballet, especially to Colonel de Basil's Ballet Russe de Monte Carlo; indeed he

---

[1] J.M. attended the Victoria Centenary Celebrations.

later wrote that, at this time, ballet was his 'deepest joy'. He had become friendly with Nadine Nicolaeva-Legat, directress of the Legat School of Russian Ballet, and through her, as well as through David and Tamara Talbot Rice, he was able to meet some of the great dancers. 'He loved the company of theatre and ballet people,' Judith later wrote. 'They kindled something in him, and when he was with them he was at his best.' But to Masefield, in the 1930s, the ballerinas and the *premiers danseurs* were not only stage stars whom it was exciting to meet; they were divinities at whose shrines he loved to worship. And the verses he wrote for *Tribute to Ballet* (1938), a collection of poems and pictures in which he collaborated with the young Norfolk artist Edward Seago,[1] testify to the ardour of his balletomania, as do several earlier poems.

> The gnome from moonland plays the Chopin air,
> The ballerina glides out of the wings,
> Like all the Aprils of forgotten Springs.
> Smiling she comes, all smile,
> All grace; forget the cruel world awhile;
> Forget vexation now and sorrow due.
> A blue cap sits coquettish in her hair.
>
> She is all youth, all beauty, all delight,
> All that a boyhood loves and manhood needs.
> What if an Empire perishes, who heeds?
> Smiling she comes, her smile
> Is all that may inspire, or beguile.
> All that our haggard folly thinks untrue.
> Upon the trouble of the moonlit strain
> She moves like living mercy bringing light.
>
> Soon, when the gnomish fingers cease to stray,
> She will be gone, still smiling, to the wings,
> To live among our unforgotten things,
> Centaur and unicorn,
> The queens in Avalon and Roland's horn,
> The mystery, the magic and the dew
> Of a tomorrow and a yesterday.

[1] J.M. and Seago had already collaborated in another illustrated book, *The Country Scene* (1937).

Yet in spite of such sophisticated interludes Masefield's heart was always in the country, and one manifestation of this was his increasing love, as he grew older, for all kinds of birds, as well as for other wild creatures. In 1933, at a nature reserve in Staffordshire, he made an impassioned speech on the subject of wildlife preservation,[1] and in his novel *The Square Peg* (1937) the plot centres round the hero's battle to establish a bird sanctuary. But he also had a special affection for the natural enemies of birds; cats were for him, as for Lewis, cherished friends and members of the family. His tender understanding of feline ways is well shown in a letter he wrote to Lewis to tell him that a beloved cat called Twid had just died. On the previous Sunday, he told him, Twid had been at his usual best, eating and drinking normally, living his day's routine, but by Wednesday he was very frail.

He drank some milk and licked at a sardine, and moved to a sheltered nest in the shrubbery, a favourite summer den of his, and passed the day there. In the evening when it was cooler . . . I stayed some time with him, keeping off the flies . . . I went out to him every half hour or so, with milk and so forth. He suffered no pain at all, of that I am certain, but I knew that he was dying . . . At half past ten, I left him there at the brink of death; but I stroked him very gently and had from him something like the ghost of a purr. Very soon after this he turned a little . . . and died very quietly from old age lying on his right side, as I have so often seen him asleep in the sun . . . I put him in a box with flowers, grass, and lavender and buried him in his summer haunt.

In the light of this letter it is not surprising that according to Judith her father was stirred to a fury of anger by an incident which occurred towards the end of his time at Pinbury; a hound belonging to the local hunt attacked and wounded one of his cats. Ever since he came to the Cotswolds – in spite of his treasured memories of the Ledbury hunt – he had felt ill at ease with the hunting set; he had much more in common with the labourers who worked on their land. Now uneasiness turned to hatred. The local gentry, on their side, may initially have

---

[1] This speech was made on 21 October 1933 at the Hawksmoor Nature Reserve and Bird Sanctuary near Cheadle. The reserve had been presented to the National Trust by its founder, J.R.B. Masefield, a cousin of J.M.'s and a well-known Staffordshire naturalist.

been flattered to feel that the Poet Laureate, the famed author of *Reynard the Fox*, with his links with royalty, had chosen to live among them, but relations had begun to sour when, after two years, he published a novel, *Eggs and Baker*, which included a cruel portrait of a heartless landowner. And then, after the cat episode, when *The Square Peg* portrayed the men of the hunting set as stupid bigots and the women as hard-eyed viragoes, it was obviously going to be impossible for the Masefields to stay on in Gloucestershire. By the end of 1938 they had found an alternative home, once more near Oxford, and in the spring of 1939 the family departed from Pinbury, on the pretext that in case of war they dare not risk being cut off by snow. But some say that they were asked to leave.

3

Ever since the Lollingdon days Masefield had loved the upper valley of the Thames, and it must have seemed almost like coming home when after leaving Pinbury he and the family moved into a house called Burcote Brook in the village of Clifton Hampden near Dorchester (about eight miles south of Oxford and four from Abingdon). He was obviously in happy good humour when, in anticipation of the move, he wrote to H.W. Nevinson: 'We are soon to be on the banks of the Thames. We look out on the river and on Wittenham Clumps, and the new Suffragan Bishop of Dorchester will be within a mile to snatch us from the gulfs of Erastianism, Aryanism, and Socinianism, ever lying in wait to devour.'

Burcote Brook, or 'Burcote' as it was usually called,[1] the house which was to be Masefield's home for nearly thirty years – in fact for the rest of his life – was Edwardian in style, and somewhat resembled Hill Crest, although statelier and more rambling, with a wing that contained a billiards room and a garage.[2] French windows opened on to lawns running down to the river, and the grounds (or rather the estate, for

---

[1] Although close to the village of Burcot, the name of the house was always spelt with a final 'e'.

[2] A short time after J.M.'s death Burcote Brook was burnt to the ground. Since 1970 a home for the disabled, the Masefield Leonard Cheshire Home, has been built on the site.

more than fifteen acres went with the house) included a good deal of tangled woodland. To Masefield's joy there were tall trees with a rookery, willows by the boathouse where king-fishers flashed, and thickets where nightingales nested.

Very soon after the move John and Constance found them-selves alone at Burcote, for shortly after the outbreak of war Judith took up war work in Oxford, and Lewis, as a conscien-tious objector, enlisted in the R.A.M.C. and was sent to the Middle East. So the two settled down to a quiet wartime routine. Once again, as at Lollingdon, they were proud of growing their own vegetables, and as before they kept hens and ducks. Masefield was by now sixty, and at Burcote the pattern of his days was a regular one. By nature an early riser, he worked at his best in the mornings, and it was then that he usually resorted to the outdoor study that he established for himself among the trees. He seems to have been quite undeterred by the cold and damp. When a friend sent him 'a most beautiful warm and friendly rug', he told her that it would be worn as a kilt when he sat in his 'shivering cold shed'.

During the war years, in his woodland hideout, Masefield wrote a great variety of verse and prose. Through his friendship with the Talbot Rices he had acquired a lively interest in Byzantium, and he expressed this in two historical novels, *Basilissa: A Tale of the Empress Theodora*, and *Conquer*, a story of the Nika Rebellion. Three of his other wartime books resulted from a new yearning to dwell upon his own childhood and youth. *In the Mill* was an account of his time in the Yonkers carpet factory, and of his discovery that poetry was 'the law of his being', *New Chum* described his first term on the *Conway*, and *Wonderings* was a long meditation in verse based upon his memories of his life between the ages of one and six.

Two more books which he wrote at this time were directly connected with the war. In the first, *The Nine Days Wonder*, which has sometimes been compared to *Gallipoli*, he told in prose the story of the Dunkirk evacuation.[1] In the second, *A Generation Risen*, he paid tribute in a series of short poems to

1 *The Nine Days Wonder* was the latter part of a book describing the Anglo-French advance in Belgium and the retreat to Dunkirk which J.M. wrote in 1940. For security reasons the complete book was not published at the time, but in 1973 it was published in full as *The Twenty-Five Days*.

some of the young people who had 'come forward to save the nation in her danger'.[1] These verses showed a striking ability on Masefield's part to enter into the hearts and minds of the young who were enmeshed in mechanized warfare; in each he showed youth and courage under the threat of sudden death. One of the army poems is entitled 'Tanks in the Snow':

> Like obscene scaly saurs out of the mud,
> The fossil saurs, from fossil mud, they crawl,
> They gnash the scintilled snow to spirted scud
> They wallow roaring, stinking as they sprawl.
> Out of the sliteye in the carapace
> A gunsnout perks beneath a hidden face.
>
> Within that knobby iron hot with gas
> Men sick with stench observe and shoot and drive,
> They cheer their reptile as a thing alive
> And visit Death as though he were a lass.

In the context of Masefield's own life, *A Generation Risen* has a unique poignancy. It was published in December 1942, only a few months after Lewis, the adored 'Lew', had been killed by artillery fire in the African desert. Two tributes to Lewis, one by his mother, the other by his father, reflect something of the grief his parents suffered. Constance, in her anguish, was almost defiant when she wrote to thank friends for their sympathy; she would not accept what she felt were misrepresentations of Lewis's character. 'Many people are so kind, but they say the wrong thing,' she declared to William Rothenstein.

Our Lew seems at our elbow indignantly denying so much as false sentiment. He had a very healthy critical outlook on much of English thought, and he would have spurned words such as 'supreme sacrifice'. He was glad to fight Hitler I feel sure, but was very glad that fighting, for him, meant caring for life.

We had the very highest opinion of his mind and art (music) and he was a wonderful companion. One never seemed to think of him as immature.

Five years later Masefield wrote of his son in a different vein, with quiet dignity and restraint, in an introduction to Lewis's

---

[1] Like *The Country Scene* and *Tribute to Ballet* this book combined verses by J.M. with illustrations by Edward Seago.

hitherto unpublished second novel *All Passion Left Behind*. As he followed Lewis through childhood, boyhood, and manhood, he described with much tenderness his son's likes, dislikes, abilities, skills, hobbies, and ways of thought; he also conjectured what he might have grown into, had he lived.

He was one of great ideals, and lofty ambitions . . . He was not a reformer nor a man with a doctrine. He was wise; and would have done his best work in the manner of the Chinese sage, by the giving of good counsel, by the saying of something which would have brought good action, by making a right way apparent.

Only in the final summing up, where nothing but superlatives would do, is there a glimpse of the ageing father's unbearable heartbreak: 'He was the most delightful, the wisest, and the best man whom I have known well.'

4

No account of the latter part of Masefield's life would be complete without mention of his letter-writing. As he grew older it was a real blessing to him that he was thus able to maintain – at long range – a number of friendships which stimulated and cheered him. His faithfulness as a writer of letters was exemplified by his correspondence with Florence Lamont, which continued, in all, over a period of thirty-six years. From the time of their first meeting in 1916 until her death in 1952, he poured out his thoughts and ideas to her, and his letters finally totalled over two thousand. But this correspondence was unique, for it reflected not only personal affection and many shared interests but the intimate and enduring bonds between the families of two friends of the same generation.

The many other friendships-by-letter which delighted Masefield in his old age were not written against a background of long-standing family links. They were all of them with women much younger than himself who were his devoted admirers, and they were, in a sense, love-letters, or to coin a more accurate term 'affection-letters', for there was nothing clandestine about these friendships. When one or other of the ladies in question came to visit him, as they occasionally did, Constance welcomed them kindly.

His letters to these ladies, penned in his fine and regular hand, and often carefully sealed, were always phrased with courteous respect. When he greeted them on their birthdays, which he did without fail, the graciousness of his good wishes was mixed with tenderness; when he enquired after a sick parent, or offered condolence on a bereavement, his sympathy was from the heart. It is very clear that these relationships brought him profound consolation. 'Your letters show me how very precious your friendship is,' he wrote to Lucie Nicoll, the beautiful widow of a Hampshire farmer, after lamenting that so much of 'the old happy social intercourse and the meeting of friend with friend' had vanished away. To Joyce King, an earnest, artistic lady who edited the *Malvern Gazette*, he wrote, 'Many, many thanks for all the friendship your heart gives me,' and to Suzanne Fay, when she became engaged, he wrote begging that their exchange of letters should not be interrupted: 'When one comes to be ninety-three next birthday (one really forgets the exact figure but it is about that) a young friend seems like a bright morning or a rising star, or the Hope of the World.'

Each of Masefield's correspondents was leading an active and interesting life, into which he entered with enthusiasm and gentle paternal concern. This was especially so in the case of Rose Bruford, whom he had first met long ago at the Oxford Recitations, when she was a shy young drama student. His correspondence with her had begun in 1923, and it continued for forty-four years – until his death. During this time Miss Bruford, a brilliant speaker of verse, became Masefield's favourite protégée: in 1932 he wrote to her 'You have indeed become one of the best of living speakers.' Later, in 1950, he encouraged her to start a training college for verse-speaking and dramatic art, and gave her every kind of help with this successful venture.

Lucie Nicoll's work, running the family farm, which included a dairy herd of 250 cows, as well as much arable land, fascinated Masefield continually. Each year, as the vagaries of weather brought her the usual anxieties, he declared his admiration for her courage and efficiency as a farm manager. He wished, so he once told her, that he himself had trained as a farmer, and he evidently liked to pick up odds and ends of farming lore.

I know (I don't know how) that white clover seed is the hardest crop of all to gather, and how you gather it I do not pretend to guess. Perhaps you have a special geared cutter like a carpet-cleaner. There is a big clover, a sort of giant white clover, with a flush of pink in each blossom, which lays me low, always; is yours that sort?

If so, you must some day let me see the crop before you cut; and if you are quick, you will get a snap-shot of me swooning with rapture, and be able to get half a guinea for it from any illustrated weekly paper.

Another lady with whom Masefield corresponded steadily during the last fourteen years of his life was Audrey Napier-Smith, a violinist with the Hallé Orchestra in Manchester. In 1953 she had written to him to express her admiration and gratitude for his play *Melloney Holtspur* which had just been broadcast. This touched him because he had always felt that the play had been misunderstood. As their correspondence got under way he discovered that Miss Napier-Smith, who had served during the war in the Women's Royal Naval Service, was very knowledgeable about ships, and eager to know more. She also read a lot, and her taste in books often coincided with his. Many of the long letters which he wrote to her each week contained comments on his own favourite reading. In response to her discerning questions he expanded upon Chaucer, Shakespeare, Keats, Shelley, Browning, Blake, Swinburne, and Thomas Gray; on Dickens, Mark Twain, Victor Hugo, Trollope, Thackeray, du Maurier, and Oscar Wilde. He discoursed at length on Dr. Johnson, Rossetti, and William Morris. She also encouraged him to relive the past, so the letters abounded in reminiscences of Yeats, Synge, Hardy, Housman, Brooke, and innumerable others.

Masefield took a lively interest in Miss Napier-Smith's professional work. He himself had never been musical in the orthodox sense. Yet in 1941 he had written

> Though books delight me, sometimes music seems
> As sure a gateway to a world of dreams.

And towards the end of his life, when his sight was failing, he found solace in listening to classical recordings. Music was for him 'a form of fluid poetry full of inner meaning . . . a language that was spoken in some far away Celestial Hall of sound'.

5

The decade following the war began for Masefield with a spate of new activities and official duties. For a time he made frequent trips to London, especially to the Royal Academy of Dramatic Art, where he tried to promote 'story telling' as a branch of drama, and to the newly-launched National Book League, of which he was the first President. Early in 1949, however, when he was seventy, his busy round was brought suddenly to a stop, for he fell seriously ill. Influenza led to pneumonia, and the gravity of his condition may be judged from a message which appeared in *The Times* after the crisis was over:

Dr. and Mrs. John Masefield[1] thank all the countless friends who by message, letters and gifts of all kinds have cheered long weeks of sickness and anxiety. Of those who have prayed for their welfare publicly and privately, here and elsewhere, they think with the most heartfelt gladness.

But the long weeks of sickness and anxiety were by no means over. Only a few months later Masefield was again stricken, this time with appendicitis, and the operation was a precarious one because of the state of his heart. When at last he was home again he wrote – in his thankfulness – some verses entitled 'In Praise of Nurses', as a tribute to the nurses of the Acland Nursing Home who had cared for him. But they also convey something of what he had just been through.

> Man, in his gallant power, goes in pride,
> Confident, self-sufficient, gleaming-eyed,
> Till, with its poison on an unseen point
> A sickness strikes and all his strengths disjoint.
> Then, helpless, useless, hideous, stinking, mad,
> He lies bereft of what he was and had,
> Incapable of effort, limb and brain,
> A living fog of fantasies of pain.

[1] From about this time J.M. was often referred to as 'Dr. Masefield'.

And yet, today, as ever, since man was,
Even mad Man a healing impulse has.
Doctors there are, whose wisdoms know and check
The deadly things that bring the body's wreck,
Who minish agony, relieve and heal
Evils once mortal in Man's commonweal.
All honour Doctors; let me honour those
Who tend the patient when the doctor goes.

Daily and nightly, little praised or paid,
Those ordered, lovely spirits bring their aid,
Cheering the tired when the pain is grim,
Restoring power to the helpless limb.

Watching through darkness, driving away fear
When madness brings her many spectres near;
Cleansing the foul, and smiling through the pique
Of nerves unstrung or overstrained or weak,
Bringing to all a knowledge, hardly won,
Of body's peace and spirit's unison;
And blessing pillows with a touch that brings
Some little ease to all man's broken strings.[1]

Masefield's convalescence was slow. Even by the following
spring he was still very weak. And when at last he was up and
about once more he was a changed man, a really old man – his
face deeply lined, his silvery-white hair thinning, his figure
stouter – and he was much less mobile. From now on he no
longer drove a car, and he was told that he must cut down
drastically on his visits to London.

Yet in some ways he showed amazing resilience. Although
he published little during the 1950s his creative impetus was
irrepressible. He still wrote regularly every morning, though
no longer in his outdoor shed; the living room with the french
windows was now his study. He wrote mostly poetry not prose,
but an exception was *So Long to Learn*, a book in which he gave
a vivid and humble account of his life as a writer. Yet another
sign of his indomitable vitality was a pioneer publishing experiment in which he took part towards the end of the 1950s, not
long after his eightieth birthday: it was a bold and imaginative

---

1 These verses, published in *The Bluebells and Other Verse* (1961) were dedicated to
Mary Clifford, Laura Franklin, Helen McKenna, Phyllis Simmonds, and Joanna
Wills.

venture for one who set so much store by the spoken word. With the sponsorship of the American Academy of Poets he presented a new narrative poem, *The Story of Ossian*, in audible form, as a long-playing record instead of a book; in sonorous tones he recited the long epic himself.

In the 1950s daily life at Burcote was not at all easy. John and Constance managed as best they could, with the help of a housekeeper, but shopping was difficult now, so Constance wrote to Masefield's sister Norah, 'because Jan can't drive the car, and I am shy of shopping alone, now that I am a bit deaf'. This last remark was an understatement; Constance's deafness was much worse. Nevertheless in extreme old age she mellowed and her asperity softened – at ninety she made a very favourable impression when she spoke at the local Women's Institute. She also showed initiative and courage. When the weather was fine she still pottered about the garden, and as an indoor interest she started learning Russian.

In the autumn of 1959, however, she sank into her last lingering illness. Masefield insisted on 'helping' the nurse who cared for her, and he was continually at her bedside until on 18 February 1960 she died, after contracting pneumonia, at the age of ninety-three. In *The Times* her death was announced in words that were obviously written by Masefield himself; she had died 'very peacefully after a long illness . . . the inspiration and joy of all who knew her'. Also published in *The Times*, in a different vein, was an appreciation from an anonymous friend which included a pithy summing up: 'She was a blue-stocking and an intellectual, if one can use such a misguided term about a lady who was simply intelligent.'

6

Without Constance, Masefield's life at Burcote became increasingly solitary, and in the neighbourhood he was now regarded as a recluse. The reporters who sometimes came to interview him often found him curt, and other visitors were not encouraged unless they were special friends who had come a long way, such as Corliss Lamont and Helen MacLachlan (daughter of the MacLachlans who had befriended him in Yonkers). To one Oxford friend who suggested coming over, the reply was simply 'Better not'. Yet to those who realized what it meant for Masefield to be free from the strain of watching Constance die he seemed almost light-hearted. Judith, who was by now in her fifties, and who took to living at Burcote after her mother's death, has said that she likes to remember her father as 'laughing merry', 'brim full of the enjoyment of life', and 'a fount of good stories'.

Judith acted as hostess when visitors came, but she had no enthusiasm for the domestic arts, and everything else was left to a succession of housekeepers. The house became more and more run down, though Masefield, who all through his life had been accustomed to living in a certain amount of discomfort, and had long since acquired ascetic habits – he liked a simple diet and abstained from alcohol and tobacco – does not seem to have noticed, or if he noticed he did not mind.

Every day he continued to write. 'I must keep my hand in at poetry. If one doesn't work at it all the time, one's skill would disappear.' During the 1960s his Laureate verses included not only the usual tributes to royalty but also a number of obituaries; the most spontaneous of these was written after the assassination of President Kennedy:

> All generous hearts lament the leader killed
> The young chief with the smile, the radiant face,
> The winning way that turned a wondrous race
> Into sublimest pathways, leading on.

> Grant to us Life that though the man be gone
> The promise of his spirit be fulfilled.

Another obituary verse, on the occasion of T.S. Eliot's burial, and headed 'East Coker', showed that he was able to rise above a personal dislike, for he had never felt in sympathy with Eliot.

> Here, whence his forbears sprang, a man is laid
> As dust, in quiet earth, whose written word
> Helped many thousands broken and dismayed
> Among the ruins of triumphant wrong.
> May many an English flower and little bird
> (Primrose and robin redbreast unafraid)
> Gladden this garden where his rest is made
> And Christmas song respond, and Easter song.

Apart from his writing, Masefield in old age had a multitude of occupations. There were *The Times'* crosswords, and chess problems, and poker-patience, and billiards, and of course the books from the London Library as well as his own perennial favourites. But in his eighties he found reading increasingly difficult, for cataract was developing. He also began to be troubled by deafness. His life at this difficult time was however brightened and eased by the understanding and support of Dr. Isabel Little, the Oxford doctor who had attended Constance and who latterly became his own doctor. He also relied on a devoted friend, Kathleen Barmby (the daughter of a Radley master) who had already been helping the Masefields while Constance was alive. For Masefield the widower she acted as 'driver and odd-job-helper', coming out from Oxford at least three times each week, and when there were official functions to be attended she drove him wherever necessary and then played the part of lady-in-waiting.

During the last seven years of Masefield's life there were quite a number of such occasions, for honours were heaped upon the aged Laureate, and he also helped to celebrate the memory of various literary figures.[1] In 1961 he was one of the first five recipients of a new honour, Companion of Literature,[2] and in the same year he received the William Foyle Poetry Prize for his book *The Bluebells and Other Verse*. In 1964 the National Book League gave him a prize for writers over sixty-five, for his book *Old Raiger and Other Verse*. Yet this book was not his last – his vitality as a writer was inexhaustible. He was eighty-eight when his final book, *In Glad Thanksgiving*, was published, and just before that he had declared that he had enough ideas for another twenty years of work.

7

I had not meant to utter to men's ears
The holy things from which my spirit bleeds,
But I have done with sorrow, and Death nears,
And (being old) none cares (if any heeds).

---

[1] At Highgate in 1961 J.M. spoke at the reinterment of the body of S.C. Coleridge, and in 1963 at a ceremony when Yeats's rooms in Woburn Place were opened as a Yeats memorial.

[2] Instituted by the Royal Society of Literature.

But in a dream the glory that was She
Shone in my spirit and enlightened me.
.   .   .   .

Without, the leaves fly at the wind's desire,
A tawny owl bewails the grief in him,
The quarter moon wests silver to the sea.
One hour more, and She will be with me ...

What more to say, but that I dearly wait
Commanding Death's tense whisper at the gate.

The idea of a heavenly 'She', a 'She'

> ... of excellence untold
> In robes unutterably bright

appears again and again in Masefield's poetry, especially that of his final years. Some, doubtless, would see no more in this than a lonely widower's idealization of his wife. Others, in Masefield's case, might attribute it to the nostalgia for his long-lost mother that had haunted him all his life, or to the trauma of his frustrated adoration for Elizabeth Robins. But we must remember that Masefield was profoundly a lover of Dante. When he speaks of the spirit of a dying man as bleeding from the *holy* things, the whole matter seems to be lifted on to a plane far above that of the merely psychological. The parallel with the ending of the *Paradiso* is striking. Masefield's passion for beauty was one of his most deeply-rooted characteristics – for beauty in nature, art, poetry, women. His Beatrice, his Madonna, had been revealed to him in many different forms. But in the end, so it appears, he began to look steadily beyond the transitory.

One can certainly argue that he had become aware, probably unconsciously, of a need to venerate an eternal figure of womanly perfection, a figure of absolute purity, tenderness, and goodness. But how startled, indeed scandalized, he would have been (for he was violently prejudiced against anything that he considered essentially Roman Catholic) if it had been suggested to him that the object of his yearning was the Virgin Mary. Nevertheless if there was, in fact, such a yearning in him, it would have been entirely in keeping with his other gropings towards the Christian traditions of the age of Dante, the age of his beloved Chaucer, the age of the undivided Church.

✺

EPILOGUE

_____

When death finally threatened, Masefield could have chosen
to try to postpone it, but he did not. A very trivial accident
had been the cause which led up to this crisis. A split toe-nail
had gone septic, and this had brought on gangrene in the foot,
which then spread relentlessly up the leg. Amputation might
have saved his life, but this he refused to sanction. Before long
he had to be drugged, yet till almost the end his mind was as
clear as ever. Death came on 12 May 1967 when he was almost
eighty-nine.

Cremation was according to his wishes, but the disposal of
his ashes was not; they were deposited, with appropriate ritual
and literary acclaim, in the Poets' Corner at Westminister
Abbey. Perhaps no one had come across the typewritten verse
in which he expressed the wish that his ashes should be scattered
in the open air. Or perhaps, even if it was found, the demands
of his fame had taken precedence. This is what he had written,
to his 'Heirs, Administrators and Assigns':

> Let no religious rite be done or read
> In any place for me when I am dead,
> But burn my body into ash, and scatter
> The ash in secret into running water,
> Or on the windy down, and let none see;
> And then thank God that there's an end of me.

But had he been really so sure, in his heart of hearts, that the
scattering of his ashes would have been 'an end' of him? There
is a mass of evidence in his writings, especially in some of his
letters of condolence, of a conviction that a new kind of life
persists after physical death.

Masefield's beliefs on death were disparate; the strongest of
them, dating from his youth and from his early readings in

eastern religion, was a belief in some kind of reincarnation, some kind of ineffable fulfilment beyond the grave. In 1953, after Florence Lamont died, he wrote to one of her sons, 'As I grow older, I feel even more strongly that there is much that cannot die in each human life; and that that undying thing goes on in radiance to other service with new energy.' Then in 1960, five months after he lost Constance, he expressed the same ideas more fully when he wrote to Joyce King at a time of bereavement:

Alas; death is a part of life here; a change we pass through. But, surely, something in us is great, aware of greatness, and so undying. I feel sure that we have all lived before, and known our loves and delights before, and receive what we have earned, in love and kindness.

I cannot but believe this, and that life-bonds are renewed and maintained; surely all the dear bonds . . . Hope on. We could not hope, if there were not a World of Fulfilled Hope, the gleams of which shine down on us.

The theme of a relationship between the departed and the living, especially between those who had been closely linked in love, recurs often in Masefield's published writings, but in the compassion for the grief of others which animated his letters of sympathy it can be seen at its clearest, as for instance in a letter to Audrey Napier-Smith, written shortly after her mother died, and not very long before his own life came to an end. 'Death', he wrote,

is a part of the eternity in which we move; an eternity of chance in the three divine progressions of Power, Order and Beauty, to which the stars are subject. It may be agony of pain to the human heart from whom the beloved is sundered, the pain of the survivor [which] all who live have to know. But to the heart that has done with the body what release, what rest . . .

Yet that freed heart has the consecrated affections, who shall say how old, how deep, how nurtured through Time? The freed heart (who can doubt) still loves, guards, blesses, helps, guides . . . unfettered by an ailing body, seeing what we cannot see, prompting by ways we cannot know.

Selected Books by John Masefield

The most recent bibliography of John Masefield's work is *John Masefield, O.M. – A Bibliography* by Geoffrey Handley-Taylor (Cranbrook Tower Press, 1960), while *John Masefield's England* by Fraser Drew (Associated University Presses, 1973) includes listings not only of his books of poetry, novels, plays, and miscellaneous works, but of his prefaces, forewords, introductions, and contributions to periodicals. The latter book also gives lists of Masefield bibliographies, critical studies and memoirs, and of articles about him in books and periodicals.

All works listed below were published by William Heinemann Ltd. in London, and by The Macmillan Company in New York, unless otherwise stated.

I. POEMS, VERSE PLAYS, AND VOLUMES OF POEMS

Salt-Water Ballads (London: Grant Richards, 1902; New York: The Macmillan Company, 1913)

Ballads (London: Elkin Mathews, 1903)

Ballads and Poems (London: Elkin Mathews, 1910)

The Everlasting Mercy (London: Sidgwick and Jackson, Ltd., 1911; New York: The Macmillan Company, 1912 [with *The Widow in the Bye Street*])

The Widow in the Bye Street (London: Sidgwick and Jackson, Ltd.; New York: The Macmillan Company, 1912)

The Story of a Round-House and Other Poems (New York, 1912)

The Daffodil Fields (London and New York, 1913)

Dauber: A Poem (London, 1913)

Philip the King and Other Poems (London and New York, 1914)

Good Friday (Letchworth: Garden City Press; New York: The Macmillan Company, 1916 [in *Good Friday and Other Poems*])

Sonnets (New York, 1916)

Sonnets and Poems (Letchworth: Garden City Press, 1916)

Lollingdon Downs and Other Poems, with Sonnets (London and New York, 1917 [in U.S. *Lollingdon Downs and Other Poems*])

Rosas (London and New York, 1918 [in U.K. in *A Poem and Two Plays*])

Collected Poems and Plays, 2 vols. (New York, 1918)

Reynard the Fox: or the Ghost Heath Run (London and New York, 1919)

Animula (London: The Chiswick Press, 1920)

Enslaved and Other Poems (London and New York, 1920)

Right Royal (London and New York, 1920)

King Cole (London and New York, 1921)

The Dream (London and New York, 1922)

Selected Poems (London, 1922; New York, 1923)

A King's Daughter: A Tragedy in Verse (London and New York, 1923)

Collected Poems (London, 1923; New York, revised edn., 1935)

Sonnets of Good Cheer (London and Bath: the Mendip Press, 1926)

Tristan and Isolt: A Play in Verse (London and New York, 1927)

The Coming of Christ (London and New York, 1928)

Midsummer Night and Other Tales in Verse (London and New York, 1928)

Easter: A Play for Singers (London and New York, 1929)

South and East (London: The Medici Society; New York: The Macmillan Company, 1929)

The Wanderer of Liverpool (London and New York, 1930)

Minnie Maylow's Story and Other Tales and Scenes (London and New York, 1931)

A Tale of Troy (London: 1932; New York, 1931)

A Letter from Pontus and Other Verse (London and New York, 1936)

The Country Scene (London: William Collins Sons & Co. Ltd., 1937)

Tribute to Ballet (London: William Collins Sons & Co. Ltd.; New York: The Macmillan Company, 1938)

Some Verses to Some Germans (London and New York, 1939)

Some Memories of W. B. Yeats (Dundrum: The Cuala Press; New York: The Macmillan Company, 1940)

Gautama the Enlightened and Other Verse (London and New York, 1941)

Natalie Maisie and Pavilastukay (London and New York, 1942)

Land Workers (London: 1942; New York: 1943)

A Generation Risen (London: William Collins Sons & Co. Ltd., 1942; New York: The Macmillan Company, 1943)

Wonderings (Between One and Six Years) (London and New York, 1943)

On the Hill (London, 1949)

The Story of Ossian (London and New York, 1959)

The Bluebells and Other Verse (London and New York, 1961)

Old Raiger and Other Verse (London, 1964; New York, 1965)

In Glad Thanksgiving (London and New York, 1967)

II. NOVELS

Captain Margaret: A Romance (London: Grant Richards, 1908; Philadelphia: J. B. Lippincott Company, 1909)

Multitude and Solitude (London: Grant Richards, 1909; New York: Mitchell Kennerley, 1910)

Martin Hyde: The Duke's Messenger (London: Wells Gardner, Darton and Co. Ltd.; Boston: Little, Brown, and Company, 1910)

Lost Endeavour (London: Thomas Nelson and Sons, 1910; New York: The Macmillan Company, 1917)

The Street of Today (London: J. M. Dent & Sons Ltd.; New York: E. P. Dutton & Company, 1911)

Jim Davis (London: Wells Gardner, Darton & Co. Ltd., 1911; New York: Frederick A. Stokes Company, 1912)

Sard Harker (London and New York, 1924)

Odtaa (London and New York, 1926)

The Midnight Folk (London and New York, 1927)

The Hawbucks (London and New York, 1929)

The Bird of Dawning (London and New York, 1933)

The Taking of the Gry (London and New York, 1934)

The Box of Delights: or When the Wolves were Running (London and New York, 1935)

Victorious Troy: or The Hurrying Angel (London and New York, 1935)

Eggs and Baker (London and New York, 1936)

The Square Peg: or The Gun Fella (London and New York, 1937)

Dead Ned (London and New York, 1938)

Live and Kicking Ned (London and New York, 1939)

Basilissa: A Tale of the Empress Theodora (London and New York, 1940)

Conquer. A Tale of the Nika Rebellion in Byzantium (London and New York, 1941)

Badon Parchments (London, 1947)

III. PROSE PLAYS

The Tragedy of Nan and Other Plays (London: Grant Richards; New York: Mitchell Kennerley, 1909)

The Tragedy of Pompey the Great (London: Sidgwick and Jackson, Ltd., 1910; New York: The Macmillan Company, 1914)

The Faithful: A Tragedy in Three Acts (London and New York, 1915)

The Locked Chest; The Sweeps of '98 (Letchworth: Garden City Press; New York: The Macmillan Company, 1916)

Melloney Holtspur (London and New York, 1922)

The Trial of Jesus (London and New York, 1925)

The End and Beginning (London and New York, 1933)
A Play of St. George (London and New York, 1948)

IV. MISCELLANEOUS PROSE

A Mainsail Haul (London: Elkin Mathews, 1905; New York: The Macmillan Company, 1913)
Sea Life in Nelson's Time (London: Methuen & Co., 1905)
On the Spanish Main (London: Methuen & Co., 1906)
A Tarpaulin Muster (London: Grant Richards, 1907; New York: B. W. Dodge and Company, 1908)
My Faith in Woman Suffrage (London: The Woman's Press, 1910)
A Book of Discoveries (London: Wells Gardner, Darton and Co., Ltd.; New York: Frederick A. Stokes Company, 1910)
William Shakespeare (London: Williams and Norgate; New York: Henry Holt and Company, 1911)
Gallipoli (London and New York, 1916)
The Old Front Line (London and New York, 1917)
The War and the Future (New York, 1918)
St. George and the Dragon (London, 1919)
The Battle of the Somme (London, 1919)
The Taking of Helen (London and New York, 1923)
The Taking of Helen and Other Prose Selections (New York, 1924)
Recent Prose (London, 1924; New York, 1933)
Shakespeare and Spiritual Life (Oxford: the Clarendon Press, 1924)
With the Living Voice (London, 1925)
Oxford Recitations (New York, 1928)
The Conway from her Foundation to the Present Day (London and New York, 1933)
The Nine Days Wonder (London and New York, 1941)
In the Mill (London and New York, 1941)
New Chum (London, 1944; New York, 1945)
A Macbeth Production (London, 1945; New York, 1946)
Thanks Before Going (London, 1946; New York, 1947)
St. Katherine of Ledbury and Other Ledbury Papers (London, 1951)
So Long to Learn: Chapters of an Autobiography (London and New York, 1952)
Grace Before Ploughing: Fragments of Autobiography (London and New York, 1966)

Notes

In the following notes, for the sake of brevity, I have referred to John Masefield as J.M., and have also used initials for the following: C.R.Ashbee (C.R.A.); Janet Ashbee (J.A.); Laurence Binyon (L.B.); Rupert Brooke (R.B.); Miss Kathleen Barmby (K.B.); H. Granville-Barker (H.G.-B.); Miss Ann Hanford-Flood (A.H.-F.); Corliss Lamont (C.L.); Mrs. Florence Lamont (F.L.); Lillah McCarthy (L.M.); Harry Masefield (H.M.); H.W.Nevinson (H.W.N.); Elizabeth Robins (E.R.); Sir William Rothenstein (W.R.); Jack B. Yeats (J.B.Y.); W.B. Yeats (W.B.Y.). The following members of J.M.'s family are referred to by their first names: Constance, Judith, Lewis, Ethel, Norah. The full names of others interviewed or quoted, cited here by their surnames only, are given in the list of acknowledgements at p.xiii. Other abbreviations and short forms are given below.

PRINCIPAL SOURCES CITED OR QUOTED

I. BY JOHN MASEFIELD   *Cited as*

Published work (Heinemann editions except where stated)

    Collected Poems (1923)   *CP*
        All poems quoted or referred to (written prior to 1923) are from this volume and follow its text, unless otherwise stated.
    In the Mill (1941)   *IM*
    New Chum (1944)   *NC*
    So Long to Learn: Chapters of an Autobiography (1952)   *SLL*
    Articles in the *Manchester Guardian*   *MG*

Unpublished material
    (i) The Bodleian Library   Bod.
        Masefield collection includes letters to Constance, J.B.Y., H.W.N., C.Belliss; First World War note-   W.W.I
        book; notes and drafts of early reminiscences   N and D

(ii) Humanities Research Center, University of Texas HRC
Extensive Masefield archive

(iii) Berg Collection, New York Public Library   BC
Masefield collection includes journal of *Gilcruix*
voyage, two booklets of verses for Myra Bartlett,
letters to E. Marsh, Lady Gregory, and E.R., and
holograph account of J.M.'s life from birth to
marriage written for E.R. in 1910   E.R. 1910

(iv) Columbia University Libraries   CUL
Letters to Constance (1915–17) and others

(v) Houghton Library, Harvard University   HL
Letters to F.L., J.B.Y., W.R.

(vi) Yale University Library
Letters to Joyce King

(vii) King's College Library, Cambridge
Letters to R.B., C.R.A., J.A.

(viii) University of Sussex Library
J.M. notes in E.R.'s *Votes for Women*

(ix) In private hands
Letters to Ethel, Norah, H.M., and Ethel trans- Ethel
scripts of pre-1897 verses, in the possession of Mr. trans.
and Mrs. Hilary Magnus
    Letters to H.M. in the possession of Mr. J.B.
Masefield
    Letters to Rose Bruford, in her possession
    Letters to Lucie Nicoll in the possession of Mrs.
Betty Seymour Price
    Letters to L.B. in the possession of Mrs. Basil
Gray
    Letters to A.H.-F. in the possession of Mr.
Compton Whitworth
    Letters to Laurence Whistler in his possession
    Letters to W.B.Y. in the possession of Senator
M. Yeats
    Notes and drafts of early reminiscences in the N and D
possession of K.B.

II. OTHER SOURCES

Published   *Cited as*

C. Lamont, *Remembering John Masefield* (Kaye and
Ward, London, 1972)   *RJM*

page

78 'first success' / 'John M. Synge', p. 191

79 'learned his *métier* . . .' / ibid.

'There was something . . .' / *SLL*, p.154.

'Someone ought . . . its great passionate . . .' / ibid., p.155.

'The Yeatses are . . .' / letter to Constance, 5 April 1903.

'You know darling . . .' / ibid., 12 April 1903.

80 'About this question of age . . .' / ibid., 7 April 1903.

'We were up late . . .' / ibid., undated.

'We stand . . .' / ibid., 17 April 1903.

80n 'a wonderful she . . .' / ibid.

81 'I am now going to . . . And if I can . . .' / letter to Mrs. J.B.Y., undated.

'He is going to introduce me . . .' / letter to Constance, undated.

81–2 'a simple story . . .' / ibid., 3 May 1903.

82 'Have got job . . .' / letter to Ethel, undated.

'Aunt Emily asked . . .' / Constance letter to J.M., 10 April 1903.

'Your Aunt Constance . . .' / recollection of Miss D. Holmes.

83 'gurgled with pleasure . . .' / letter to Constance, 4 May 1903.

'A registrar . . .' / *The Street of Today* (1911), p.237.

'Insolent and sneering . . .' / letter to Constance, 26 May 1903.

'We were down there . . .' / letter to H. Ross, undated.

84 'It was very good of you . . .' / letter to J.B.Y., undated.

85 'I thought my last night . . .' / letter to Constance, 22 July 1903.

86 'a page of reviewing 20 books . . .' / letter to J.A., January 1903.

'24 books to review at once' / ibid. (c. August 1903).

'over 80 books to review . . .' / letter to C.R.A., 22 November 1905.

'the shortest and most incisive . . .' / Gilbert Thomas, *John Masefield* (1932), p.17.

'But for you . . .' / letter to W.R., 25 June 1910.

'John Masefield has got a wife . . .' / Ashbee journal, September 1904.

87 'She uses Jan . . .' / ibid.

'We are mightily plagued . . .' / letter to J.B.Y., undated.

88 'Churchwarden Gothic . . .' / letter from J.A. to C.R.A., January 1905.

page
88   'fairly sodden . . .' / letter to J.B.Y., undated.
89   *The Buccaneer* / letter to Norah, 23 February 1903.
        The Wrecker's Corpse / letter to J.B.Y., undated.
        'not really work at all' / *SLL*, p.172.
89–90   'I have left Manchester . . .' / 'I never heard . . .' / letter to
        H. Ross, 17 April 1905.
90   'a female girl . . .' / ibid., undated.
        'Dear Madam . . .' / ibid.
91   'A thieving pirate . . .' / letter to J.A., 30 April 1905.
        'Good God . . .' / letter to H. Ross, undated.
92   'When I from Campden town . . .' / letter to J.A., 4 April
        1905.
93   'I'm afraid I can't possibly . . .' / letter to Ethel and H. Ross,
        1 September 1906.
        'They hold a sing-song . . .' / letter to J.B.Y., undated.
93   'a mill of prose drama . . .' / letter to W.R., 12 December
        1905.
93n   'I did not do anything . . .' / Dan H. Lawrence (ed.),
        Bernard Shaw, Collected Letters (1972), p.607.
94   'I never saw . . .' / letter to Lady Gregory, 9 January 1907.
        'one of those aberrations . . .' / letter from G.B. Shaw to
        J.M., undated (postmark 27 July 1907), Bod.
95   'an intense and moving beauty' / L.M., *Myself and my
        Friends* (1933), p.105.
        'I don't *think* . . .' / Constance letter to J.M., undated.

CHAPTER SIX

Maida Hill West: Judith, Introduction to *RJM*; F.T. Grant
Richards, *Author Hunting* (1934); H. Pyle, *Jack B. Yeats* (1970); letters
to Constance, Judith, A.H.-F., H.M., Ashbees; Constance's letters to
J.M.; recollections of Judith. Elizabeth Robins: L. Edel, *Henry
James, The Treacherous Years* (1969); D. MacCarthy, *The Court
Theatre 1904–1907* (1907); E. Robins, *Votes for Women* (1907), *My
Little Sister* (1912); *My Faith in Woman Suffrage* (1910); *The Street of
Today* (1911); L. McCarthy, *Myself and My Friends* (1933); letters to
E.R.; E.R.'s letters to J.M.; J.M.'s notes in E.R.'s copy of *Votes for
Women. The Everlasting Mercy* and J.M.'s celebrity: *SLL*; Introduction
to *The Everlasting Mercy and The Widow in the Bye Street* (N.Y. 1912);
Ronald Ross, *Memoirs* (1923); E. Marsh, *A Number of People* (1939);
G. Keynes (ed.), *The Letters of Rupert Brooke* (1968); C. Hassall,
Edward Marsh (1959), *Rupert Brooke* (1964); R.H. Ross, *The Georgian
Revolt* (1967); F. Swinnterton, *The Georgian Literary Scene* (1935);

M. Beerbohm, *Fifty Caricatures* (1913); J.C. Squire, *Collected Parodies* (1921); D. Felicitas Corrigan, *Siegfried Sassoon – Poet's Pilgrimage* (1973); letters to R.B., E. Marsh, J.B.Y., H.M. Hampstead and Great Hampden: *Isabel Fry*; J.C. Squire (pseudonym 'Solomon Eagle'), 'Books in General', *New Statesman*, 7 June 1913; letters to J.B.Y., Ethel, H.G.-B.; recollections of Judith.

page

96   'I have just been painted . . .' / letter to A.H.-F., 8 April 1909.

'starving poet' / Ashbee journal, September 1904.

98   'a lovely little farm . . .' / letter to A.H.-F., 8 April 1909.

'On Sunday April 3 . . .' / H.V. Marrot (ed.), *Life and Letters of John Galsworthy* (1935), p.280.

'Children make life . . .' / letter to C.R.A., 23 November 1910.

'Children are about . . .' / letter to H.M., 9 October 1913.

'A poem is like . . .' / letter to J.A., 19 March 1907.

100   'She is my genius . . .' / letter to E.R., undated.

101   'unable to talk sense . . .' / ibid., 16 February 1910.

'gentle, soft, frail . . .' / quoted in L. Edel, *Henry James – The Treacherous Years*, p.29.

102   'Your letters . . .' / E.R. letter to J.M., 25 January 1910.

'I keep thinking . . . You must write the story . . .' / letter to E.R., 26 November 1909.

'If I can be of any help' / ibid., 29 November 1909.

103   'I wonder if anybody . . .' / ibid., 27 January 1910.

'Oh dear! Why will he . . .' / E.R.'s note on J.M.'s letter to her, 18 February 1910.

'delirious . . .' / E.R. to J.M., 26 February 1910.

105   'The spring is beginning' / *SLL*, p.186.

'in the freshness . . . followed by the . . . like Piers Plowman . . .' / Introduction to *The Everlasting Mercy and The Widow in the Bye Street* (U.S. 1912).

'the incredible and the impossible . . . I will write . . .' / *SLL*, p.187.

109   'incomparably the finest . . .' / *Daily Chronicle*, 29 November 1912.

'certainly one of the . . .' / G. Thomas, 'The Poetry of John Masefield', *Everyman*, 22 November 1912.

'rugged strength . . .' / *Evening Standard*, 3 February 1913.

'Masefield boom' / *Morning Post*, 7 February 1913.

'As for fame . . .' / letter to J.B.Y., 24 October 1912.

CHAPTER SEVEN

Lollingdon: *St. George and the Dragon* (1919); *Lollingdon Downs and Other Poems, with Sonnets* (1917); C. Hassall, *Rupert Brooke*; B. Curtis Brown, *Isabel Fry*; C.E. Montague, *Disenchantment* (1922); letters to Ethel, H.M.; Constance's 1915 diary. Arc-en-Barrois: J. Magill, *The Red Cross* (1926); J. Hone, *The Life of Henry Tonks* (1939); E.M. Forster, *Goldsworthy Lowes Dickinson* (1934); D. Proctor (ed.), *Autobiography of Goldsworthy Lowes Dickinson* (1973); letters to Constance, Judith, Ethel, H.M.; Constance's 1915 diary; letters from the British Red Cross Society archivist to the author. French hospitals: letters to Constance, Ethel, H.M., F. Sidgwick, Lady Ottoline

Morrell, W.R., E.V. Lucas, Miss Wheelwright. Gallipoli: *Gallipoli* (1916); Sir Ian Hamilton, *Gallipoli Diary* (1920); E. Ashmead Bartlett, *The Uncensored Dardanelles* (1928); C. Mackenzie, *Gallipoli Memories* (1929); J. North, *Gallipoli – The Fading Vision* (1936); H.W.N., *Fire of Life* (1935); 'Motor Launches for the Wounded', *The Times*, 20 August 1915; 'Mr' Masefield's Gift', Constance's letter to *The Times*, 27 August 1915; letters to Constance, Judith, Lewis, H.M., F.L., W.R., E.V. Lucas, E. Marsh, Miss Wheelwright; letters from the Red Cross Society archivist to the author. Projected U.S. lecture tour: L. Masterman, *C.F.G. Masterman* (1939); G.W.E. Russell, *Arthur Stanton* (1917); letters to C. Belliss, J.B. Pond Jr. (Univ. of Iowa); Constance's diaries, 1916, 1916–17.

page

117 eight centuries old / *St. George and the Dragon*, p.13.

  'a sort of moat . . . a good bird and flower place' / letter to Ethel, 5 June 1914.

118 'one is said to be able . . .' / letter to H.M., 18 February 1914.

  'the two days . . .' / Constance's diary, 14 July 1915.

  'the Austro-Serbian business' / *St. George and the Dragon*, p.13.

119 'their chargers . . .' / ibid.

  'He is uncertain . . . He has declared . . .' / Constance's diary, 21 January 1915.

  'When we were saying . . .' / ibid., 14 January 1915.

120 'Much as I love Isabel . . .' / Constance letter to J.M., undated.

  'When she is here . . .' / Constance's diary, 2 February 1915.

  'a simple, arduous life' / 'I feel she wants . . .' / 'it was getting beyond . . .' / ibid., 12 February 1915.

  'Well we shall see . . . It is . . .' / ibid.

  'the ways of hens' / ibid., 16 February 1915.

  'all sorts of queer lore . . .' / ibid., 27 February 1915.

  'more like a nice farmer . . .' / ibid., 13 February 1915.

121 'hang unconsciously . . .' / C.E. Montague, *Disenchantment*, p.62.

  'I envy Jan his work . . .' / Constance's diary, 12 February 1915.

122 'It is very stormy . . .' / ibid., 14 January 1915.

  'Tonight he has fallen . . .' / ibid., 8 February 1915.

  'Oh dear . . .' / ibid.

123 'first of war' / 'mud to the eyes . . .' / letter to Constance, 3 March 1915.

  'brave and good and fine . . .' / ibid., 5 March 1915.

page
123   'all right . . .' / letter to Constance, 4 March 1915.
       'One man merely had . . .' / ibid., 15 March 1915.
       The worst time . . . / ibid., 7 March 1915.
124   'The relief . . .' / ibid., 15 March 1915.
       'What our *blessés* . . .' / ibid., 29 March 1915.
       'Many of our men . . .' / ibid., 12 March 1915.
       'No one comes back . . .' / ibid., 13 March 1915.
       'I'm very well . . .' / ibid., 5 March 1915.
125   'Don't worry . . .' / ibid., 12 March 1915.
       'My dearest Con wife . . .' / ibid., 17 March 1915.
       '*du bon cœur* . . .' / ibid., 8 March 1915.
       'I'm a bit vexed . . .' / ibid., 2 April 1915.
       'They have an impossible . . .' / 'I like neither them . . .' /
         ibid., 17 March 1915.
126   'The really hard . . .' / ibid., 7 March 1915.
       'It is a fearful thing . . . We must see . . .' / ibid., 1 April
         1915.
       'lady probationers' / 'They pet . . .' / ibid.
       'the only woman here . . .' / ibid., 9 March 1915.
       'a rough kind' / 'quite first rate . . .' / ibid., 6 March
         1915.
       'In May some time . . . they want me . . .' / ibid., 17 March
         1915.
127   'My beloved Con . . .' / ibid., 14 March 1915.
       'I'm afraid the instinct . . .' / ibid., 6 April 1915.
       'Wood is very cheap . . .' / ibid., 26 March 1915.
       'One must not say . . .' / ibid., 17 March 1915.
128   'I daren't think . . .' / 'I think a lot about the future . . . Will
         wars go on . . .' / Constance's diary, 5 March 1915.
       'Goldie is awfully logical . . .' / ibid.
       'Goldie and those other . . .' / letter to Constance, 8 March
         1915.
       'We literary men . . .' / ibid., 28 March 1915.
       'I don't think that people . . .' / ibid., 9 March 1915.
129   'When I first heard sabots . . .' / ibid., 5 April 1915.
       'I don't feel that . . . They are guilty . . .' / ibid., 2 April
         1915.
       'One longs for these . . .' / ibid., 10 April 1915.
       'in about a year . . .' / ibid., 29 March 1915.
       'France is not . . .' / ibid., 9 April 1915.
       'I didn't know quite . . .' / 'But one night . . . The days that
         followed . . .' / Constance's diary, 14 July 1915.

CHAPTER EIGHT

New York and the East Coast: letters to Constance, W.B.Y.; Constance's letters to J.M.; Constance's 1916 diary; L. O'Connor letter to J.M. (BC); J.B. Pond Lyceum Bureau brochure 'First American Tour of John Masefield, The Sailor Poet'; 'A Lyric Poet . . .' *New York Tribune*, 23 January 1916; 'John Masefield, Poetic Explorer', *Evening Post*, 29 January 1916; 'Masefield again in America', *The Literary Digest*, 5 February 1916; Fraser Drew, 'A Gift of Books', *The Literary Review*, Summer 1973. Mid-West: letters to Constance, Mrs. Vaughn Moody; L. Untermeyer, *Modern American Poetry* (1925). Last month of tour: letters to Constance, Mrs. A.P. Saunders; Constance's 1916 diary; letters from the J.B. Pond Lyceum Bureau to A.P. Saunders; letter from J.B. Pond Jr. to J.M., 3 June 1958.

146 'as though they were going . . . I never saw . . .' / letter to
   Constance, 8 February 1916.

   'It was a very good way . . .' / 'No music . . .' / ibid.

   'the enemy' / 'a sort of limited . . . all very rich . . .' /
   'I felt myself . . .' / ibid., 4 February 1916.

147 'A lot of queer food . . .' / ibid.

   'Oh God, you don't know . . . Hundreds of . . .' / 'picturesque' / 'fearful hag' / 'Pittsburgh extends . . .' / 'I would
   like . . .' / 'and she'll be there . . .' / ibid., 6 February
   1916.

148 'We careered . . .' / ibid., 10 February 1916.

   'they might, and very likely would be . . .' / J.M. report
   dated 5 February 1916.

   'Chicago is still . . . But till then . . .' / letter to Constance,
   12 February 1916.

   'bowling along . . . Oh my dear . . . I never saw . . .' / ibid.,
   14 February 1916.

149 'as fierce a town . . .' / 'feeling was high' / ibid., 16 February
   1916.

   'hard-mouthed terror . . . Now Mr. Masefield . . .' / ibid.,
   6 February 1916.

   'four slimy female reporters . . .' / ibid., 3 February 1916.

   'they weren't quite so bad . . .' / 'a big noisy smoky city . . .' /
   ibid., 16 February 1916.

   'absence of civic sense' / 'I never felt it much . . .' / ibid.,
   18 February 1916.

150 'after being bedevilled . . .' / 'O God . . .' / 'I saw one
   monstrous . . .' / ibid.

   'I don't know why . . .' / ibid., 12 February 1916.

   'carnal, hard . . .' / ibid., 21 February 1916.

   'a very nice . . .' / ibid.

150–1 'which was the very devil . . .' / 'for a dish of soup . . .' /
   'seemed to give . . .' / 'I daresay . . .' / 'a highly popular
   . . .' / ibid., 19 February 1916.

151 'The gentle friendly . . .' / ibid.

   'This land . . .' / ibid., 11 February 1916.

   'Generally speaking . . .' / ibid., 28 January 1916.

   'Youth never asks . . .' / ibid., 11 February 1916.

   'The fall itself . . .' / 'this vast bulk . . . and floats around
   . . .' / ibid., 23 February 1916. The account of Niagara
   was published in 'Letters', *Recent Prose* (1924).

152 'Whatever the falls . . .' / ibid.

CHAPTER NINE

Gallipoli: Foreign Office correspondence on J.M.'s assignment (PRO. FO 371/2835); *Gallipoli* (1916); Foreword to *The Battle of the Somme* (1919); H.W.N., *Fire of Life* (1935); letters to W.R., H.W.N.; letters to J.M. from Constance, Sir Ian Hamilton (Bod.). U.S. relief work in France: Foreign Office correspondence on J.M.'s appointment (PRO. FO 395/3); 'List of American Relief Organizations in France' (TS. Bod.); 'The Harvest of the Night', *Harpers Monthly Magazine*, May 1917; J.M. letter, 'An Anglo-American Entente', *Daily Chronicle*, 29 January 1917; letters to Constance, H.M.; recollections of Lady Phipps. Projected book on the Battle of the Somme: Lord Newton, *Retrospection* (1941); Letters to Constance; Constance letters to J.M. Somme battlefield: N. Lytton, *The Press and the General Staff* (1920); letters to Constance, Judith, Lewis, F.L., H. Walpole, Agnes Fry. J.M. and his family: W.W.I notebook (Bod.); letters and postcards to Constance, Judith, Lewis, Mrs. V. Moody; Constance letters to J.M., E. Marsh; *Isabel Fry*; Earl of Oxford and Asquith, *Memories and Reflections*, Vol. II. 1918 U.S. tour: J.M. interview, *New York Times Magazine*, 27 January 1918; 'John Masefield in New Haven', *Yale University Library Gazette*, April 1958; letters to Constance, Lewis, J.B. Pond Jr., Miss Horniman, H.W.N., Mrs. V. Moody, Mrs. E.B. Reed, F.L.; J.B. Pond Lyceum Bureau letters to A.P. Saunders. Armistice period: letters to Constance, H.M., H.W.N., H. Walpole, L.P. Bell; Constance's 1920 diary.

page

158   'the second grand event . . .' / *Gallipoli*, p. 4.

159   'Someday . . .' / letter to W.R., 9 November 1916.

'The fact is we shan't know . . .' / Sir Ian Hamilton letter to J.M., 18 July 1916.

'like wildfire' / Constance letter to J.M., 11 October 1916.

'a brilliant poetic sketch' / H.W.N., *Fire of Life*, p.344.

'the supreme *Gallipoli*' / 'That is war service . . .' / E. Marsh note to Constance, quoted by her in a letter to J.M., 3 October 1916.

'A very delicate mission' / 'a big scheme . . .' / letter to H.M., 16 August 1916.

160   'it is dreadful . . .' / letter to Constance, 1 September 1916.

'a very beautiful thing' / 'face making' / ibid., 3 September 1916.

'really an adaptation . . .' / ibid., 4 September 1916.

'I don't find . . . They are all . . .' / ibid., 7 September 1916.

'jolly, bachelory . . .' / ibid., 6 September 1916.

'though by no means quiet' / ibid., 1 September 1916.

'living in motorcars . . .' / ibid., 13 September 1916.

'Being in the air . . .' / ibid., 15 September 1916.

160–1   'like a town . . .' / 'The hills outside . . .' / ibid., 13 September 1916.

'places run by Americans' / 'other works' / ibid., 28 September 1916.

'beautiful human souls, with that best sort . . .' / ibid., 29 September 1916.

'had no language . . .' / ibid., 30 September 1916.

'What a row I shall have . . .' / ibid., 22 October 1916.

162   'When I get back . . .' / ibid., 6 October 1916.

'spangled staff officers' / ibid., 14 October 1916.

163   'an amusing clever . . .' / 'rather amusing' / 'a sort of black hat' / ibid., 15 October 1916.

163n   'What is that fellow . . .' / Lord Newton, *Retrospection* (1941), p.224.

163   'Lord Esher . . . said that I am wanted . . .' / 'There is loneliness . . . Think it over' / letter to Constance, 9 October 1916.

page

173   'perhaps some . . .' / *The Battle of the Somme*, p.2.

        'I must apologize . . . It was simply . . .' / letter to Miss Horniman, 10 March 1918.

        'turned to other work . . .' / letter to F.L., 24 September 1917.

174   'talking to soldiers' / letter to H.M., 16 November 1917.

        'Jan had to be away . . .' / 'We had our own bonfire . . .' / Constance's diary, 20 February 1920.

175   'Now we have peace . . .' / letter to H.M., 16 November 1918.

CHAPTER TEN

The Masefields at Boars Hill: pocket-diary 1922; letters to C. Belliss, F.L., H.W.N.; recollections of Judith, Henry Smith; Introduction to Lewis's *The Passion Left Behind* (1947); *A Foundation Day Address* (1921); M.B. Rix, *Boars Hill Oxford* (1970); 'Fire in Mr. John Masefield's Study', *The Times*, 3 May 1928. Boars Hill friends and acquaintances: R. Graves, *Goodbye to All That* (1929); *RJM*; L. McCarthy, *Myself and My Friends* (1933); J. Smith and A. Toynbee (eds.), *Gilbert Murray: An Unfinished Autobiography* (1960); Julian Huxley, *Memories* (1970); Cecil Roberts, *The Years of Promise* (1968); C. Hollis, *The Seven Ages* (1974); M. Praz, *The House of Life* (1958); C.B. Purdom (ed.), *The Shaw Barker Letters* (1956); 'On Rigging Model Ships' in *Thanks Before Going* (1947); letters to L.B., Blunt, R. Graves, Nancy Graves, L. Hutchinson, L.T. Nicholl, S. Sassoon; R. Graves letter to Constance; Constance's diaries 1915, 1920; recollections of Blunt, Coghill, E. Gillett, Muir, Miss Jean Smith, Miss Ethne Thompson. Post-war writings: 'Fox-hunting' in *Recent Prose* (1924); T.C. Chubb, 'Some Recollections of John Masefield', *Mark Twain Journal*, Summer 1969; J. Guest (ed.), *Ambrosia and Small Beer* (1964), pp.48–9; pocket-diary 1919; undated letter to H.W.N. *re King Cole* [August 1922]. J.M.'s theatrical productions: Basil Maine, *The Best of Me* (1937); Julian Huxley, *Memories* (1970); Sibyl Thorndike, 'The Theatre and Gilbert Murray', in *Gilbert Murray: An Unfinished Autobiography*; 'A Country House Theatre', *Country Life*, 8 August 1925; letters to G.D. Barlow, C. Belliss, H. Walpole, Mrs. V. Moody, L. Quartermaine; recollections of Cobb, Coghill, Muir, Richards; programmes for productions of *King Lear*, *Macbeth*, *The Alchemist*, *Esther*, *Measure for Measure*, *Twelfth Night*, *The Young King*, *Evil*, *Gruach*, *Boadicea*, *Tristan and Isolt*, *The Two Angry Women of Abingdon*, *Meleager*. Oxford Recitations: *With the Living Voice* (1925); *Oxford Recitations* (N.Y. 1928);

Minnie Maylow's Story and Other Tales and Scenes (1931); Marion Cole, *Fogie* (1967); George Buchanan on J.M., *The Times*, 22 May 1967; letters to L.B., L. Abercrombie; G.B. Shaw postcard to J.M., 7 July 1924 (CUL); recollections of Bruford, Brown, Carina Robins, Coghill, Lady Fairfax-Lucy. Religious drama: *SLL*; G. Weales, *Religion in Modern English Drama* (1961); R. Jasper, *George Bell: Bishop of Chichester* (1967); L. Irvine, *The Canterbury Adventure* (1959); *RJM*; G.R. Wilson Knight; *Neglected Powers* (1971); report of J.M.'s speech at Aberdeen University, *Aberdeen Press and Journal*, 21 March 1922; review of *The Trial of Jesus*, *Morning Post* (signed S.R.L.), 21 March 1932.

page

179   'quite remote . . .' / Constance's diary, 25 February 1920.
'wild Berkshire . . .' / *The Passion Left Behind*, p.6.

180   'out in his shack . . .' / Constance's diary, 5 March 1920.
'The bright colour . . . the thrill of the horn . . .' / 'Fox-Hunting', *Recent Prose*, p.160.

181   'I hope the poem . . . He has the gift . . . He could never be . . .' / Constance's diary, 5 March 1920.

182   'a rather wooden-looking . . .' / 'a woman . . .' / 'in the manner . . .' / *The House of Life*, p.258.
'There was often . . .' / Muir recollections.

183   'the very soul . . .' / *New York Times Magazine*, 27 January 1918.

184   'a tender-hearted . . .' / 'not got enough . . .' / 'Nancy is a strange . . .' / Constance's diary, 20 February 1920.
'charming family' / 'We attach . . .' / letter to R. Graves, 22 April 1920.
'I myself back . . .' / 'He has mirth . . .' / letter to L.T. Nicholl, 7 April 1919.
'as mad as a hatter. Some days he . . . "the greatest . . ."' / 'a jolly simple . . .' / Constance's diary, 20 February 1920.

185   'collegy streets . . . one is seldom . . .' / letter to L. Hutchinson, undated.
'a gray town . . .' / 'A vagrant, I . . .' / 'Shopping in Oxford', *Gautama the Enlightened and Other Verse* (1941).

186   'With squeaky wit . . .' / pocket-diary, 28 June 1922.
'with the living voice' / title of the address given by J.M. to the Scottish Association for the Speaking of Verse (1925).

187   'designed to brighten . . .' / Preface to *Poems and Plays of John Masefield*, Vol. I (N.Y. 1918).
'The simple souls . . . Euripides . . .' / letter to L.B., undated.

CHAPTER ELEVEN

Appointment as Laureate: letters to Ramsay MacDonald (PRO. 30/69/2/10 Pt. 2), J.B.Y., C. Sansom, draft of letter to Lord Chamberlain, 8 May 1930 (HRC); letters to J.M. from Ramsay MacDonald (PRO. ibid.), A.E. Housman, W.B.Y., Lady Gregory; recollections of Sir Nevile Butler, C. Sansom; Fraser Drew, *John Masefield's England* (1973); K. Hopkins, *The Poets Laureate* (1954); D. Marquand, *Ramsay MacDonald* (1977); H. Maas (ed.), *The Letters of A.E. Housman* (1971). Press comments on appointment: *The Times*, *The Observer*, *The Sunday Times*, *New York Times*; press reports of J.M. interviews in *Westminster Gazette*, *Evening News*, *Scotsman*, *Daily Herald*. Laureate poetry, speeches etc.: verses in *The Times* (as given below); drafts of letters to King George VI (HRC); letter to A.H.-F.; reports in *Hereford Times*, *Ledbury Reporter and Guardian*, *The Cadet*. Honours and responsibilities: *SLL*; letters to L.B., Edmund Blunden, Mrs. Gwyneth B. Edmunds, Gilbert Murray, Prof. I.A. Richards (draft), Sir Osbert Sitwell, Muriel Walthen, Sir Clive Wigram (draft).

CHAPTER TWELVE

1930s at Pinbury: J.M.'s pocket-diaries, 1935, 1938; letters to Ethel, H.M., L.B., Lucie Nicoll; recollections of Prudence Barker, K.B., Mr. Nial Charlton, Prof. N. Coghill, Mrs. P. Diamand, Mrs. L.

Franklin, Lord Gore-Booth, Mrs. A. Heavens, Mrs. Oldridge, Whistler; programme for Oxford Summer Diversions (1939); 'Pauntley: Aims and Methods of the Home' (Foreword by J.M.); B. Smith, *The Cotswolds* (1976). Travels during 1930s: letters to H.M., H.W.N., Nicoll, J.R.B. Masefield, Talbot Rice; recollections of Miss Caroline Gurney; 'The English Poet Laureate at Athens University', *Athens Times*, 18 April 1931; 'Britain's Poet Laureate talks about Poetry', *New York Times Magazine*, 22 January 1933. Burcote: *RJM*; letters to H.W.N., C. Belliss, E. Seago; recollections of Judith, Prudence Barker, K.B., Lord Gore-Booth, MacLachlan, Oldridge. Illness and last years: Judith's Introduction to *RJM*; 'Profile: John Masefield, O.M.', *The Observer*, 28 October 1945; 'John Masefield, O.M.', *The Sunday Times*, 23 December 1951; J.H.B. Peel, 'John Masefield at Eighty', *The Sunday Times*, 1 June 1958; 'Masefield's New Epic: *The Story of Ossian*', *The Times*, 23 April 1959; 'Poet Laureate', *Guardian*, 9 August 1960; J.H.B. Peel, 'John Masefield at 87', *Evening Standard*, 31 August 1965; 'The First Ten Years [of the Rose Bruford Training College of Speech and Drama]' (1960); recollections of Judith, C.L., K.B., Bruford, Franklin, MacLachlan, Mr. J.B. Masefield, Sir Peter Masefield, Oldridge, Sharpe.

page

205 'paused on the line . . .' / Constance letter to C.L., 12 October 1932, *RJM*, p.39.

205n 'It is no longer . . .' / letter to L.B., undated.

206 'rescue hide and seek' / recollections of Barker.
'gorgeous rags' / recollections of Oldridge.

207 'I do think beauty . . .' / recollections of Coghill.
'My two haven't married . . .' / Constance letter to Nicoll, undated.

208 'My son comes home . . .' / letter to J.A., undated.
'Deep deep the drift . . .' / pocket-diary, 22 December 1938.

209 'deepest joy' / letter to Kay Ambrose, undated (Bod.).
'He loved the company . . .' / recollection of Judith.
'The gnome from moonland . . .' / 'Ballet Russe I', *A Letter from Pontus and Other Verse* (1936).

210 'He drank some milk . . .' / letter to Lewis, 5 June 1942.

211 'We are soon to be . . .' / letter to H.W.N., undated.

212 'a most beautiful . . .' / letter to C. Belliss, undated (annotated '28 Sept. 1940').
'the law of his being' / cf. *IM*, p.98.

213 'Many people are so kind . . .' / 'Our Lew . . .' / Constance letter to W.R., 20 June 1942.

EPILOGUE

Index

J.M. = John Masefield.